CORPORATE STRATEGY

Other books in The McGraw-Hill Executive MBA Series include:

FINANCE AND ACCOUNTING FOR NONFINANCIAL MANAGERS
MERGERS AND ACQUISITIONS
SALES MANAGEMENT

CORPORATE STRATEGY

THE McGRAW-HILL EXECUTIVE MBA SERIES

JOHN L. COLLEY, JR.
JACQUELINE L. DOYLE
ROBERT D. HARDIE

McGraw-Hill

New York   Chicago   San Francisco   Lisbon
London   Madrid   Mexico City   Milan   New Delhi
San Juan   Seoul   Singapore   Sydney   Toronto

Library of Congress Cataloging-in-Publication Data

Colley, John L., Jr.
    Corporate Strategy/by John L. Colley, Jr. and Jacqueline L. Doyle and Robert D. Hardie.
        p. cm.
    Includes bibliographical references and index.
    ISBN 0-07-137265-2
    1. Strategic planning. 2. Strategic planning—United States. 3. Conglomerate
corporations—Management. 4. Conglomerate corporations—United States—
Management. I. Doyle, Jacqueline. II. Hardie, Robert D. III. Title.

HD30.28 .C64313 2001
658.4'012—dc21   2001018694
                                                                      CIP

McGraw-Hill
A Division of The McGraw·Hill Companies

1 2 3 4 5 6 7 8 9 0   AGM/AGM   0 9 8 7 6 5 4 3 2 1

ISBN 0-07-137265-2

Printed and bound by Quebecor/Martinsburg.

McGraw-Hill books are available at special quantity discounts to use as premiums and
sales promotions, or for use in corporate training programs. For more information, please
write to the Director of Special Sales, Professional Publishing, McGraw-Hill, Two Penn
Plaza, New York, NY 10121-2298. Or contact your local bookstore.

 This book is printed on recycled, acid-free paper containing a minimum of 50%
recycled, de-inked fiber.

CONTENTS

PART FIVE

STRATEGIC RESTRUCTURING FOR SHAREHOLDER VALUE   211

Preface

Management strategies are essential to business success in the relatively chaotic environment caused by the restructuring of American industry. This restructuring has been, and continues to be, taking place primarily within the context of a specific scheme of industrial organization—namely, a corporation composed of various business units or operating divisions. During the last three decades, the basic strategies of American industry have evolved continually and have been adjusted to respond to competitive and financial pressures. During this time, many changes in the diversified corporation have taken place.

For perspective, let us examine the 1970s and 1980s. Those decades were identified as being a sustained period during which large corporations tended to diversify into different businesses. They did so to placate financial analysts' preferences for risk aversion, which were, in turn, brought on by concepts from "portfolio theory." This theory was one of risk management, promoting the concept that a diversified company was less at risk from market downturns than a single, focused business, because numerous industries were unlikely to experience problems simultaneously. As a result, most of the Fortune 1,000 U.S. companies became diversified and decentralized.

Naturally, these diversified companies embraced a decentralized form of operations for planning and control. The breadth of a typical corporation's business operations precluded anyone from completely understanding all of the operations. This situation led to a natural division of labor: the corporate staff was responsible primarily for deciding on and financing the portfolio of businesses to be included in the company holdings, and the various division managers were responsible for all aspects of their respective operations.

After operating in this mode for many years—the so-called old economy—American businesses saw the late 1980s usher in the beginning of a period of new trends in industrial organization. At that time, financial analysts began to profess that they found the diversified businesses difficult to "understand." They feared that having many business units provided companies with opportunities to mask their risks or troubles. The successes of more prosperous business units would "hide" the deficiencies of less prosperous ones. These concerns about diversification emerged gradually, accelerated in the nineties, and have become major impediments to most diversified, decentralized corporations in the twenty-first century.

In today's corporate world, financial analysts and institutional investors characteristically afford focused and pure-play (read "narrow product category") companies the opportunity to achieve much higher stock price multiples than diversified companies. As a result, CEOs and boards of directors of many public companies have been led to unwind much of the diversification previously cherished. This impetus had led, in recent years, to a continuous stream of divestitures, as companies have lessened the diversification within their portfolios at the behest of the financial community. These divestitures often have resulted in improved operating results and, concomitantly, higher returns on shareholder investment.

The second major exogenous factor that had upset the status quo of the "old economy" was the explosion in the 1990s of the "new economy," centered on the high-technology, telecommunications, computer, and Internet-related businesses. The careful equilibrium that had existed in the financial markets and in the consumer and industrial markets for a century was pushed aside by a new breed of "technocrats" who marshaled formidable technological advances in electronics to create whole new industries. Their success, in turn, first attracted the attention of venture capitalists and then large numbers of mainstream investors, who saw a means for participating in a new economy perceived to possess almost unlimited upside potential.

This development had changed the strategic perceptions of risk and return for virtually every CEO of a major U.S. corporation. The CEO had to decide whether his or her business was threatened by the new technologies as well as whether the company should attempt to capitalize on the new developments in its normal competitive environments. The century of stability and predictability of competitive pressures, relative market shares, and labor and material costs had spawned generations of risk-averse managers. Many managers were willing and eager to substitute planning for risk. Multiyear contracts with labor unions and suppliers were attempts to remove major risks from pricing decisions. The new economy offered the prospects of almost unlimited returns on investment, at the cost of a level of risk and uncertainty unknown for generations. The strategies of the old economy were shaken and subjected to scrutiny as never before. Would the company be left behind? Should the company make major investments in the new economy and, if so, how? The world of the CEO of many old-economy companies had permanently changed overnight, because the new environment was far-reaching and enduring.

These important trends in new technology coexist with the still-surviving range of corporate portfolio diversity in U.S. corporations today.

Recognizing that fact, we write this book to address the key strategic issues related to the management of the multidivisional organization. The strategic interface between parent corporations and operating divisions is discussed, with strong emphasis being placed on analytical and financial relationships among them. Corporate strategies are examined in the context of questions concerning the appropriateness of various divisions (and potential acquisitions) for inclusion in the corporate portfolio of businesses. Also addressed is the need for corporate strategies to encompass the allocation of resources among the businesses of the portfolio.

The many strategic issues faced by diversified, decentralized, multidivisional companies are illustrated in the hypothetical Pelican Corporation case studies following Chapter 11. This company consists of 10 divisions, each of which presents one or more strategic dilemmas to its parent company, Pelican. These divisions, as do most divisions in a large, multidivisional firm, include both larger firms and considerably smaller firms, raising the strategic issue of whether size matters in the end. Some divisions are high-technology firms, while others make products that are almost commodities; some divisions conduct business in very cyclical markets while others do so in more stable growth situations; and some divisions lose money while others are extremely profitable.

Divisional strategies, to be successful, require management to have extensive understanding of competitors and realistic product, marketing, and pricing strategies, based on the division's role in its competitive environment and the corporate portfolio. In this context, particular emphasis is placed in this book on improvement in labor productivity as a critical, continuing competitive factor. Overshadowing all of this are the concerns and opportunities provided by the new dichotomy in America's economy.

The issue of corporate growth is relevant to firms operating in either the new economy or the old economy. In a free-enterprise, competitive environment, there is no substitute for the energizing phenomenon of growth. It is our belief that all strategic issues can be dealt with more effectively in a growth environment than in a stagnant one. And so our basic premise, for all businesses, is that the strategic-planning process begins with managers devising strategies for growth, followed by addressing the concomitant issues their firms face.

Finally, we want to recognize the crucial importance of each of two aspects of corporate strategy. First, the strategic planning process begins with decisions regarding the firm's strategic goals and objectives, followed by the formulation of strategies for their attainment. Second, plans must be devised for implementing the strategies and managing the myriad of detailed actions that are required to execute the strategies effectively. In many ways this strategic-planning process in the business world is analogous to the longing for the "ultimate weapon" that has characterized military leaders throughout history. In seeking "sustainable competitive advantages," commanders have hoped to acquire access to a weapon so unique that it would tip the battle in their favor.

Unfortunately, this hope has, for the most part, been futile. Consider the small number of ultimate weapons we recall throughout military history, and the relatively short time during which they afforded the fortunate a competitive advantage. From the spear, bow and arrow, crossbow, long bow, gunpowder, and firearms, to machine guns, artillery, tanks, and nuclear weapons, the competitive advantage lasted only until opponents internalized the advantages of each weapon and copied them. Even with all of the science and technology involved with nuclear weapons, the competitive advantage only was sustainable for three years.

On the other hand, consider the success of the Greek phalanx, the Roman legion, Ghengis Khan's cavalry, modern military logistics, and the ever-present use of alliances to rein in those who appeared too powerful. It is apparent that, for the most part, history has belonged to the "organizers and implementers" and only for fleeting periods to those with some undefendable ultimate weapon. So it is with business. Unique strategies are few and can seldom be perpetuated for very long. Even patents expire at the end of some specified time interval.

As a result, in our system of free enterprise and competition, with unprecedented capabilities for communication, ideas don't remain proprietary for very long. Competitors become aware of the strategies of others from suppliers, customers, industry connections, former employees, and especially from the CEOs' statements in the annual reports of most public companies. Surely, success in the business environment is dependent on the derivation of effective strategies, but it is at least equally dependent on superior ability to execute the strategies. Those firms with superior strategies and the ability to execute them are the big winners in the free enterprise system. This dual theme of strategy formulation and concomitant superior execution is reinforced throughout the chapters and case studies of this book.

Thus, we emphasize the dual needs to manage change effectively and to move decisively in implementation decisions. In fact, the entire process of strategic planning and execution is dependent for success on the ability of CEOs to lead change and execute decisions swiftly and decisively. We learn from the master of understanding and explaining human nature, Niccolò Machiavelli, that these traits are essential for the "prince" who wishes to defend and expand his realm (read business). Machiavelli wrote, in 1532, that "there is nothing more difficult to execute, nor more dubious of success, nor more dangerous to administer than to introduce a new order of things,"[1] thus warning of the difficulties of implementing changes. He also wrote that, "in taking a state its conqueror should weigh all the harmful things he must do and do them all at once so as not to have to repeat them every day, and in not repeating them to be able to make men feel

---

1 Niccolò Machiavelli, *The Prince* (1531), from *The Portable Machiavelli*, edited and translated by Peter Bondanella and Mark Musa, Viking Penguin, New York, 1979, 94.

secure and to win them over to the benefits he bestows upon them."[2] Our experience reinforces this notion that when some tough decision must be implemented, it is far better to take the action swiftly and decisively, thus getting the period of unrest over as rapidly as possible and allowing the people affected to get on with their activities and establish a new routine.

We now move on to explaining these issues in greater detail, with many subtleties illustrated by the examples in the case studies.

John L. Colley, Jr.
Jacqueline L. Doyle
Robert D. Hardie

---

2 Machiavelli, 106–107.

Acknowledgments

We are grateful to the University of Virginia, the Darden Graduate School of Business Administration, and the Darden School Foundation for their extensive support, which made this project possible.

It is a great pleasure for us to also acknowledge the support and assistance of a number of administrators, faculty colleagues, and students. The Darden School's Research Committee was a steady supporter of this project, along with Jim Freeland, Associate Dean of the Faculty. We especially acknowledge the Darden School's permission to include materials in the book which were previously copyrighted by the school. We also thank our faculty colleague, Wallace Stettinius, for his wisdom about management and his encouragement of this book project. We especially thank Conan Owen for his insightful role in the development and analysis of the Pelican series of case studies.

We also thank the following present and former students who assisted with various parts of the effort:

Jack Benson	Rachel Korkowski	Tony Ruffine
Douglas Comstock	Hiroshi Kubota	Marc Ruggiano
Eileen Filliben	David Martin	Shiro Sakamoto
Paul Fowler	Yoshihiro Matsuzaki	David Santley
Tia Garner	Daniel McCarthy	Winston Shearon
Timothy Heaps	Panos Midis	Jack Woodfin
Sherman Henderson	Kari Pitkin	Takashi Yamaguchi
Maurice Kelley	Pilar Rivera-Cruz	Debra Zehner
Martin King	Vitalijs Rubsteins	

We are grateful to all of our students, both graduate students at the Darden School and executives, who encouraged us to pursue the topics in this book over many years. They stimulated our curiosity, broadened our thinking, and compelled us to continuously improve our materials and reasoning. We are extremely appreciative of these invaluable contributions.

We would also like to acknowledge the support of our assistants at the Darden School. We are grateful to Mary Darnell, Sherry Alston, and Barbara Richards for their assistance in preparing the materials contained in this book.

We would also like to thank our colleagues at McGraw-Hill for their many contributions, including Laura Libretti, who has provided us with unerring administrative guidance. We are especially grateful to Kelli Christiansen, who, to our good fortune, initiated our relationship with McGraw-Hill and contributed to the realization and betterment of this project at every turn. We thank her for her professional insight, guidance, and direction.

Finally, we are indebted to our families for their unending support. As always, they have seen us through.

John L. Colley, Jr.
Jacqueline L. Doyle
Robert D. Hardie

PART ONE

THE BASICS OF CORPORATE STRATEGY

CHAPTER 1

Introduction to
Corporate Strategy

CAPITALISM, DIVERSIFICATION, AND CORPORATE GOALS

A major strength of the U.S. free-enterprise system is the capability of major corporations to amass large sums of required investment capital. These funds come from both institutional and individual investors who purchase debt and equity instruments based on their assessments of the company's future prospects. The costs of these funds to a firm are largely dependent upon the past financial performance of the firm and the investors' and lenders' expectations of the risks inherent in projected future performance. This contingency leads to a practice in which the chief executive officers (CEOs) of corporations interested in influencing investors make public projections of their corporate goals and their strategies for achieving those goals. These projections, along with the company's past success at achieving its stated goals, allow the investment community to rationally choose preferred investments.

The most important measures of corporate performance assessment are the interrelated goals of return on investment (ROI); growth in revenues, earnings, or market share; and the adequacy of cash flow to fund the growth. The efficacy of corporate goals and performance are measured by comparisons with companies in the same industry, and, ultimately, with the wider array of investment opportunities across the spectrum of all industries.

The natural development of most corporations during the last 30 years has resulted in some degree of diversified, decentralized operations. The tendency to lower investment risk by diversifying a company's businesses and product lines has made it difficult for corporate executives to manage the myriad of operational details in a wide range of businesses. The investment community in recent years has pressured companies to become less diversified by rewarding focused companies with significantly higher multiples of stock price to earnings. In spite of this pressure, the diversified, decentralized form of corporate organization is still the dominant mode of operation of most large, public U.S. companies.

Diversification, despite all its advantages in avoiding risk, has one major disadvantage: the difficulty of achieving reasonably stable corporate results. Each industry has its inherent pattern of investment intensity, gross profit margins, degree of labor intensity, rate of new product development and introduction, prevailing rate of research and development expenses, and degree of market elasticity. Each operating unit (a division or subsidiary company) of a diversified company has a characteristic set of feasible financial results based on the industry competitive structure it faces. The performance of the divisions on the variables listed above leads to a set of boundaries that define reasonable corporate expectations with regard to return on investment, growth, and cash flow.

Achieving high returns on investment in industries that are highly investment-intensive is difficult. So is growing significantly faster than the industry's market growth rate. Finally, growing significantly faster than the market if the product or service is a commodity is almost impossible. Typically, any attempt to capture market share by reducing prices in this situation will lower the prices and margins of all of the competitors, because competitors will meet the lower prices to protect their market shares. It is also axiomatic that fast-growing businesses require injections of cash to grow capacity and to provide the necessary working capital to fund their growth.

Many focused businesses seem to have difficulties achieving high returns on investment, high relative growth rates, and self-sustaining cash flow simultaneously. If the business were to grow rapidly over a long time, it would need continuous injections of cash. If it were required to maintain some level of debt to total capital, it would invariably and continually reach points in time at which its debt would encounter limits imposed by lenders, and it would have to issue additional equity in order to continue to grow. This process would relentlessly dilute the ownership of the company and would be counterproductive from an investor standpoint.

Some businesses with market leadership through new product innovation or through patents are able to earn sufficient profit margins, and the resultant cash flow, to support almost any market growth rate. But such situations are very rare, and they are most often found in so-called high-technology, research-oriented businesses. Finally, investment-intensive businesses producing commodity products or any business facing price pressures from strong foreign competition will find it difficult to earn an attractive ROI.

These challenges, however, are offset in each situation by concomitant advantages to a company with a portfolio of businesses. In spite of their needs for cash, fast-growing businesses provide their corporate parent with the growth for which financial analysts long. Businesses with market leadership provide their parent company with high profit margins. And investment-intensive businesses, in spite of thin margins and low returns on investment, often provide steady, high levels of cash flow, resulting largely from high levels of depreciation. As a result, many companies resist pressures from the financial analysts for more focus and prefer to operate through a portfolio of business units, which brings the mix of desirable results to the corporate totals.

This advantageous combination of performance measures does not necessarily represent synergy among the businesses of the portfolio. Many companies seek synergies among operating divisions, such as supposed advantageous supplier/customer relationships created through vertical integration. The advantages would seem to be the capturing of the supplier margins, which would tend to increase the company's profits. In reality, the disadvantages inherent in attempting to achieve synergy often greatly outweigh the advantages, because of the internal squabbles that naturally arise over fair transfer prices, reasonable inventory levels, and delivery dates.

Many well-run companies have come to realize the power of the free enterprise system in resolving these situations. The divisions are left to do business with one another at their discretion, based on arm's-length relationships, without corporate edicts in regard to transfer prices or schedule dates. Division managements are left to fill their procurement needs on the open market, with a caveat that they should "buy internal," all other things being equal. Supplier divisions must compete by meeting market standards for prices and delivery. One very successful company went so far as to institute a policy that if a division did not sell more than 50 percent of its output on the open market, then another division in the same company purchasing more than 50 percent of its output would subsume it. The general notion throughout this book is that synergies are advantageous, when the free enterprise system is left to work, and the only effective rules are those provided by competition.

This book covers the topic of corporate strategy from the dual perspectives of both the parent company and the operating divisions of a diversified, decentralized corporation. The corporate challenge is to provide an effective set of consistent results over the long term from a given mix of businesses, each of which has some inherent pattern of achievable results. The divisions are charged with producing outstanding results compared to similar companies, their own past performances, and that of other well-run companies. In such a corporation, the results of the total enterprise are very much the sum of the results of the operating units.

Evidently, the only way the corporate office can make significant changes in the important performance measures of return on investment, growth, and cash flow is to make changes in the portfolio of businesses. That is, it can choose to acquire new, more desirable businesses and/or it can choose to divest less-attractive businesses. In the end, its long-term results will be determined by the mix of businesses and their potential for contributing to the crucial performance measures. Corporations that perform superbly will find ready access to equity markets, will enjoy lower interest rates than competitors, and will be able to use strong stock prices to acquire additional businesses. The overriding objective of contemporary corporate management is to enhance shareholder value. That will be the ultimate objective of the corporate strategies discussed in this book.

CORPORATE-LEVEL STRATEGY

In a diversified, decentralized corporate setting, strategy at the corporate level may be narrowed to a choice or set of choices, which are not mutually exclusive. First among these, a corporation may choose to continue operations as an ongoing enterprise with the business units currently in its portfolio. This strategy more or less commits the corporation to the pattern of results reasonably available from the current business units. If the business units compete in attractive industries and are well managed, this strategy may be viable and desirable. The growth of the company is thus committed to the limits imposed by the natural growth rates available to the several business units.

A corporation may instead opt to sell one or more of its current business units.This choice could result from a perception that these units lack long-term prospects consistent with the company's objectives. The decision could follow from environmental or other regulatory requirements that call for extensive capital investments for continued operations in one or more business units. The company may not have the cash for such investments or may not wish to commit the investment at the time. The company may not have the time or resources to focus on a particular division. Either way, selling the unit would bring in cash that could be used in what would be considered more advantageous ways. It may also improve performance relative to the company's specific goals.

A corporation may also choose to spin off one or more of its current business units. Spin-offs offer certain advantages to a company and to its shareholders, as compared to the sales of operating divisions, especially related to taxes. Spin-offs occur when management feels that greater shareholder value can be achieved by separating operations. In such a case, the shares in the newly separated business are distributed pro rata to the holders of the parent company's shares. Because this transaction is considered a substitution of one item of a stipulated value for another item of similar value, it is deemed to create no gain for either party and is, thus, a tax-free exchange. Understandably, spin-offs are becoming increasingly popular because of this advantage. This process allows the individual shareholder to decide whether to sell or hold the new stock, thus controlling the occurrence of a taxable event. Alternatively, a parent company may choose to sell one or more of its businesses, either by negotiation or by auction to the highest bidder. Naturally, a selling price in excess of the book value of the business would create a taxable event. Whether the mechanism is a sale or a spin-off, the result is the same—a leaner, more focused corporation.

Occasionally, a company may find itself in a strategic and/or operational situation from which it cannot readily extricate itself. A competitive advantage formerly enjoyed might have been neutralized by an aggressive competitor. The firm may face prohibitive labor or material costs that are uncontrollable. It may find itself "in play" as a result of an unsolicited offer for its shares. The company may find that its focused market segment is vanishing as a result of shifting consumer trends or substitute products. For these and other reasons, the corporation may conclude that shareholder interests are best served by "going out of business." The company would thus sell out to another company, and its shareholders would receive cash or stock in the acquiring company in return for their shares.

Alternatively, a company may choose to invest cash accumulations into strategic acquisitions. The management may feel that the company should proceed in a different direction and that certain focused acquisitions may enhance the competitive position of one or more of the corporation's business units. This choice precludes simply reinvesting all available cash into existing operations. These acquisitions, if carefully thought out, can improve the company's performance in regard to return on investment, growth, and/or cash flow.

Finally, a company may choose to use its cash accumulations to buy back its own shares. This option has become increasingly popular in recent years as many companies, faced with holding levels of cash beyond their reasonable operating needs, and believing their stock to be underpriced, reason that buying their own shares constitutes the best use of these funds from the shareholder's point of view. The cash accumulates as a result of an imbalance among the company's growth rate, its needs for cash, and its ability to generate cash. After debt is paid down to optimal levels, the cash in excess of internal needs normally earns less than the prevailing ROI from operations. Thus it lowers the overall average ROI for the corporation. It does so because public companies normally invest excess cash only in risk-free government bonds; The management is not expert at investments and companies are not normally formed for the purpose of investing in other companies. We note that the repurchase of shares is effectively a tax-free dividend, increasing the shareholders' investment with no tax penalty.

Many variations or combinations of these corporate-level strategies exist. All essentially constitute the types of actions feasible for the corporate management to undertake to improve performance, as measured by the increase in shareholder value. Most extended efforts to pressure business-unit managers to improve performance are fruitless. Corporate management must establish limits for business units to conform to corporate goals and forgo the common "hockey-stick" effect of promised future improvements. If a business is well-positioned in an attractive industry, and if it is well-managed, then the corporate management must accept the results. If many believe that the unit could be managed better, then a management change is in order. In the final analysis, the corporate performance is largely determined by the performance potential of the several business units.

This determination is, of course, predicated on the premise that corporate overhead is in line with that of other well-run companies. No amount of divisional excellence can overcome the negative effects of a bloated, out-of-control level of corporate overhead expenses and punitive interest charges brought on by excessive levels of corporate debt.

STRATEGIES FOR DIVISIONS AND FOCUSED COMPANIES

The term *division* will be used in this book to stand for such business designations as "subsidiaries," "business units," or stand-alone "focused companies" that may be part of a corporate portfolio. In fact, from corporation to corporation, these terms are used interchangeably. The strategic challenge in a division is quite different from that of its diversified, decentralized parent. The first major distinction between division and parent is that a division must normally obtain any needed cash from its parent company rather than the capital markets. It must prepare detailed plans for its future operations, carefully spelling out its needs for capital expenses and for working capital. It must also determine its product, marketing, and pricing strategies in a way that is consonant with overall corporate goals and objectives.

The details follow from a systematic answering of a series of strategic questions. Does the division intend to grow rapidly or slowly? Is this projected growth rate slower than the market growth rate, at the market growth rate, or faster than the market growth rate? Will the division need to have excess (for now) capacity in place to accommodate the growth? Is the division the cost leader (the low-cost producer) in its industry? Are there structural or other restrictions that limit its ability to be or become the cost leader? Are the restrictions, if any, labor related, supplier related, or management related? Is the division a leader or a follower in the marketplace? Does the division command a premium price for its product, or, does the market dictate the prices? Is the product line a "full" line or a "narrow" line? Through which channels are the products marketed?

Does the quality level of the products meet industry standards, or are the products quality leaders? The answers to these and other strategic questions help define the basic strategies of divisions. Michael Porter defined three basic, generic strategies available to any business that produces goods and services and faces a complex marketplace.[1] These generic strategies are:

- Market a differentiated product

---

1 Michael Porter *Competitive Strategy*, Free Press, New York, 1980, 34–46.

- Focus on, or dominate, a market niche
- Be the low-cost producer

A firm may choose to differentiate its products as sufficiently high in quality to command a premium price. Products can also be differentiated by the diversity of the product line, by the offering of features not matched by competitors, or by their reliability.

A firm may choose to compete in a narrow market niche, such as the standard line of bearings, or the specialty line of bearings. It may choose the lowest-cost market segment or the small (in units), highest-priced segment. It may choose to market a limited line of children's clothes, as contrasted with a full line of clothing for all segments of the population. In addition, the firm may choose a geographic niche, limiting its distribution to a well-defined region, typically prescribed by transportation economics.

A firm also may strive to be the lowest-cost producer of its products. This means that no competitor can produce and deliver an equivalent product at a lower price. To be in this situation provides a firm with many strategic advantages, including the ability to punish competitors by lowering prices, which competitors would have trouble meeting.

Finally, these alternative strategies are not mutually exclusive. Pursuing one generic strategy does not preclude a firm from simultaneously striving to implement the others, although Porter argued that most firms found the successful implementation of a single strategy a daunting task. On the other hand, some companies can set all three strategies in place and execute them effectively and simultaneously, which enables them to become the dominant firms in their industries. Some competitors, however, cannot survive the product, marketing, and pricing advantages that accrue to firms that successfully pursue the three generic strategies simultaneously.

SUMMARY

In diversified, decentralized companies, the strategic questions (problems or opportunities) at the corporate level consist of the following:

- What businesses should the firm be in?
- Should the company be "restructured" through acquisitions and/or divestitures?
- How should the company's ongoing operations be financed?
- Is the level of corporate expenses consistent with that of other well-run companies?

For operating divisions of diversified, decentralized companies, the strategic questions relate to their interfaces with their competitive marketplaces. They must determine which of the three generic strategies they will follow. Will they seek to differentiate their products, attempt to compete in a particular niche, and/or strive to be or to become the low-cost producer?

The bottom line is that the parent corporation and its divisions have very different strategic issues. The corporate office operates in one orbit, facing its set of unique problems and opportunities. The more diversified the corporation, the more difficult it is for corporate executives to understand the detailed problems and opportunities faced by its operating divisions. Division executives, on the other hand, operate in a financial structure created and managed by the corporate office. This setup allows them to create effective divisional marketing and operational strategies that will be of maximum utility in creating value for the shareholders of the parent company.

The remainder of this book addresses most aspects of corporate and divisional strategies. Our primary objective in writing this book has been to clearly set out the dichotomy between strategic issues at the corporate level and the divisional level. In Chapter 2 we begin this process by discussing the pressures that have led to an increasing emphasis on strategic planning.

Review Questions

1. How should corporate goals and objectives be set?
2. Why do most large U.S. companies operate in a diversified set of businesses?
3. What strategic choices are available to the CEO of a diversified, decentralized corporation?
4. What strategies are available to managers of focused companies or operating divisions of large companies?

CHAPTER 2

The Increasing Emphasis on Strategic Planning

THE EVALUATION PROCESS

The fundamental compelling force that leads managers to engage in strategic planning is the eventual appraisal of their performance. Stockholders evaluate the performance of companies in terms of the profits earned, the dividends paid, the market price of the company's stock, and the public image of the company and its management. Customers continually appraise a business's performance in terms of the prices charged for its products, product quality and reliability, and the ability of the organization to meet delivery dates. Vendors demand timely payment of obligations. Government agencies maintain surveillance over operational factors such as market share and pricing policies, antitrust regulations, pollution control, equal employment opportunites, and many others.

Wall Street financial analysts and investors are primarily interested in the long-term earnings of the firm, and bankers evaluate companies in terms of debt repayments, various financial ratios, cash position, and general financial strength. Financial institutions, which are significant players in the market for corporate stocks, employ analysts to guide their investments. The market price of a company's stock is a major determinant of the firm's ability to raise capital by issuing public securities. Financial analysts thus exert considerable influence over the availability of equity funding for a firm. The assessment by bankers of the risk inherent in a firm's operations directly affects the interest rate the firm must pay for borrowed funds.

IDENTIFYING THE MEASURES

What are the principal attributes that the professional evaluators prefer? Consider the most obvious measurable results (or expectations): profits, return on investment, cash flow, growth, and, finally, stability (predictability).

11

The professionals assess the adequacy of the operating results of a business through a complex evaluation of the interrelationships of these attributes. Which of the performance criteria are preferred has changed in the past, with periods in which growth, or return on investment, or then stability were preferred. The measures of financial results have gradually become more sophisticated, with transitions from "earnings" to "earnings per share" to "return on investment" to "cash flow."

The first level of assessment of a company and its management considers the earnings and the return on investment sustained over time, compared with other firms in the same industry and with general industrial performance. A business can report consistently high levels of profitability and not be able to provide internally for its cash needs, particularly in fast-growth situations. Financial analysts and bankers therefore look beyond the levels of profitability reported, to the cash the business would need to sustain its operations in the long term.

If two businesses are each highly profitable relative to comparable companies in their industries, and if both have ample cash flows to fund their operations, then professional analysts will prefer the company with the higher past or potential growth rate in sales, profits, and net worth.

Finally, among companies possessing all the favorable attributes previously described, professional analysts prefer stability, or predictability of results, to volatility.

Financial analysts guide investors in their choices of firms and in the timing of their investments. A need to forecast future profits is inherent in the process of capital formation, because investment decisions are made in the anticipation of future profits, not for past performance. Analysts must depend on top corporate managers for assistance in the process of attempting to forecast future profit levels. Corporate officers regularly provide public projections of anticipated profits and possible problems. These public pronouncements build a degree of credibility (good or bad) for the manager and the company with the investment community. The level of confidence in which the manager and his or her company is held is a major determinant of the company's stock price and its borrowing rate from banks.

Financial analysts prefer a stable and improving earnings pattern, which suggests a high degree of management control. Indeed, in any industry, some companies consistently react to factors in their competitive markets and sustain higher earnings than their competitors, with essentially similar facilities, labor, and raw material costs.

Beyond the figures, the analysts and bankers form opinions regarding the level of their confidence in a firm's management, the potential available in its market segments, its degree of diversification, and other subjective attributes that can't be quantified.

ADDITIONAL COMPLICATING FACTORS

Other factors complicate management's job and mandate careful strategic planning. These factors include the following:

1. *Size of business organizations.* The sheer size of firms, in terms of sales, products, employees, plant locations, and new capital investment requires more-detailed strategic planning to give direction to operations and to monitor performance.

2. *Product proliferation.* The increasing rate of introduction of new products and the general growth of the marketing function have compelled managers to have some method of planning and controlling their product mix. Obsolete products must be eliminated and new products brought to market in a timely fashion to ensure that the firm maintains a stable pattern of profit and cash flow.

3. *Diversification.* Recognition of the risk inherent in dependence on a single or limited product line has led many managers to seek to diversify, either by developing new products or by mergers and/or acquisitions. The need to integrate the numerous diversified activities to produce a controlled pattern of results has increased the need for detailed strategic planning.

4. *Decentralization.* The traditional functional form of management organization (e.g., marketing, finance, operations, engineering) is often unwieldy in its ability to respond in numerous markets with large numbers of product lines. Managers have come to realize that the ability to respond in specific market segments is greatly enhanced by decentralizing, by delegating complete authority to conduct a segment of the business to an autonomous general manager. This decision, in turn, makes the results of the firm, as a whole, depend largely on the sum of the results of its decentralized units. Strategic planning processes and systems provide tools to assist corporate managers in their efforts to plan and control decentralized activities.

5. *Growth of international business.* The rapid spread of business operations around the world has complicated management's strategic tasks in terms of language differences, variations in product codes and standards, facility and skill differences, currency exchange rates and movement restrictions, and legal and other constraints.

6. *Government regulation.* With large stakes at risk in automated facilities, long-range marketing strategy, and guaranteed annual wages and other supplementary unemployment benefits, businesses have to cope with increasing government regulation in

such areas as pollution abatement, safety requirements, and antitrust regulations.

SUMMARY

Each of these factors has complicated top management's job. The demands of the bankers and analysts are unchanged. Companies with strong, sustained profit performances are more readily able to obtain the capital needed for future growth. Some degree of "management of earnings" is feasible through various accounting and financial procedures, within the framework of generally accepted accounting principles. This management of earnings includes the manipulation of closing dates for various financial transactions, the definition of a variety of judgment variables, or the purchase of "sales" or "earnings" via acquisitions. Long-run dependence on such creative accounting methods has been capricious, however, and a number of apparently well-managed companies eventually have exhausted the ability to sustain such manipulations. In the long run, management must plan and control the strategic and operational factors in sufficient detail to produce the preferred results.

Placing a great deal of emphasis on strategic planning does not guarantee success or lead unerringly to the desired results. Unexpected catastrophes as well as serendipitous windfalls have befallen well-managed and poorly managed firms alike. The weight of logic, however, supports the notion that an effective strategic planning process would enhance a firm's ability to achieve favorable results.

Many companies have thus persevered in trying to implement a detailed strategic planning system, in spite of organizational resistance to change and other obstacles. The numerous details that must be managed to provide the strategic direction and operational control required for successful ongoing operations are addressed in subsequent chapters of this book.

Review Questions

1. What competitive factors compel managers to engage in strategic planning?
2. What measures do professional evaluators of corporate performance prefer?
3. What other complicating factors lead to an increasing emphasis on strategic planning?

CHAPTER 3

Strategy, the Old Economy, and the New Economy

INTRODUCTION

A book on corporate strategy in the year 2001 must address the impressive "new economy" that developed in the United States and the world in the decade of the 1990s. For most of the past 100 years, the economy of the United States largely consisted of a nucleus of large industrial companies and financial institutions, referred to as the Fortune 500 companies. For many decades, this group of corporations led the country in output, employment, new-job creation, and capital investment. Most corporate laws, governmental regulations, and rules governing monopolistic and antitrust behavior were written and administered with the "old economy" in mind.

The strategic objectives for these old-economy firms have evolved into a hierarchy of goals, led today by the need to increase shareholder value. The primary means of increasing shareholder value is to increase the profitability of the firm relative to the investment capital employed, which is usually measured by the return on shareholders' equity. A firm that outperforms its competitors on this measure normally will command a premium share price. Such a firm also will enjoy a cash-balancing growth rate greater than that of its competitors, meaning that the firm can grow faster than its competitors without having to seek cash externally. This concept is explained in detail in Chapter 9.

In previous chapters, we have discussed both aspects of corporate strategy, the notions of portfolio management for diversified, decentralized companies, and the three basic generic strategies for divisions in focused businesses. Now we introduce another complicating issue: Is there, or should there be, a difference in the strategies of the companies engaged in the new economy as opposed to the old economy?

ENTER THE NEW ECONOMY

In the 1990s, a strong new economic force exerted itself. It was led by a group of firms that specialized in telecommunications, network switching devices, Internet servers, Internet search engines, computer chips, computers, software, and cellular telephones, among others. Employees of these firms spoke a new language, replete with novel terms peculiar to the new environment. The business "rules" by which U.S. industry had maneuvered for most of the past century suddenly seemed obsolete. The stability so cherished by the financial investment community was pushed aside by these new businesses that seemed to offer unlimited potential along with unfathomable risks.

In the early 1980s, the Internet was considered a network for use mostly by the military establishment and the scientific community. Few individuals or firms considered the possibility for commercial applications of the Internet, which was publicly owned. Firms with locations around the world slowly began to understand the power of information transfer through local and wide area networks and electronic mail, and new applications developed rapidly. The Internet developed into the core of the new economy, which has numerous sectors that have become intertwined to provide seamless business, consumer, educational, and other applications for use around the world. The personal computer, a commonplace new-economy device, has provided access to the Internet and to other services as well, via a direct connection to one of the networks or through Internet Service Providers (ISPs).

THE IMPACT OF THE NEW ECONOMY

The expansive growth in real terms of new-economy products and services has been enhanced by the rapid obsolescence of products by new technological developments. The ever-increasing new demand is augmented by large sales of replacement equipment and upgrades. Industries with sales that relate to the growth of the personal computer industry have benefited extensively from this state of affairs.

A crucial problem with many companies in the new economy, however, is that many of them have scant revenues, and profits may not be expected for many years. In fact, in 2000, one firm went public without any revenues. Was the initial public offering (IPO) successful? The firm raised more than a billion dollars, with its shares more than doubling from the original price on the first day. The IPO was recognized as the largest in monetary terms to that point in time for a U.S. company that had yet to report any revenues. Shares of the stock soared the first day, reaching as high as $98 before closing at approximately $85. At that price, this firm with no revenues, no earnings, and three customers possessed a market capitalization in excess of $28 billion.

THE NEW ECONOMY: REVOLUTION OR HYPE?

The aura pervading the industries of the new economy brings to mind similar developments in the past. In these situations, a new idea or a new technology would surface that was perceived to have the potential to change the way business was conducted. The product or service would enjoy rapidly growing demand for a time, and the firm's share price would escalate, but eventually the mania would come to an end. The growth rate would slow, the firm's stock price would plummet, and the fad would subside.

In some situations, a product was not even required to create a mania. Sometimes a rumor of a cure for some medical malady or the perceived first-mover advantage into an unknown market would be enough to create a similar frenzy. These situations often resolved themselves, as investors would eventually come to understand a firm's profit potential and value its shares accordingly. The U.S. investment community has seen such manias on a number of previous occasions. Railroads, automobiles, radios, and biotechnology created impressive corporate valuations, based on projections that the introduction of these particular products would revolutionize the way business and life were conducted. Some firms in these industries failed miserably. Those firms that succeeded, however, proved to be long-term industry leaders and provided strong returns to their shareholders.

The potential of the new economy has often been compared to two such historical "movements": the tulip-bulb craze of the late 1500s and early 1600s and the radio craze of the 1920s.

The Tulip-Bulb Craze

In the late 1500s and early 1600s, tulips became very popular in Holland. Certain bulbs developed colorful stripes that caused the bulbs to command a higher price in the market, and the prices of these bulbs escalated rapidly. The frenzy over tulips grew and eventually took on an added dimension when speculation entered the tulip-bulb craze, as merchants began trying to guess which bulbs would sell best. They felt confident in purchasing extra inventory at any price to meet the public's expected demand. Concurrently, the merchants raised their prices to adjust for their rising costs. The belief was that the prices of tulips would continue to rise, and that Holland would become the worldwide source for these types of bulbs.

As the profits escalated for some, the desire to be "in the game" increased for others. Methods were developed to allow even the lowest-income classes an opportunity to participate. A call option was introduced that allowed buyers to purchase the right to buy bulbs in the future at a particular price. If the bulbs had gone up in value by the call date of the option, the owner of the call option exercised the right to the bulbs, buying them at the option price and selling them at the new market price. The investor realized the difference as profit.

The Dutch began selling anything they could to buy bulbs and participate in the mania, with hopes of getting rich quickly. Prices continued to soar, but eventually investors began to sell their investments in tulip bulbs to garner their profits. Mass selling then ensued, despite assurances from the Dutch government that the tulip markets were strong. But the fall in prices continued, bankruptcies resulted in large numbers, and tulips eventually sold for the price of onions.[1]

History indicates that very few won in the game of Tulipmania. The speculative and frenzied tulip market caused the Dutch economy to go into a major depression. Even those merchants and speculators who had profited greatly faced the depression in Holland along with everyone else. The frenzy surrounding the "new economy" at the turn of the twenty-first century caused numerous skeptics to refer to investing in Internet companies as Tulip.com.

Radio Mania

The tulip mania reflected a people swept up by the "hype" of a single product. The "radio craze" of the early 1900s more accurately foreshadowed the current mania of the Internet, not only in related stock price appreciations but also in its overall importance to American business. Eventually, both radio in the mid-1920s and the Internet in the late 1990s came to be viewed as a way of reaching every possible consumer through advertising. Revenues from the sales of radio receivers and components increased rapidly from 1922 to 1929, and the share prices of radio-related stocks surged.

As radios made their way into a large segment of American homes, the remainder served as strategic "growth potential," providing crucial "market potential" that encouraged large expenses for research and development (R&D) and for manufacturing capacity. This implied demand was similar to that created today by the number of homes that do not currently possess Internet access. Significant growth prospects typically spur any market, and such was the case with radio, especially after it was introduced into the automobile. Industries emerged up and down the supply chain in support of radio, and investors took notice.

Yet the radio boom soon crashed as a result of several factors. First, the stock market crash of 1929 destroyed the U.S. population's disposable income and the feeling of good fortune that had spurred radio purchases. In addition, many who had invested in the stock market for the first time discovered that the market could go down as well as up and that stocks could not continue to go up indefinitely. In fact, the market crash of 1929

---

1. Burton Malkiel, *A Random Walk Down Wall Street*, W.W. Norton and Company, New York, 1996.

eliminated 90 percent of the major radio manufacturer's market capitalization, taking the share price back to single digits.[2]

Greenspan and the New Economy

The future of the Internet, and the extremely high valuations realized by Internet firms, caught the attention of the U.S. government and Federal Reserve (Fed) Chairman Alan Greenspan. The Fed chairman had been cautious about the large increases in valuations, as measured by the stock-market indexes [the Dow Jones or the Standard & Poor's (S&P) 500] during the late 1990s. During an open session of the Senate Finance Committee in 1999, Greenspan was asked where he thought the new economy was headed in the long run and how much of the Internet phenomenon was based on sound fundamentals versus how much of it was based on hype.

Greenspan replied: "You wouldn't get hype working if there wasn't something fundamentally, potentially sound under it. The issue really gets to the increasing evidence that the significant part of the distribution of goods and services in this country is going to move from conventional channels into some form of Internet system, whether it is retail, goods or services, or a variety of other things. The size of that particular market is so huge that you have pie-in-the-sky types of potentials for a lot of different vehicles. And undoubtedly, some of these small companies for which stock prices are going through the roof will succeed. And they very well may justify even higher prices. The vast majority are almost sure to fail; that's the way the markets tend to work in this regard."[3] So, as Chairman Greenspan described it, inevitably many firms will move to the Internet as a way of distributing their goods and services. Some of these firms will win, and some will lose, but the ones that win may win big because the market potential is huge.

SHAREHOLDER VALUE IN THE NEW ECONOMY

Would the financial exuberance within the investment community for new-economy companies during the past decade qualify as a genuine new direction for investors, or was it simply a more recent manifestation of the "crazes" or "manias" described above? Our conclusion is that the recent run-up in the values of new-economy stocks, as illustrated by the IPO described above, fully qualifies as a "craze," down to the recent "correction" of the NASDAQ Stock Market. In the first quarter of 2001, the NASDAQ Index was down approximately 60 percent from its peak, with much of the "correction" involving funds moving from less-credible new-economy companies to

---

2. James Lardner, "Ask Radio Historians About the Internet," *U.S. News and World Report*, January 1999, 48–52.

3. CNBC Live Broadcast, "Chairman Greenspan Testifies Before the Senate Finance Committee," January 28, 1998.

other firms with stronger financial performances, mostly to companies of the old economy. The run-up in the NASDAQ Composite Index over the previous three years and the subsequent correction can be seen in Exhibit 3.1.

Regarding value creation, among premium, diversified old-economy companies, many have chosen to include in their portfolios only businesses that were either number one or number two in their respective markets. Others have chosen firms that had exemplary gross margins, showed strong returns on equity, or were undervalued based on time-tested investment analysis principles such as intrinsic value. But are these definitions applicable to the new economy? The search for excellent firms has proven to be much more difficult in the new economy because intrinsic value, market share, profits, and even revenues often do not exist for many firms.

The recent correction in the NASDAQ Stock Market reflected a refocusing by the investment community on the long-established criteria by which companies had come to be valued: profits, cash flow, and growth, as described earlier. Firms without the preferred financial performance found their stock prices hammered by the sudden refocusing of attention. This development indicated that the reaction of investors to the new-economy craze had completed the cycle from unbridled exuberance to skepticism. New-economy companies seeking capital are now being judged in much the same way as old-economy companies: by the soundness of their strategies and the attractiveness of their financial results.

STRATEGIES FOR THE NEW ECONOMY

The recent shift by both institutional and individual investors to expect strong performances by new-economy firms on conventional values suggests

EXHIBIT 3.1

NASDAQ Composite Index 1997–2000.

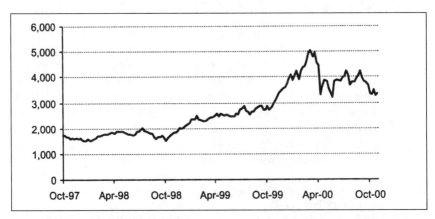

Source: The NASDAQ Stock Market.

that the expansive stock price–to–earnings multiples of new-economy stocks were unsustainable. Holding new-economy CEOs to the time-tested measures of performance has brought some semblance of rationality back to the financial markets. Now the CEO of a new-economy company must derive, implement, and articulate strategies that are clear, effective, and profitable. Let us consider some of the strategies that have been widely employed within the new economy. Although these strategies have been afforded colorful names by their advocates, all are derivatives of one or more of the three generic strategies described earlier.

The Roll-Up Strategy

One strategy employed by new-economy companies has been to acquire other high-technology firms at a rapid rate and, through that process, gain the services of talented people who might be the only "sustainable competitive advantage" in the industry. After a critical mass of talented people has been accumulated, new-economy firms then offer their shares to the public. The shares in the company can then be used to acquire (roll up) competitors to build a dominant firm in a given technological or marketing segment. This roll-up, or acquisition strategy, has been popular in both the new and old economies.

Category Killers

Some Internet retailing firms have sought to become the dominant leader in a particular market segment (category), such as the sale of books, compact discs, videos, toys, or perhaps all of the above. Expectations of this strategy include the efficient delivery of service, advantageous timing of customer payments, no retail outlets, lower inventories, and lower sales and administrative expenses. Many companies employing this strategy are under increasing pressure to become profitable.

The Direct Model

By employing the Internet, either new- or old-economy retailers can attempt to reach consumers directly, thus eliminating the distributor and the distributor's margin. The most successful direct model has been that of Dell Computers, which has created impressive shareholder value through its model of selling personal computers directly to consumers. Most of its competitors have had to follow with similar strategies.

Brand Building

Intel Corporation employed a brand-building marketing strategy with "Intel Inside." The chips of other manufacturers might be shown to be as fast and as effective as Intel chips, but many customers have come to equate the presence of an Intel chip inside their computers with higher quality. This demonstrates the power of a brand image, for which advantages may continue long after they are warranted.

Market Dominance

Another strategy is demonstrated by Microsoft's "market dominance" in the operating system market. The operating system is one of the critical components that every personal computer must have to operate, and Microsoft's products have become the standard for nearly every personal computer on the market.

Hedging

Another strategy involves attempting to be involved in as many new-economy sectors as possible, to hedge a firm's position in the industry. Only a few years ago, browsers were thought to be the key to the new economy, then portals, then business-to-consumer capabilities, then business-to-business prowess, and then bandwidth technical capability. Some firms hedge their bets by either developing technology or acquiring it in several of the new-economy sectors.

The Agnostic Approach

Some firms develop and sell products that support the basic functions of the Internet rather than any product or vendor. Cicso Systems successfully implemented this strategy, along with the other network switch providers. Other "backbone" providers, such as telecommunications firms, also supply capabilities that are essential to all Internet-related activities.

Betting on the Standards

Some firms attempt to forecast which technology standards will be adopted by the user community and by standards organizations. One firm did this with the standards for cellular phones. Once it became known that the likely standard would be adopted by the cellular phone industry and that the company was poised to capitalize on its strategy, its stock price rose more than forty times in one calendar year.

STRATEGIES UNIQUE TO THE NEW ECONOMY

The new-economy strategies we have described thus far are interesting but not especially novel. They are all variations of the generic strategies described in previous chapters, and they illustrate interesting varieties of pursuing or gaining position to pursue niches, differentiation, or being the low-cost producer. We see that the demands of the investment community are now essentially the same for both the old and new economies.

There are two trends in strategic decision making that have become predominant uniquely in the new economy. First, the majority of the firms and industries that make up the new economy have avoided vertical integration and diversification, both of which characterize many firms in the old economy. Perhaps because of the complex technologies pursued, firms in these industries have been very niche-oriented, with narrowly focused products and services. This focus reflects the difficulty in mastering even one such new-economy technology. Further, the industries have been tiered vertically from components to subassemblies to systems.

The component suppliers tend to stay out of the subassembly and systems businesses, and the systems producers have stayed out of the component businesses. This industry structure has had advantages for both parties. Component developers can move rapidly along in developing radically new devices, with the assurance that the systems developers will adopt superior components as soon as they are available. Systems suppliers are free to adopt superior new components, without hesitation, because they have no heavy capital investments (read "sunk costs") in component manufacturing facilities. A few companies have attempted to vertically integrate, producing their own components, but most such strategies have eventually placed the company in an untenable competitive position.

This mode of industry structure began in the electronics industry, with all elements of the industry benefiting from the structure and providing decades of continuous development of a myriad of new and continuously improving products. Almost all of the sectors of the new economy are similarly structured. Specialized firms continue to develop and market monitors, software, modems, hard drives, chips, memory devices, and so on, with other specialized firms assembling the computers. Both sets of manufacturers benefit, consumers benefit, and the financial analysts prefer the focused companies. There is a free flow of the latest technologies into the products we buy. The relative power and other capabilities of the computers we purchase are enhanced by the new technological developments and the lower relative prices that derive from effective competition in both tiers of the industry. And finally, the investment community more readily understands the focused firms.

The second strategic trend unique to the new economy was the use of very early IPOs of stock to raise capital to finance the expensive development of the many new technologies. The conventional approach to financing such activities had been through venture capitalists, who have been willing to assume the considerable risks attendant to new technologies in return for large proportions of equity in these firms. The dot-com mania described previously provided an alternative avenue for emerging firms to raise large amounts of capital. Given the unparalleled appetite of the investing public for shares in these emerging industries, and with the

willing help of investment bankers, new-economy firms were able to go
directly to the investing public to raise capital. Such efforts were eventually so successful that some firms found themselves raising more capital
than they thought they needed, as we saw in the example of the high-flying
IPO described previously. The recent correction in the NASDAQ Stock
Market, however, has damaged the early IPO as a viable strategy. New-
economy firms are thus in the position of having to depend more on venture capitalists for needed funds, making the new economy look more and
more like the old economy.

SUMMARY

The revolutionary high-technology products of the new economy have
changed the way we work, shop, and live. Products have always come and
gone, and firms have emerged and vanished. Many firms once listed on the
Fortune· 500 have disappeared, replaced by firms with better products,
strategies, and business models. There is a relentless turnover among the
successful firms; a birth-and-death process involving the survival of the
fittest, in consonance with the best traditions of our capitalist, free-enterprise
system. This volatility has been and will continue to be even more pro-
nounced among the firms in the high-technology sector.

There will doubtless be some impressive winners in the new economy. Because it is not clear how many winners will be in a particular sector,
it is important for a new-economy firm to be a leader among its competitors. Financial analysts addressing the new economy have applied the old-
economy adage of the importance of a business being number one or number two in its respective markets. New-economy managers trying to focus
in a rapidly changing marketplace are using time-tested principles and concepts from the mature old economy. The mania has passed, the hype has sub-
sided, and traditional wisdom seems to have prevailed for the time being.
In the final analysis, we have found that there are few differences between
the strategies successfully employed in the new economy and the old economy. In Chapter 4, we will discuss the strategic planning process that is
essential, regardless of the "economy" within which a firm competes.

Review Questions

1. Is there, or should there be, a difference in the strategies of companies engaged in the new economy as opposed to the old
   economy?
2. Is the new economy truly a revolution, or is it simply "hype"?
3. How does the structure of high-technology industries contribute
   to the continuous development of new-economy companies?

CHAPTER 4

The Strategic Planning Process

INTRODUCTION

This chapter covers concepts and terminology related to corporate strategy formulation and implementation. The strategic-planning phase of corporate strategy formulation consists of looking toward the future, providing direction to the firm in terms of the businesses in which the firm chooses to be engaged, and setting appropriate goals and objectives. Strategic planning must be augmented by a detailed operational planning system that enhances the likelihood that the firm's operating units will achieve the desired results. With appropriate goals and objectives set and strategies for achieving them in place, the firm must decide how to organize to provide the best environment for achieving the strategic goals and objectives through the implementation of the strategy.

The CEO of a company must define the authority relationships through which the business will be conducted. This task involves delegating responsibility for certain aspects of the business to specific individuals or organizational components. A functional organization usually denotes highly centralized control of the business. In such an organization, the marketing of all of the firm's products is the responsibility of a marketing executive whose department generates the company's operating revenues. Similarly, the manager of manufacturing or operations is responsible for the delivery of all of the products or services of the firm and thus manages most of the firm's assets and costs. The engineering and finance functions are also conducted centrally. In a centralized, functional organization, revenues and costs are not considered jointly except at the level of the president. The responsibility for profits in such an organization clearly resides with the president, who must rely on a combination of sales efforts to produce revenues and expense budgets for cost control to provide a total result that generates a profit for the organization.

The size and complexity of operations have led many companies to decentralize the management of the enterprise into a number of profit centers, which then tend to be functionally organized. In such an organization, the profit-center manager and his or her staff have the responsibility for conducting the firm's business in a segment of the company's markets. The CEO determines the broad direction for the company, sets goals and objectives for the divisions, and makes changes in top-level executive personnel when necessary. The overall company profitability is dependent on the performance of the divisions. The functionally organized firm usually is referred to as a *decentralized organization*, and the divisions are sometimes described as *profit centers*.

Companies or divisions that engage in long-running projects, or those that have several different product lines within a profit center, may use a project, product-line, or matrix organization structure. In these types of organizations, specialized managers are designated to coordinate the activities of the functional departments with regard to a given project or product line. These specialized managers report to the general manager and are expected to plan for and monitor functional operations to ensure the profitable operation of their product-line segments of the business.

Many companies find it necessary to change and adjust their organizations from time to time. The CEO attempts to accommodate customers, the management talent available, the environment, and internal problems. He or she must appoint people to manage the organizational activities created as well as continually appraise their performance relative to agreed-upon goals and objectives. Finally, a control system must be in place to compare results with plans and ensure that appropriate corrective actions are taken when objectives are not being met.

THE STRATEGIC PLANNING PROCESS

Businesses operate through a continuous strategic planning process of setting goals, assessing performance, taking corrective action, and monitoring results to ensure improved performance. Management must detect problems and identify new opportunities through an effective control system and/or through their personal knowledge of the business, as illustrated in Exhibit 4.1.

When a symptom of a problem or a new business opportunity is detected, management must ensure its careful definition, which requires a detailed insight into the workings of the business. The creative portion of the decision-making process involves deriving feasible alternative strategies to capitalize on the opportunities or counteract the problems that have been identified. The more alternatives that can be put forth for investigation, the more effective the action taken is likely to be. Conversely, if the number of alternatives explored is limited, the best approach to the situation might be overlooked.

E X H I B I T   4.1

The strategic planning process.

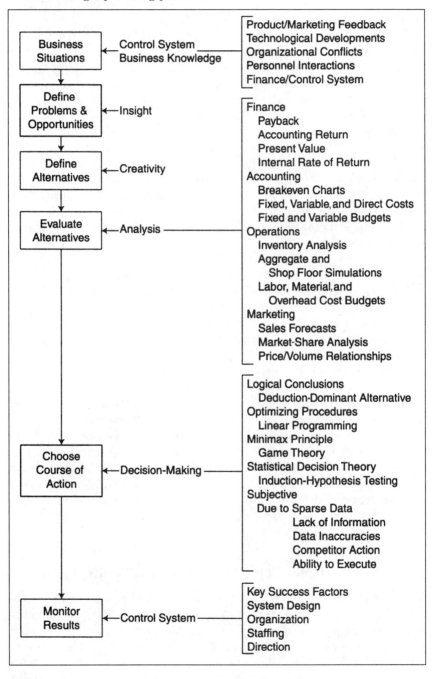

Each of the alternative courses of action must be analyzed to determine its advantages and disadvantages and its economic cost and effectiveness. The additional revenues, likely costs, and necessary investment must be estimated and the likely results calculated.

The manager must choose a course of action with which to react to the problem or opportunity. There are many ways to make this decision, including reacting to an overwhelming set of circumstances with ample backup data, conducting an in-depth analysis of relevant data, or literally playing a hunch. Governmental authorities may require a pollution-abatement investment if a facility is to continue operating. A proposal for a new tool may provide a sufficient cost reduction to recover the investment in a year. In such cases, the manager has little difficulty choosing a course of action. In other cases, where the preferred course is not evident, the process of analysis is more difficult and risky. In many situations, there is never going to be enough data, and the manager must speculate about the future actions of customers and competitors. Occasionally, the manager may guess correctly on the external factors and misjudge the ability of the organization to execute the plan.

Lower-level and more straightforward decisions are more apt to be accompanied by sufficient data to support the use of analytical tools and techniques. Conversely, higher-level, more strategic decisions normally are made in an environment of insufficient data and the inability to estimate accurately the actions of competitors, trends in the market, or the organization's ability to execute the strategy. These are the defining strategic decisions for corporations. The ability to handle these situations is what determines whether CEOs are effective or ineffective. CEOs who can consistently make successful strategic decisions in these situations are priceless.

The final task in the process of strategy formulation and implementation is to ensure that actions happen as they have been planned. The manager must determine the key success factors for the organization and provide for the continuous monitoring of results through effective control systems. He or she must rely on the existing control system and his or her knowledge of the business to address the myriad of complicating factors and achieve the desired results. This brings us back to the detection of problems or opportunities, which begins again the process of strategy formulation and implementation.

ESTABLISHING CORPORATE STRATEGIC GOALS

To establish achievable corporate goals and objectives, we must first consider the ultimate reason for a corporation's existence. Corporations primarily exist to provide investors an adequate return on their investment. With this in mind, let us revisit the most obvious measurable results as given in Chapter 1. They were, in a logical sequence based on precedence relationships, profits, return on investment, cash flow, growth, and stability (or predictability). Although the emphasis on one or more of these measures may lessen or intensify over time, they collectively represent the most important measures for corporate performance. The most obvious answer to the question of which result to prefer is that we would want to maximize all of them.

As pointed out in Chapter 1, external agencies that appraise the performance of public companies gradually have become more sophisticated in the measures they prefer, with transitions from profits (earnings), to earnings per share, to ROI, to cash flow. The fundamental problem for the diversified, decentralized corporation is to manage the results of operations to achieve both high levels of each performance measure and balance among them. This challenge is heightened by the numerous complicating factors cited in Chapter 1.

Because trying to achieve synergy among the divisions (or business units) is assumed to be at least as troublesome as it is constructive, corporate results are tied to the sum of the results of the several divisions. Each division has an individual set of desirable and achievable goals with respect to profits, ROI, and growth, and if corporate results don't meet the expectations of corporate executives, the only feasible remedy is to change the mix of divisions in the corporate portfolio through acquisitions and/or divestitures.

Consider the corporate expectation for profits. If each division or operating unit is performing in an outstanding fashion compared to competitors or comparable companies, corporate edicts attempting to increase profits are likely to be counterproductive. If the level of profits emanating from each unit is as strong as can reasonably be expected, then the total corporate profit level is as strong as it is likely to get with the given portfolio of divisions.

Let us consider ROI. Again, the current operating divisions compete in a set of industries and markets with characteristic degrees of asset intensity and requirements for working capital. If each division is performing at an outstanding level with regard to asset management, compared to competitors and comparable companies, then the total corporate assets, and the concomitant return on assets, are as strong as they are apt to get.

We also need to consider growth, given that each operating division faces a competitive situation in which its industry has some prevailing growth rate. The industry may be a "mature" one, in which the growth is closely tied to the rate of population growth, such as the appliance industry or the soap industry. In such a situation, invariably the best strategy is to hold a division's market share by growing at the market rate. In the case of the fast-growing industries, such as the computer industry or the cellular phone industry, the division may choose to grow at a rate less than, equal to, or greater than the market rate. If a division in a fast-growing industry chooses to grow at less than the market rate for any reason, the value of the division arguably would diminish over time; the better strategy would be to sell the division immediately, because its value is likely to decline in the future. If the division grows at the market rate or faster (increasing market share), the parent company will need to provide the cash needed to fund the rapid growth.

What total corporate performance can reasonably be expected? The resulting corporate performance on each measure will be the sum of the results from the divisions, or a sort of weighted average of the divisions in certain measures, combined with the cost of the corporate office. The key question for corporate management is, "How will this composite set of financial results play with the external evaluators of the company's performance?"

Considering these results, together with their assessment of the company's long-term prospects, the financial analysts will have an important role in determining the price at which the company's stock will trade. If the company wishes to increase the valuation of its shares, it must improve its performance with regard to the key performance factors, and changing the businesses in its portfolio would be the most likely method for doing that. The company would trade away or sell one or more of the divisions that are performing less effectively than others and/or acquire additional businesses whose performance would enhance the corporate results.

And finally, what stock price multiple should be sought? Many investment managers seek to lessen the risk in their portfolios by holding shares in a variety of industries. The shares of the leading performer within each industry are likely to be in demand, leading to stock price multiples greater than the averages within their industries. As a result, the first decision for the management of a firm is whether it will strive to be a leader or a follower within its industry. A straightforward comparison of the company's results to those of its competitors will reveal the inherent stock price likely to follow from its existing portfolio of operating units.

A very small number of diversified, decentralized companies transcend these stock price levels because their performances are truly outstanding, compared to the many thousands of public companies. These companies enjoy multiples of share price–to–earnings greater than 20, meaning investors pay more than 20 times the earnings per share of the company to purchase and own the stock. A general rule of thumb is that these stock price levels are awarded only to firms that consistently, over a long time period, earn returns on equity greater than 20 percent and grow earnings per share at a rate greater than 15 percent per year, compounded. Very few diversified old-economy firms consistently exceed both of these criteria and achieve stock price multiples greater than 20. As we described in Chapter 3, the irrational exuberance on the part of investors for shares in new-economy firms has disappeared, at least for now, and those companies will, for the most part, have to meet the performance criteria that have been developed by investors over many decades.

The conclusion is that, at the corporate level, a company must choose its fundamental goals with regard to aspirations for its share price. Then, it must choose to compete in a set of businesses from which the desired level of performance can be expected. Finally, it must ensure, through its strategic planning control system, that the divisions perform to their potentials. Major adjustments to the company's performance can most often be achieved only by altering the makeup of the company (i.e., restructuring).

SETTING PROFIT CENTER GOALS AND OBJECTIVES

Establishing overall, long-term objectives and strategy is the first step in any focused company or division planning exercise. Strategies can be offensive or defensive. Offensively, they can be directed at capturing market share from competitors, opening new markets, or expanding existing ones. Alternatively, they can be devised to protect the existing situation and defend against competition. Strategy must be formulated with recognition of existing outside influences, including those brought on by the overall economic situation of the company and its industry. Strategy formulation also must recognize an organization's strengths and weaknesses. Finally, strategies should reflect the personal interests and desires of the company's owners and management.

Translating Strategic Objectives into Planning Goals

A company's strategic objectives are usually expressed in general terms. Before an operational plan can be developed, these strategic objectives must be refined into planning goals. The process of converting strategic objectives into planning goals is illustrated in Exhibit 4.2. Are the derived goals realistic and attainable with a reasonable degree of risk? Consider the planning goal in Exhibit 4.2 of improving return on assets from 12.8 percent to 20.0 percent. Management must question the means by which the return on assets would be improved. What specific new products, advertising programs, inventory-reduction programs, scheduling developments, and/or new facilities (perhaps automation) will be developed to bring about the improved results? After sufficient examination to ensure that each goal is feasible, management adopts a set of planning goals for input into the next stage of the planning process.

Return on Investment

To devise more detailed operational goals, a return-on-asset goal would be separated into two factors: the profit on sales and the sales-to-assets ratio, also called the *asset turnover rate*. Thus:

$$\frac{Profit}{Assets} = \frac{Profit}{Sales} \times \frac{Sales}{Assets}$$

In a long-range plan, the improvement in return on assets projected in Exhibit 4.2 would be scheduled in detail, year by year, as shown in Exhibit 4.3.

The components of the return-on-sales ratio and the turnover rate then must be planned in greater detail. Profit as a percentage of sales is highly dependent on the extent of competition in the industry, the degree of labor intensity, characteristic wage and material costs, and overhead costs. The turnover rate for a product line is largely a function of the output per dollar of capital achievable in a given industry. Thus, the more capital-intensive any industry, the more difficult it is to achieve a high turnover rate. On the other hand, within a given industry, the relative turnover rate among the competing companies is manageable through the organization's scheduling efficiency, inventory control, wage and work-rule systems, facility utilization, workforce levels, and so forth.

Cash Flow

A profit center's operating results and the changes in its financial structure can be summarized to provide a measure of the firm's cash flow. The profit after tax that is retained in the business (not paid out in dividends) and depreciation are typical sources of cash. Planned capital expenditures and

E X H I B I T   4.2

Translation of strategic objectives into planning goals.

Strategic Objectives	Planning Goals
1. To improve return on assets	1. Increase return on net assets (after taxes) from 12.8% to 20%
2. To increase overall profit	2. Increase overall profit margin from 4% to 7%
3. To increase sales by: (a) Improving market penetration in existing markets (b) Opening up new markets, diversification	3. (a) Product A: increase market penetration from 15% to 20% Product B: increase market penetration from 20% to 25% (b) Move product from development to production (planned market penetration, 5%) Purchase a company in the XYZ industry
4. To increase manufacturing productivity	4. Purchase new equipment Establish a methods engineering department
5. To improve management–union relationships	5. Establish new industrial relations department and examine management's approach to labor problems

EXHIBIT 4.3

Projected return on investment.

Year	Return on Sales, %	Turnover Rate	Return on Assets, %
1	8.0	1.6	12.8
2	8.5	1.7	14.5
3	9.0	1.8	16.2
4	9.5	1.9	18.0
5	10.0	2.0	20.0

additional working capital required for growth in sales require cash. The "sources" must be greater than the "uses" if a firm is to have a positive cash flow. It is possible for a successful and profitable business to reach an untenable cash position if the new capital required to support growth is greater than the cash generated. Analytical relationships among cash flow, growth, and investments are developed in Chapter 9. These relationships should aid in the establishment of feasible, self-reinforcing sets of operating goals.

THE COMPARISON PROCESS

How are realistic goals set? For the most part, goals must be derived from internal comparisons of one operating unit with another, with past performance, or by external comparisons with similar businesses. Comparing operating results to goals provides an indication of the level of current performance. If results are below expectations, management must decide whether the business is being run poorly or whether the goals themselves are unrealistic. The comparison process must assess the strategic position of the business as well as the details of operating performance.

As shown in Exhibit 4.1, the control stage of the strategic planning process compares results with goals or targets and notes exceptions for corrective action. Control activities take place throughout the organization at an overall level and at a detailed level in each department. At a profit-center level, control must be exercised to ensure that the product, marketing/pricing, and manufacturing strategies are realistic and provide a framework for successful business operations. With the proper strategies in place, the organization still faces the more difficult task of controlling the numerous and interrelated low-level details that are essential to providing a consistently profitable operation. The terms *labor cost control, materials control, production control, inventory control, quality control,* and *facilities control* are used widely to designate organizations, systems, or procedures intended to aid management in this task.

PRODUCT, MARKET, AND PRICING STRATEGIES

As mentioned previously, the top level of management control occurs at the corporate or profit-center level where management must assess the relative performance of the three basic business functions: marketing, engineering, and manufacturing. When the product, marketing, and pricing strategies are properly synchronized with the cost base, a business is under "control" from a top-level standpoint. If a business is known to be in trouble, or if trouble is suspected as a result of an assessment of performance, analysis must provide a means for determining whether the essential functions are providing their respective contributions to success:

- Engineering must provide product leadership.
- Marketing must provide marketplace leadership.
- Manufacturing/operations must provide cost and quality leadership.

No amount of manufacturing or operations methods work, materials selection, quality control, or marketing expertise can offset the deleterious effects of a poorly designed product. Similarly, a well-engineered product that is manufactured effectively, at a low cost, can be "given away" in the market place by an inept marketing function. And finally, superb engineering and marketing cannot offset poor manufacturing or operations, where the majority of costs, assets, and people are found.

A COST-EFFECTIVENESS ANALYSIS

Management must have an orderly framework to assist in the assignment of responsibility for profit problems to the functions. A graphical procedure illustrates an approach to this circuitous problem. A firm must view its products in comparison with competitors' products on scales of the cost to the customer and product effectiveness.

In Exhibit 4.4, the customer would prefer a product at point A to one at point B, because he or she would choose strictly on price if the products were considered equally effective. The customer would also prefer C to B, because the more effective product would be preferred if both products were equally priced.

In every industry a product must meet some minimum standards of safety and reliability, so a line should be added to each graph to represent the codes and standards that prescribe the minimum level of product effectiveness that can be marketed. There is some lowest feasible cost at which any given level of product effectiveness can be delivered consistently, and this minimum cost rises as a producer markets a more effective product. These two considerations are shown in Exhibit 4.5.

The top-level planning and control sequence begins with the determination of the product, market, and pricing strategies. Does the management intend to be a leader or a follower in the market served? Will the organiza-

E X H I B I T 4.4

Customer preference diagram.

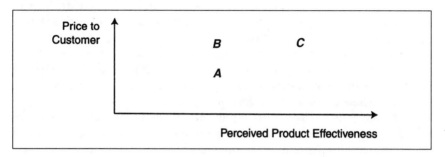

E X H I B I T 4.5

Effect of manufacturing constraints.

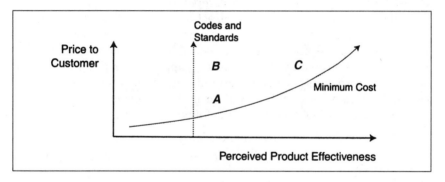

tion work toward the marketing of a superior product that will sell at a premium price? Is the product intended to be equally as effective as competitors' products? Does the management expect to segment the market and strive to gain a dominant market share of the differentiated segment, whether it is the discount-house segment, the low-priced segment, or the high-quality segment? Regardless of the product, market, and pricing strategies chosen, the role of manufacturing or operations is to produce the required product at a lower cost than that of competitors.

If management believes that product-line profitability is unsatisfactory, it must first determine the following:

1. Is the product engineered to meet the strategic intent?
2. If yes, is the marketing function as effective as competitors'?

If the answer is Yes to both questions, then resolution of the profitability problem will be with manufacturing or operations and the management of costs and assets.

Problem: A High Cost Base

Exhibit 4.6 reflects the additional factors of production costs and product effectiveness. If a firm's product is intended to be as effective as those of competitors, the firm faces strict price competition. Any operational inefficiency will lead to reduced profit margins. A firm with costs at point *B* in Exhibit 4.6 obviously will face reduced profit margins on sales when it must meet competitors' prices in the marketplace. If the firm attempts to maintain its profit margin on sales, it will be forced to sell at higher prices, and this increase will lead to a loss of market share.

Management can confirm or reinforce its suspicion of the existence of a high cost base or excess assets by examining such aggregate performance measures as sales per employee, material costs or cost of goods sold as a percentage of sales, value added, and overall wage costs, and comparing them with those of competitors. In today's information age, many databases are available by subscription or without cost on the Internet to assist a firm in analyzing how its operating performance and level of capital investments compare with those of competitors.

If the cost base is out of control, actions must be taken to correct the problem, and unacceptable performance often leads to management changes. Providing the specifics for success is the job of middle management, because top management can only evaluate results, approve or reject proposals, or change the managers involved. If top management is forced to resort to edicts, that step is a sign of failure at the middle-management level.

Such edicts often take any of the following forms:

1. Large layoffs of salaried and hourly personnel
2. Freezes on hiring to allow attrition to reduce the employment level

E X H I B I T   4.6

Sources of price differences.

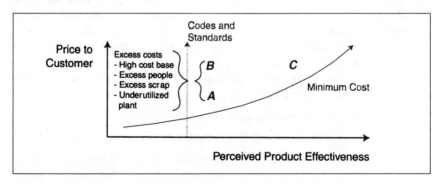

3. Mandatory reductions in inventory levels
4. Freezes on capital expenditures

Such painful actions are often seen by the work force as unpopular manifestations of top management's authority when, in fact, they are brought on by middle-management failures at the operational level.

To continue the discussion of the cost-effectiveness analysis, we recognize that problems with excess costs may exist with a product intended for the high-quality, high-priced segment of the market. These costs include excess labor costs, caused by high wage rates or inefficiencies, excess material usage, scrap, or high overhead costs. Exhibit 4.7 shows the results. The excess costs experienced at point D will reduce the profitability of the firm relative to that of competitors.

Problems: Overdesign and/or Overmanufacture

The organization that is pursuing a product-leadership strategy with the production of a superior product that commands a premium price may also face a second type of cost problem. If the customers have difficulty accepting the product's superiority, then a situation exists as shown in Exhibit 4.8. The customer may not accept the use of more-precise designs, higher-cost materials, superior facilities, or meticulous workmanship as providing a superior product. If the product does not warrant a premium price, the overdesigned or overproduced product results in excess costs for the firm at point E. An equivalent product provided by a competitor that has costs at point C will command that segment of the market. If the extra engineering, quality control, superior materials, and other quality factors, designed and manufactured into the product do not result in the product's being perceived as superior, then they are simply excess costs and must be eliminated.

E X H I B I T   4.7

Sources of price differences (b).

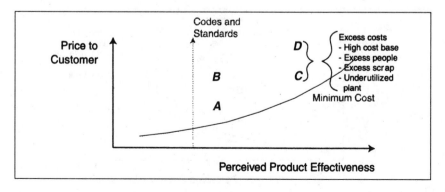

E X H I B I T   4.8

Sources of price differences (*c*).

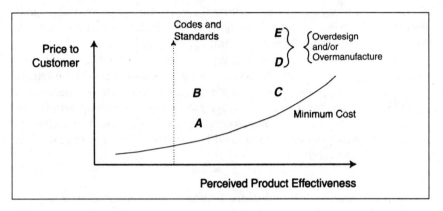

The Most Difficult Situation: A Mix of the Two Problems

Finally, the situation may reflect a bit of each of these unfortunate situations. The company may face a mix of a high cost base confounded by overdesign and/or overmanufacture. The firm then faces the situation illustrated in Exhibit 4.9.

MANAGEMENT ACTION

Top management must continually assess whether the causes of the design and manufacturing problems are capable of being overcome by the management personnel in place or whether more forceful action is required.

E X H I B I T   4.9

Sources of price differences (*d*).

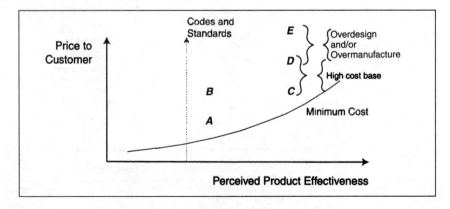

These judgments are made difficult by the lack of complete knowledge of competitors' costs and profits for a given product line, by the lack of specific knowledge of the marketplace on the part of the top corporate managers, and by a tendency of the operating managers involved to insist that the current team can make the necessary improvements.

In the long run, a firm must strive to deliver products that the customers want and for which they are willing to pay, produced at a cost lower than those of its competitors. Top-level problems of these types often must be corrected by drastic actions by management, including reorganizing, changing managers, mandating work-force reductions to bring productivity into line, and/or directing a change in product or market strategy. The importance of productivity improvement to effective competition will be covered in Chapters 5, 6, and 7 in Part Two.

DETAILED OPERATING CONTROLS

As stated earlier, when the product, market, and pricing strategies are properly synchronized with the cost base, a business is under "control" from a top-level standpoint. Management must then plan and control many detailed aspects of the firm's operations. The large number of related detailed measurements requires that operations managers have a special temperament to cope with them on a positive basis, because manufacturing or operations is the crucial hub of the control problem. In most businesses, the majority of the people, assets, and costs are managed by the manufacturing or operations organizations. Therefore, most of the control organizations, systems, and procedures are found in the manufacturing or operations function. Top managers realize that if they are to achieve outstanding profit performance relative to competitors, they cannot succeed with an out-of-control operations function.

SUMMARY

In this chapter, we have covered the strategic planning process and the two levels of inherent planning and control problems. The top level of management must determine first whether the company is in the most appropriate businesses and correct any deficiencies by restructuring through acquisitions and/or divestitures. At the profit-center level, an operating unit (division) must determine if it is in the right business with a correct strategic approach and with a reasonable possibility for success. No amount of lower-level skills, experience, dedication, or energy can compensate for "being in the wrong ballpark." The result will be similar to a forfeited ball game. On the other hand, when the broad strategic factors are in order, the managers at the operating level must still win the marketplace by "out-executing" the competition.

In Part Two, we turn our attention to a crucial measure of execution for most firms—productivity. We will address the importance of productivity and its improvement, define these measures, and examine their relationship to overall firm performance in both the old and new economies.

Review Questions

1. What options in organizing are available to managers to carry out their strategic plans?
2. What does the strategic planning process entail?
3. What is the primary reason for the existence of a business?
4. What are the differences between corporate and profit center goals and objectives?
5. How does the niche or segment in which a business competes influence the derivation of reasonable goals and objectives?

PART TWO

THE STRATEGIC IMPORTANCE OF PRODUCTIVITY

CHAPTER 5

Productivity Improvement and Competitiveness

INTRODUCTION

The concept of productivity improvement and its relationship to competitiveness is one of the most compelling aspects of corporate strategy. Competing organizations typically have access to the same or similar production technology, and thus, in most situations, competitive advantage does not result from the availability or proprietary nature of technology. Similarly, most competing firms also have access to the same or comparable suppliers of raw materials and finished parts. Consequently, the costs of purchased materials are rarely a source of sustainable competitive advantage. On the other hand, the remaining direct costs; sales, general, and administrative (SG&A) costs; other overhead costs; and corporate expenses largely consist of the "cost of people" (employees). These costs provide opportunities for creating sustainable competitive advantages.

Several elements make up the cost of people, including wage rates, benefits, ancillary costs (e.g., space, equipment, travel), compensation other than wages and salaries, and finally, the level of output achieved during the time people work. Together, these elements are among the most important aspects of competition in both manufacturing and service environments. We also should recognize that the greater the degree of labor intensity in a firm's products, the more important the cost of people becomes to the firm's cost competitiveness.

One of the three generic strategies described earlier is to be the low-cost producer; the other two (market niche and product differentiation) are market-oriented. The emphasis on being the low-cost producer, however, is an internal phenomenon, following the notion that nothing prevents a company or operation from being the low-cost producer except the creativity, persistence, and management skill of the CEO and his or her team. For most organizations, achieving the status of low-cost producer would require an organizationwide focus on productivity, particularly employee productivity.

We are reasonably certain that the managers of the construction of the pyramids in Egypt were concerned about productivity. The first record of formal attempts to measure work in the interest of productivity improvement, however, wasn't until the writings of Frederick W. Taylor, who originated time studies of work around the turn of the twentieth century.[1] These methods of work measurement were gradually introduced into a wide variety of production contexts, from job shops to assembly lines. Several systems for defining work and the time required to accomplish it were developed and refined, and over the years a variety of means of defining productivity and tracking its improvement evolved.

This chapter, together with Chapters 6 and 7, addresses the conceptual underpinnings of a strategic emphasis on employee productivity. We discuss the nature of the problem, some well-known concepts related to the measurement of productivity, and some new comparison processes that assist management in measuring its relative effectiveness at achieving outstanding levels of productivity. We also discuss the all-important behavioral aspects of managing the workforce. These include the situation-explicit inclination of employees either to resist attempts to improve productivity or to assist willingly and energetically in achieving productivity gains.

THE MEASUREMENT OF PRODUCTIVITY

Managers use a variety of measures to assess the level of productivity within their organizations, as well as among their competitors. Gathering data for and managing these metrics typically is done at various levels of the organization, and it ordinarily follows from the organization's reporting structure. As we consider higher and higher levels within the organization, the definitions of productivity employed often change correspondingly.

Productivity involves a measure describing how well an organization converts its resource inputs into profit-generating outputs. Many measures of productivity are used in assessing the performance of operations, firms, and economies. Here, we will focus on a single factor in the measure of productivity: employee productivity. When managers analyze productivity, organizations have numerous choices for the measures of outputs (some measure of the production of goods and/or services achieved) and inputs (some measure of labor used), which are employed as the numerator and denominator, respectively, of a ratio measure of productivity, for example. Productivity equals labor hours divided by units produced. We would expect that the choices would vary, depending on the context of the use of the measure, especially as we move from the level of the production or service facility to that of an economy.

---

1. F.W. Taylor, *The Principles of Scientific Management*, Harper & Row, New York, 1911.

When examining the internal operations of a firm, managers might prefer to employ measures of activities of output—for example, the number of times an operation is performed, the number of products produced, the number of transactions completed, or the number of services delivered. One example of this type of measurement is a large bank holding company's use of "millions of transactions per full-time-equivalent employee per month" as the bankwide measure of productivity. The bank's management has tracked this performance measure for many years and through numerous acquisitions to ensure that productivity has increased continually.

When a firm formulates its strategic goals and objectives, and compares its operations to those of its competitors, managers must use publicly available measures. Data that report the level of transaction, service, or even production volume are not readily available in most competitive situations. Even when the production of automobiles is regularly reported in units, the number of units cannot be used as a measure of effective output for purposes of measuring productivity because of the major differences in cost and complexity among the different makes and models of automobiles. The measure of labor productivity we employ in this book is revenues (i.e., dollars) per employee. When examining banking operations, we substitute total assets for revenues. There are several advantages to using such aggregate measures.

The emphasis on productivity is often associated primarily with lower-level, direct workers. In the strategic context, productivity should be considered as the relative level of effectiveness among competitors of all of a firm's employees, from the CEO to the lowest-level worker. Employment level as a measure of input is advantageous, particularly when compared to labor dollars spent, because it is comparable across industry players, it is uninfluenced by regional wage differentials, and it is not affected by accounting allocations of employment costs. Furthermore, it avoids the need to account for compensation in addition to wages or salaries. We assume that the tasks within a group of competitors are sufficiently similar that the ability to accomplish given levels of output represents equivalent demands for resource inputs. Some firms will simply be better at accomplishing these tasks. Similarly, firms may be advantaged or disadvantaged by regional wage differentials. Firms located in high-wage neighborhoods will face a tougher job of cost improvement, but the difference is similar to a rate variance in cost accounting as opposed to a usage variance. The firm that achieves an outstanding level of revenues per employee enjoys the higher level of productivity, regardless of the wage differentials.

Finally, the level of employment transcends a variety of corporate practices in regard to allocating the cost of employees to corporate or divisional budgets, to line or staff designations, or to definitions of direct labor versus indirect labor. The choice of the total number of employees as the measure of labor input nullifies these otherwise complicating factors. If we set out to measure factory productivity, we may be deluded into believing we are achieving productivity improvements when, in fact, we are adding computer software specialists to prepare computer instructions for automatic machines at a rate faster than the reduction in direct factory workers. This illusion of improvement would occur if computer personnel were considered members of the corporate or indirect staff, rather than direct factory workers. All of these contradictions are avoided by using the total number of employees, from the CEO to the entry-level worker.

Having established the importance of labor productivity and a means of measuring it, we will dedicate the remainder of this chapter to examining three concepts related to labor productivity. Two of these are familiar in the field of corporate strategy: economies of scale, and the learning or experience curve. The third is a new concept we introduce that addresses the issues of the need for the continuous improvement of employee productivity. We call this concept *economies of growth.*

ECONOMIES OF SCALE

Economies of scale have long been a staple of economics literature. The term *scale economies* has generally been used to describe the process by which larger firms are able to spread their fixed and semifixed costs over a larger volume of products or services, leading to lower average costs per unit of output. In many industries, it was proven and widely understood that "scale" alone could provide a competitive advantage through lower costs, putting pressure on smaller competitors.

Firms may achieve economies in costs and productivity factors as their size increases, and diseconomies may set in as firms pass the most efficient (lowest-cost, highest-productivity) size. This results in the classical U-shaped curve of economic theory, which is illustrated in Exhibit 5.1 for a sample of 36 bank holding companies for a five-year period. Not all industries demonstrate diseconomies: for some, costs continue to decrease as volume increases. Often this trend has been made possible by the capability of computer-based information systems which assist in efficiently controlling larger and larger organizations.

Our focus on the number of employees as a single-factor productivity measure leads us to define and demonstrate the use of scale economies in this context. We will do this specifically in the next chapter and repeatedly in the cases related to the divisions of the Pelican Corporation later in the book. As an illustration, Exhibit 5.1 demonstrates the presence of significant economies of scale in labor in a sample of firms from the bank holding company industry. Notice the classic upturn of the curve as diseconomies occur.

LEARNING CURVE–EXPERIENCE CURVE THEORY

In the 1930s, a manager at the Wright-Patterson Air Force base in Dayton, Ohio, published a paper reporting a new phenomenon: the learning curve.

EXHIBIT 5.1

Economies of scale in bank holding companies.

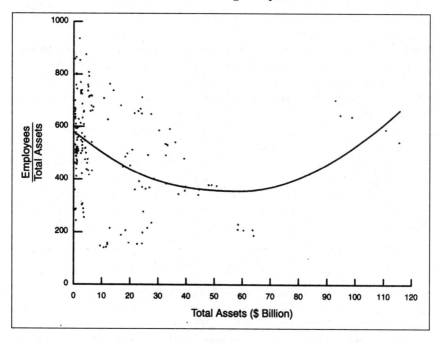

Later applications of the concept were sometimes referred to as "progress functions" and "experience curves," with the latter finding prominence in the field of business strategy. The learning curve concept used mathematics to represent the observed improvement in production times as tasks were accomplished over and over again. These improvements came to be expected in work settings in which repetitive tasks were involved, and the standard formulations of the relationships between units produced and the rate of improvement in productivity became widely used in industry. Firms that were not able to achieve improvements found themselves at a severe competitive disadvantage.

The magnitude of the learning curve improvement was seen to diminish in a systematic way as the number of repetitions increased. Learning curve–experience curve theory proposes a predictable relationship: a constant percent improvement in labor hours for each doubling of cumulative volume of output. Traditionally, an 80 percent learning curve denotes a 20 percent improvement for each doubling of cumulative volume. Improvement usually applies to the measure of productivity—

for example, labor hours per unit of output, the labor cost per unit (in constant dollars), or the total variable cost per unit (in constant dollars). Transforming the units of both productivity and cumulative output into logarithms creates a linear relationship. Exhibit 5.2 presents a learning curve found in a large U.S. service operation. The learning rate for this curve was 90 percent.

In addition to ensuring that the productivity gains of the learning curve occurred, managers and strategic planners also have given emphasis to the rate at which their firms captured these gains relative to their competition. Because the productivity gains depend on two factors—the learning rate and the cumulative number of products made or services delivered—each of these variables has been given attention. In addressing the learning rate, managers have endeavored to increase the slope of the curve, capturing more improvement with each doubling of the cumulative output of the organization.

Alternatively, managers aiming to move their groups down a given curve faster have focused on increasing production volume. In a competitive context, this endeavor regularly involves increasing market share at the expense of one's competitors. A common method of achieving this goal has involved cutting prices in order to take advantage of price elasticity.

ECONOMIES OF GROWTH

We introduce in this book a new concept in productivity improvement, the phenomenon we call *economies of growth*.[2] This notion is the product of the authors' ongoing interest in and research into productivity improvement, which can be related to the fundamentals of learning curve and experience curve theory. This powerful concept extends the previous notions regarding productivity to include the positive impact of the sheer growth of a firm on its prospects for improving productivity. Previous work first established that the mere measurement of the work accomplished in a given time would improve productivity. Then, it was observed that repetitiveness (accomplishing the same tasks over and over again) also enhanced productivity. Economists noted the effect of "scale" on output per worker, and scale economies became a readily understood means of achieving productivity advantages over competitors. Now, we introduce the newest observed productivity relationship: economies of growth.

In recognizing economies of growth, we seek a strong and statistically significant relationship between the growth rate of a firm and the growth rate of its productivity. The concept of economies of growth was recognized during an exploration of the differences between growing firms and stagnant firms in the context of the learning curve. In the specific organization studied, productivity improvement was occurring, following the

---

2. Jacqueline L. Doyle, *Economies of Growth: A Study of Corporate and Productivity Growth Rates in Two Service Industries*, an unpublished dissertation submitted in partial fulfillment of the requirements for the degree of Doctor of Philosophy in Business Administration, The Darden School of Business Administration, The University of Virginia, Charlottesville, 1995.

E X H I B I T   5.2

Example of the learning curve in a service business.

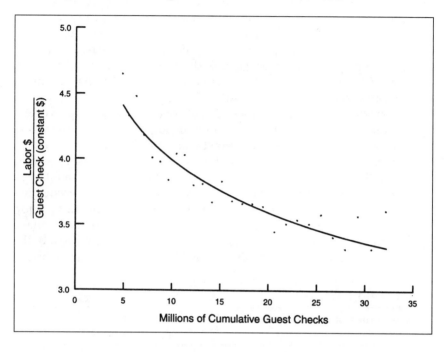

general pattern of a learning curve, with the labor requirements per unit of output declining as the cumulative number of units completed increased. As the complement of workers in the organization accumulated experience, the number of labor hours required to perform each unit of service declined. This decline effectively increased the labor capacity of the group. Because the availability of increased demand existed for the product of this organization, the group was able to grow its production volume without a proportional growth in its work force. Concurrently, the organization was able to capture the advantages of the reduced per-unit labor requirements, and because its operations were labor-intensive, it benefited substantially over time from the resultant cost reductions.

The circumstances of this situation also bring to light the possibility of an alternative scenario—one in which the opportunity for growth is absent. Considering the organization described above, stagnant growth could have come about as a result of a lack of demand, a lack of physical capacity, or the group's unwillingness to increase its output. With the improvements in productivity described previously, management would have faced a situation of excess labor capacity. The resulting options for management would have included reducing the work force commensurate with the labor-requirements reduction, or maintaining a constant work force and forgoing the benefits of the reduction, that is, reduced costs. If management elected to pursue the first of these options and proceeded with a reduction in the number of workers, management effectively would have delivered the message that, through performance improvement, employees had contributed to the elimination of some of their own jobs. In selecting the latter of the two options, however, management would have created the potential for idleness or underutilization of the work force. Neither of the two options appears to compel a continuing pursuit of improvement on the part of the workers.

Considering these alternative scenarios of productivity improvement under conditions of different growth rates in output, we began to explore the relationship between corporate growth rates and the rate of productivity improvement in various industries of the U.S. economy. Our hypothesis, which has been borne out repeatedly, was that there is indeed a relationship between a firm's rate of growth and the rate at which its productivity improves. In particular, we have found that faster-growing firms enjoy, on average, faster rates of improvement in labor productivity. We have termed these advantages *economies of growth*. A simple illustration of the basic growth economies relationship, again illustrated by a group of banks,

E X H I B I T   5.3

Economies of growth in bank holding companies.

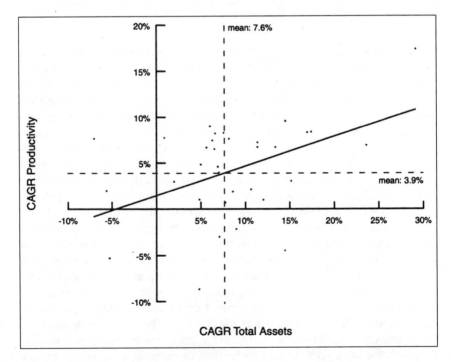

is shown in Exhibit 5.3. For the same sample of bank holding companies that we examined for economies of scale in labor, *economies of growth* were found to be highly significant using rates of productivity improvement and asset growth over the same five-year period.

The premises of economies of growth include a number of elements related to work force motivation and human nature. First, growth creates a secure and stimulating work environment. Workers with growing workloads increase productivity by focusing on important tasks, by shedding unnecessary activities, by creating new ways of accomplishing more, and by seeking best practices through shared learning across the firm. It is also a fact that in growth environments, productivity improvement and employment expansion can occur simultaneously. On the other hand, stagnant and declining environments can create resistance toward productivity improvement. In such environments, productivity improvement can occur only through declining employment rolls. In situations of stagnant or declining growth, productivity improvements would result in a need for fewer workers to accomplish a given amount of work. Acting in their own best interest, workers are reluctant to "downsize" themselves out of a job. Thus, productivity improvements are generally more difficult to achieve in operations with stagnant or declining output.

The dynamic situations accompanying acquisitions, divestitures, and organizational changes or restructurings create prime opportunities for firms to adjust productivity levels. In these circumstances, management often takes advantage of the period of corporate redefinition to reduce employment rolls. Frequently, this pruning occurs among the ranks of middle management, particularly in the case of mergers where line workers are retained to maintain production and service levels.

SUMMARY

In today's dynamic environment, the U.S. economy continues a long-term shift toward services and away from manufacturing, spurred on by the growth in the new economy. With this shift, the management of labor productivity and its improvement have become ever more important. We have recognized that labor productivity—and the related cost of people—is one of the dominant competitive playing fields for the many firms striving to lower costs. For these firms in particular, labor productivity and its improvement are strategically important in their quest to win orders in the marketplace.

In this chapter, we reviewed two well-known concepts related to labor productivity: economies of scale and the learning curve. We also introduced the concept of economies of growth, which recognizes the relationship between a firm's growth rate and its rate of improvement in labor productivity. In the next chapter, we will examine the presence of this new concept in both the old and new economies.

1. Why is the productivity of a firm's work force so important strategically?
2. What factors influence employees' willingness to support efforts to increase productivity?
3. Why should productivity measures include all of a firm's employees, as opposed to only the direct production workers?
4. What factors enhance or impede a firm's ability to enjoy economies of scale?
5. What circumstances lead to learning curve effects in business' operations?
6. How do growth economies differ from scale economies or learning curve effects?

CHAPTER 6

Productivity
Improvement in the
Old and New Economies

GROWTH ECONOMIES IN THE OLD ECONOMY

Productivity and its improvement are crucial strategic elements of competitive effectiveness in most industries, and thus necessary components of a firm's strategic planning process. We discussed in the previous chapter that the cost of all of a firm's employees constitutes a common competitive battleground for the status of low-cost producer. Focusing on this vital theme, we recognized several valuable strategic concepts.

We now continue our discussion of one of these, the new concept of economies of growth, which like the others, relates to labor productivity. Economies of growth are found when faster-growing firms demonstrate higher rates of productivity improvement than slower-growing firms. Thus, growth provides an advantage when economies of growth are present. This advantage of higher rates of improvement or growth in labor productivity aids firms in gaining on competitors in their quest for a more productive work force, and consequently, lower costs. For firms that already lead the field in productivity levels, growth economies aid in distancing them further from the lagging competition. On the other hand, firms not taking advantage of growth economies will find themselves losing valuable ground in labor productivity relative to the competition.

Using revenues as the measure of size and revenues per employee as the measure of productivity, the analyses reported in Chapter 5 were extended to include numerous additional industries. The compound average growth rate over a five-year period was used to measure the rate of change of each variable. Strong, positive relationships between revenue growth and productivity growth were found in 14 different industries. These results led us to suspect that these relationships were likely to be found in the mainstream of U.S. industry.

ECONOMIES OF GROWTH IN THE FORTUNE 500 COMPANIES

We examined the companies listed in the Fortune 500 for the year 2000 and found strong economies of growth among this set of the largest U.S. firms (see Exhibit 6.1). We see from the trend line that the growth rate of productivity over the five-year period examined (1994–1998) increased, on average, as the rate of corporate growth increased. The final number of companies examined was actually 379, after eliminating the firms for which data were not available for all of the five years 1994 to 1998. The results, shown in Exhibit 6.1, substantiated economies of growth as a cross-industry and economywide phenomenon.

Two additional relationships of interest were found among the companies in the Fortune 500 list for the year 2000. First, there was a significant relationship between productivity growth rate and market-value (market-capitalization) growth rate, which is shown in Exhibit 6.2. As one might expect, there was also a significant relationship between corporate growth rate and the growth rate of market value, with market-value growth rates increasing for larger corporate growth rates.

Exhibits 6.1 and 6.2 reveal new insights into the critical strategic aspect of "managing an effective work force," with the obvious conclusion that in the mainstream of U.S. industry, those companies that manage the productivity of their work forces most effectively have a strong head start toward premium share prices and market value (often referred to as the firm's *market capitalization*). The final relationship mentioned, which we chose not to present in graphical form, showed an uncommonly strong relationship between revenue growth and market-value growth, which confirms long-standing premises of the investment community.

ECONOMIES OF GROWTH IN THE NEW ECONOMY

A related question was whether these relationships among productivity growth, revenue growth, and the growth in market value of the firm also would characterize the new economy of high technology and ebusinesses. We therefore set out to identify the most important or the most successful companies in each of several sectors of the high-technology, ebusiness segment of the U.S. economy so that we could test for the presence of growth economies. Several guidelines were established to identify the sample of companies to represent the new economy. The first of these guidelines was to include only those firms that were clearly part of the high-technologies communications sector. This limitation excluded many firms that might have used new technologies to gain a competitive advantage in their respective

E X H I B I T   6.1

Economies of growth in the Fortune 500, 1994–1998.

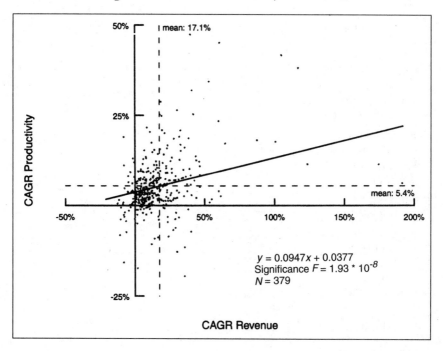

CAGR Revenue

industries but did not exist primarily to develop and market high-technology, computer-related, and communications products and/or services.

Our objective was to identify a set of companies that could represent the high-technology, ebusiness sector in much the same way that the Fortune 500 list of the largest U.S. companies represents the core of the old economy. Standard & Poor's Compustat database was used to identify a set of high-technology, ebusiness firms based on the following guidelines. For selection, firms had to have all of the following characteristics:

- Have data available for each year from 1994 to 1998
- Be headquartered in the United States
- Have at least $500 million in revenues in 1998
- Be included in the Compustat sectors of high-technology, communications firms.

The appendix to this chapter identifies the seven sectors and lists the firms in each sector, 129 in total, that met the criteria noted above.

The relationships among our variables of interest, productivity growth, revenue growth, and the growth in market value, were analyzed. First, we found the relationship between productivity growth and revenue growth—

Market value and productivity growth in the Fortune 500, 1994–1998.

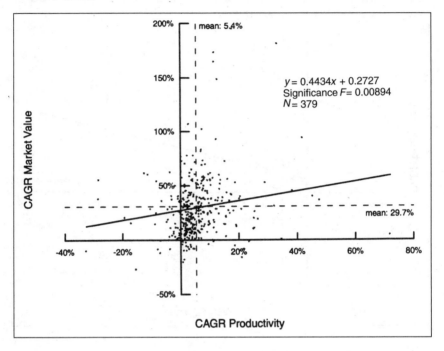

CAGR Productivity

economies of growth—to be present among the 129 new economy firms for the period 1994 to 1998. This relationship is shown in Exhibit 6.3. We also found that the relationship between market value growth and productivity growth was significant, as shown in Exhibit 6.4. Finally, a third analysis examined the growth in market value and revenue growth. This relationship was again found highly significant, which is consistent with the prevailing logic of the financial markets, that higher growth rates in market value accompany higher revenue growth rates. As expected, increased share prices, and hence market values, typically accompany strong growth in revenues in new-economy companies.

SUMMARY OF THE RESULTS FOR THE OLD-ECONOMY AND NEW-ECONOMY SECTORS

The relationships identified here reinforce the notions that faster-growing firms should be able to capture strategically important efficiencies through more rapidly improving productivity, and that more productive workers (and the attendant lower costs) should contribute to increases in market capitalization and shareholder value.

EXHIBIT 6.3

Economies of growth in the new economy, 1994–1998.

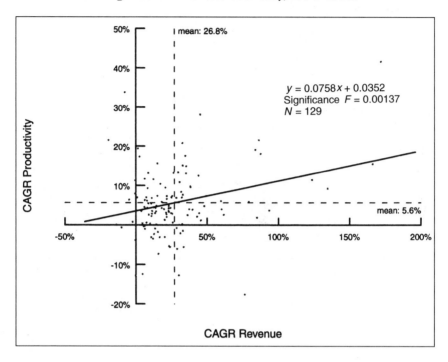

$$y = 0.0758x + 0.0352$$
Significance $F = 0.00137$
$N = 129$

mean: 26.8%

mean: 5.6%

CAGR Productivity

CAGR Revenue

The most important conclusion of this chapter is that this series of relationships—revenue growth's relationship to productivity growth, and productivity growth's relationship to growth in market value—are equally pervasive in both the old economy and the new economy. This also suggests that the same valuation methods already are being applied by the financial/investment community to the analyses of companies of both the old and new economies. These conclusions reinforce one of the major strategic premises of this book, which is that in the long run, successful companies must manage the basics. They must have specific goals and objectives that all employees can understand; they must have in place viable strategies for achieving the goals; and finally, they must outexecute the competition. These precepts are the rules for engagement in all companies, in all industries, in both the old economy and the new economy, and in the recent past and into the future.

The relationships presented in this chapter demonstrate the robustness of the concept of growth economies and their importance to managers throughout the U.S. economy. In the next chapter, we provide a more detailed look at competitive analysis, along with other conclusions related to the crucial strategic competitive factor of employee productivity.

E X H I B I T   6.4

Market value and productivity growth in the new economy, 1994–1998.

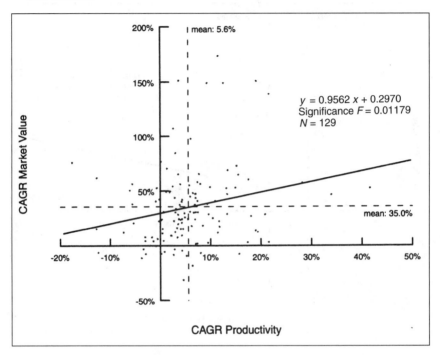

$y = 0.9562 x + 0.2970$
Significance $F = 0.01179$
$N = 129$

CAGR Productivity

Review Questions

1. What is the significance of strong growth economies among the Fortune 500 U.S. companies?
2. Similarly, what is the significance of the presence of strong growth economies among the leading firms in the new economy?
3. In both sets of companies, what is the strategic importance of the strong relationship between productivity growth rates and the growth rates of the market values of the shares of publicly traded firms?

Appendix 6A: New-Economy Firms by Sector

Equipment/Communications (networking)

3COM Corp.	Brightpoint Inc.	Harris Corp.
ADC Telecomm	Cable Design Tech CP	Motorola Inc.
Andrew Corp.	Cabletron Systems	Pittway Corp/DE-CLA
Anixter Intl Inc.	Cisco Systems Inc.	Qualcomm Inc.
Antec Corp.	General Instruments Corp	Scientific Atlanta Inc.
Audivox Corp.–CLA	General Motors CL H	Tellabs Inc.

Computers (Software/Services)

Adobe Systems Inc.	Informix Corp.	Parametric Technology Corp.
America Online Inc.	Intergraph Corp.	Peoplesoft Inc.
AMS	Intuit Inc.	Sterling Software Inc.
Autodesk Inc.	Mentor Graphics Corp.	Sybase Inc.
BMC Software Inc.	Microsoft Corp.	Symantec Corp.
Cadence Design Sys Inc.	Networks Associates Inc.	Synopsis Inc.
Computer Associates Intl.	Novell Inc.	Unisys Corp.
Compuware Corp.	Oracle Corp.	Veritas Software Co.
Electronics Arts Inc.		

Telephone and Telephone Long Distance

Alltel Corp.	GTE Corp.	Telephone & Data
AT&T Corp.	Intermedia Comm Inc.	U.S. West Inc.
Broadwing Inc.	NTL Inc.	Verizon Inc.
BellSouth Corp.	SBC Communications Inc.	(formerly Bell Atlantic)
Centurytel Inc.		

Computer Peripheral/Electronic Instrument

Dynatech Corp.	PE Corp Biosystems	Storage Technology CP
EMC Corp/MA	Perkinelmer Inc.	Tektronix Inc.
Honeywell Inc.	Quantum Corp-Cons	Thermo Instrument Systems
Hutchinson Tech.	Read-Rite Corp.	Western Digital Corp.
Iomega Corp.	Seagate Techonolgy	

Semiconductor Electronics and Equipment

Adaptec Inc.	Integrated Device Tech Inc.	Maxim Integrated Products
Advanced Micro Devices	Intel Corp.	Micron Technology Inc.
Altera Corp.	Intl Rectifier Corp.	National Semiconductor Corp.

Analog Devices	KLA-TENCOR Corp.	Novellus Systems Inc.
Applied Materials Inc.	LAM Research Corp.	Teradyne Inc.
Atmel Corp.	Linear Technology Corp.	Texas Instruments Inc.
Cirrus Logic Inc.	LSI Logic Corp.	Xilinx Inc.
Cypress Semiconductor Corp.		

Computer Systems and Data Processing

Analysts International Corp.	First Data Corp.	Paychex Inc.
Automatic Data Processing	Fiserv Inc.	Policy Management Systems
Cambridge TechPartner	Gartner Group Inc.	Pomeroy Computer Res Inc.
Ceridian Corp.	Gerber Scientific Inc.	Safeguard Scientific Inc.
Ciber Inc.	Government Technology	Savoir Technology Group Inc.
Comdisco Inc.	Inacom Corp.	SED International Hldgs Inc.
Compucom System Inc.	Keane Inc.	Shared Medical Systems
Computer Sciences Corp.	Merisel Inc.	Corp.
Electronic Data Syst Corp.	National Computer Sys Inc.	Software Spectrum Inc.
Equifax Inc.	National Data Corp.	SungardData Systems Inc.

Computer (Hardware)

Apple Computer Inc.	Gateway Inc.	Micron Electronics Inc.
Compaq Computer Corp.	Hewlet-Packard CO	Silicon Graphics Inc.
Dell Computer Corp.	IBM Corp.	Sun Microsystems Inc.

Source: Compustat PC Plus Database

CHAPTER 7

Productivity and Competitive Analysis

INTRODUCTION

Competitive analysis is critical for managers formulating corporate and divisional strategies. Executives and planners must be aware of the levels of and trends in performance of their competitors to determine the best directions for their divisions and parent corporations. They also must be capable of critically assessing their own organization's performance, over time, relative to its competitive peers.

Competitive analyses are typically based on historical data, which allows managers to review how their firm has compared to competitors in the past. Current data are more difficult to come by, and future performance must be estimated. Managers and planners use the information gathered in the process of competitive analysis to develop strategic plans and to set realistic goals and objectives. The analysis should focus on those performance measures that are central to gaining competitive advantage in the business's marketplace. We will concentrate here on measures that are significant in most competitive settings.

We discuss several related methods of competitive analysis in this chapter, two of which were introduced in Chapter 5: economies of scale and economies of growth. We begin here with a recognition of the value of a simple rank ordering of comparable firms on various measures of interest and discuss at length two-way performance mapping, which we illustrate with two performance measures, introduced in the economies-of-growth analysis: a firm's corporate growth rate and its labor-productivity growth rate.

A GENERIC FIRST STEP

A straightforward first step in competitive analysis is to develop ordinal rankings of a group of comparable firms for each element in a set of given performance measures. For example, with an identified performance measure, such as revenues, the firms being compared are listed in rank order, from the largest to the smallest. Listing the comparable firms in rank order on such variables as return on sales, gross margin percentage, and asset turnover provides valuable comparisons. The development of such lists requires that a group of comparable firms first must be identified. Such a group might consist of firms in the same industry or firms from different industries facing similar competitive environments. At least some of the firms examined should make up a competitive circle—businesses competing for orders in the same or overlapping markets. For the identified firms, performance measures vital to competitiveness should be tracked on a regular basis. (Chapter 8 provides detailed descriptions of a number of useful performance measures.) These rankings aid managers in understanding how their firms compare to the competition, assist them in recognizing their organizations' strengths and weaknesses, and provide guidance in the goal-setting process.

Some managers have demeaned this process and discounted its results for failing to provide a rich review of the actual circumstances of the competitive environment. No doubt, every figure has a story behind it, and qualitative details or perceptions might enrich our understanding of a given competitive situation. More often than not, however, those who are most critical of the comparison process represent organizations ranking at or near the bottom of their peer groups. Strong organizations want to "keep score" and never lose sight of the necessity for continuous improvement, and an organization can't measure its improvement if it doesn't know its relative effectiveness.

The rank orderings of firms on a number of attributes may be refined slightly to aid in the goal-setting process. We recommend dividing the list of ranked firms into four equal groups of firms, with each of the separating values called a *quartile*. From the divided list, managers may readily determine the quarter within which their firms are positioned, as well as which competitors are in similar situations to their own. A powerful motivator to which all members of the organization can relate is to have the goal of performing above the top quartile, or in the top quarter, for each of the key performance indicators of the firm and its industry. In the spirit of continuous improvement, after a level of performance in the top quarter is reached on any measure, the goal should be redefined to be reaching number one or number two among the comparable companies.

ECONOMIES OF SCALE IN LABOR

Earlier chapters established that the productivity of a firm's work force is a decisive contributor to competitiveness in most situations. We can use an analysis of economies of scale in labor to determine both the levels of productivity among a set of comparable firms and whether or not the sizes of the firms significantly influence the productivity levels. We can then determine the level of productivity a firm "should" be achieving to meet the industry average, taking into account the size of the firm. This measure then should be compared to the actual productivity level of the firm to determine whether the firm's performance meets, exceeds, or falls short of its expected level.

To determine whether or not economies of scale in labor are present, a regression analysis can be performed using data from a set of comparable firms. For each year of analysis, two elements of data for each of the firms in the sample are needed: scale (size) and labor productivity, measured as input per unit of output. Revenue dollars are used as a measure of scale and employees per million dollars revenue as the labor-productivity measure. As noted in Chapter 5, in banking institutions total assets are substituted for revenues because total assets normally are used to measure the size and growth of banks.

An example of economies of scale is shown in Exhibit 7.1. The illustration is based on actual data from a mature, old-economy U.S. industry, where all of the 18 competitors were constituents of the Fortune 500. Five years of data were gathered and plotted for each of the firms, and the regression model was found to be highly significant. We are interested in the

E X H I B I T 7.1

Economies of scale.

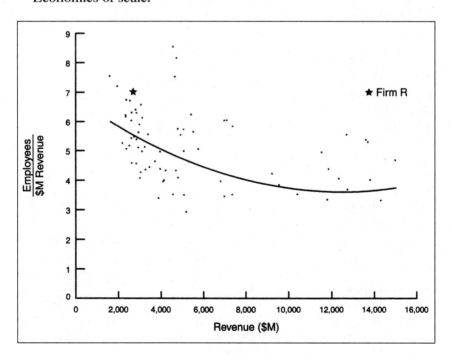

performance of Firm R, the smallest of the 18 comparable firms. We would expect that the smallest firm would have lower-than-average productivity as a result of the presence of economies of scale. But what level of productivity would be reasonable to expect for Firm R, given the economies of scale? The fitted regression line answers this question for us.

The line represents the productivity values that are expected for the range of firm sizes, based on the sample of firms used in the analysis. Accordingly, we use the equation for the line to determine the expected productivity value for a given size firm. As shown in the Exhibit 7.1, Firm R reported revenues of approximately $2.7 billion and labor productivity of 7.0 employees per million dollars of revenue. If we drop down vertically to the line from the point representing Firm R, we will find the productivity level expected for a firm with $2.7 billion in sales to be approximately 5.5 employees per million dollars of revenue. As an alternative to estimating the number of employees per million dollars of revenues from the plotted graph, the expected number could be calculated from the fitted equation. In either case, Firm R's productivity level is above (or worse than) this expected value.

It is important to recognize that all of the firms in the competitive circle must compete with one another regardless of their sizes. Scale economies may explain a smaller firm's lower productivity level, but they do not influence the fact that the larger, more-efficient firms, which have found ways to gain an advantage from their size, remain the smaller firm's competition. Firm R must compete with the firms demonstrating productivity in the range of 3.0 employees per million dollars revenue, productivity that is over twice as effective as its own.

ECONOMIES OF GROWTH

The economies-of-growth analysis allows us to examine the rate at which the productivity levels of these firms have been changing over time—to review trends in improvement deterioration. The economies-of-growth analysis also reveals whether a firm's corporate growth rate influences the rate at which labor productivity changes. Similar to our analysis of economies of scale, the analysis of economies of growth allows us to determine the rate at which the productivity of a given firm "should" be improving to meet the industry average, taking into account the growth rate of the firm. We then may compare that level to the actual performance of the firm.

We can determine whether or not economies of growth are present by performing a regression analysis on data from a set of comparable firms. For the period of the analysis, we need two elements of data for each of the firms in the sample: the corporate growth rate and the labor productivity growth rate. As noted in Chapter 5, we define the corporate growth rate to be the compound annual growth rate (CAGR) in revenues and the labor-productivity growth rate to be the compound annual growth rate of revenues per employee. Note that our measure of productivity for economies of growth is the inverse of the measure used for the economies-of-scale analysis.

Exhibit 7.2 provides a graphical illustration of economies of growth. In this industry, the competitors produce precision-measuring instruments. Five years of data were gathered, the growth rates were calculated and plotted for each of the firms, and the model was found to be highly significant. We are interested in the performance of Riviera Corporation (a case study presented later in Part 4), which is one of the slower-growing firms in the group of comparables. We would expect that a slower-growing firm would have a lower-than-average productivity growth rate because of the presence of economies of growth, but we do not yet know what level of productivity growth should reasonably be expected of Riviera given the industry trend. As we saw with the economies-of-scale discussion previously, the fitted regression line will provide the answer.

The line represents the productivity growth rate values that are expected for the range of corporate growth rates shown, based on the sample of firms used in the analysis. As a result, we use the equation for the line to determine the productivity growth rate value expected for a given growth rate of sales. We can see from the figure that Riviera has a very small growth rate of sales during the five years analyzed. In fact, Riviera's compound annual growth rate of revenues rounds to zero, while its compound annual growth rate of labor productivity was 9 percent. If we drop down vertically to the line from

E X H I B I T   7.2

Economies of growth.

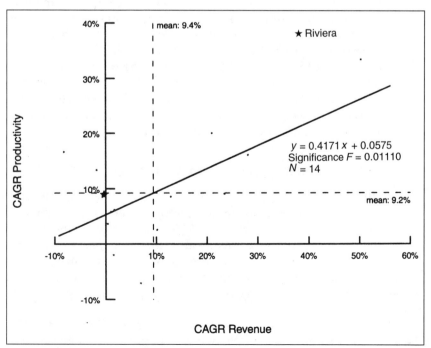

the point representing Riviera, we will find the productivity growth rate expected for a firm with no average growth in sales to be about 5 percent. Riviera's actual productivity growth rate is substantially better than this expected value. Thus, Riviera is improving its labor productivity faster than the industry trend would predict for a firm with effectively no growth in sales over five years. Its productivity growth rate, however, is slightly below the industry average of 9.2 percent.

Once again, it is valuable to recognize that all of the firms in the identified circle remain competitors regardless of their growth rates. Economies of growth may explain why a slower-growing firm would demonstrate a slower rate of productivity growth than the faster-growing one, but they do not change the competitive reality that the slower-growing firms must contend with the faster-growing firms in the marketplace. Even for those firms such as Riviera, with a productivity growth rate that exceeds expectations, managers must be cognizant of their actual productivity growth rate and how it compares with the same measure for the firm's competitors.

Economies of scale and economies of growth are separate phenomena related to productivity. Economies of scale provide a static picture of how firms in the industry have been performing. In the context previously highlighted, economies of scale provide a view of the competitive landscape based on labor productivity. Economies of growth, on the other hand, provide a glimpse of the dynamics of the direction in which firms are headed, based on their past records of improvement (or decline). Some industries demonstrate significant economies of scale and virtually nonexistent economies of growth, and other industries have the converse being true. When both effects are present, we find a confluence of events that managers should recognize. In such a situation, growth leads to economies of scale and improved productivity levels (when firms have not passed the size at which diseconomies arise). Faster growth produces economies of growth and faster improvement in productivity. The two are a powerful, mutually reinforcing combination. In industries in which both are at work, growing firms will have the advantage in productivity improvement, and slow-growing or stagnant firms should beware.

TWO-WAY PERFORMANCE MAPPING

Two-way performance mapping is another general method of competitive analysis that may be used with any two performance measures. It allows managers to review their organizations' histories relative to their peers' on the chosen two measures simultaneously. Mapping the two measures in a graphic format creates four quadrants into which the firms can be divided. We will demonstrate this technique using the measures employed in the economies-of-growth analysis—corporate growth and growth rate of labor productivity.

Particularly when economies of growth are not present in an industry, we recommend the use of the two-way performance mapping as a means of comparing firms' rates of productivity improvement. With this method, the average of a group of competitors is used as a straightforward and convenient dividing point. It is always useful to determine how many and which competitors are above (or below) average, as well as their relative rankings on a given measure.

As shown in Exhibit 7.3, the axes of the graph should be drawn in the same orientation that they were for the economies-of-growth analysis, with corporate growth rate serving as the horizontal axis and labor productivity growth rate as the vertical axis. The axes also should be drawn at the industry-average values. Thus, the horizontal axis, representing corporate growth rate, will cross the vertical axis at the industry average value of labor productivity growth, dividing the firms with above-average productivity growth (above the horizontal axis) from those with slower-than-average productivity growth (below the horizontal axis). Similarly, the vertical axis, labor productivity growth, will cross the horizontal axis at the average value of corporate growth rate, separating firms with above-average growth rates (to the right) from those with below-average growth rates (to the left). This creates a convenient system of four quadrants.

Detailed Example

An example of this type of two-way performance mapping is shown in Exhibit 7.3. The illustration is based on actual data from the same entrenched, industrial U.S. industry for which we saw economies of scale in labor earlier in the chapter. The identification of the firms is based on size (revenue dollars), with Firm A being the largest and Firm R the smallest. We can see from the figure that the industry-average corporate growth rate is 10 percent, and the industry-average productivity growth rate is 10.85 percent, as shown in the top half of Exhibit 7.3. The growth rates were calculated over a five-year period. The bottom half of Exhibit 7.3 provides data on the CAGR of revenues and the CAGR of productivity for each company.

As we saw earlier, economies of scale in labor were found to be present in this industry, with diseconomies setting in for the largest of the firms. Economies of growth were not statistically significant, however, which makes performance mapping particularly effective for this industry. An examination of the quadrants in Exhibit 7.3 provides some insight into why the economies of growth were not present.

Firms in Quadrant I, which showed above-average corporate growth rates and above-average productivity growth rates, had been successful in growing both of these measures. Of the four companies in this quadrant, only one had eliminated jobs over the five years examined; the other three had created jobs. As a general rule, jobs have been eliminated when the CAGR of productivity exceeds the CAGR of revenues. Jobs have been created when revenues have grown faster than productivity. Firms in Quadrant II had rapidly-growing revenues, but they had not taken advantage of the opportunity for growth in productivity. All three of the firms in

EXHIBIT 7.3

Two-way performance map for an entrenched manufacturing
industry.

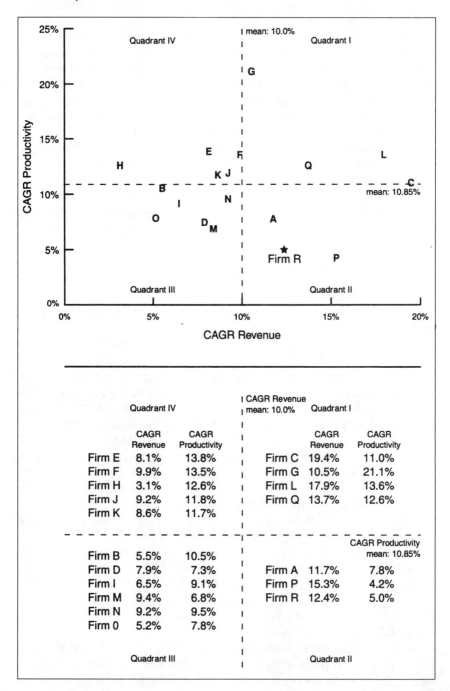

		CAGR Revenue mean: 10.0%		
Quadrant IV			**Quadrant I**	
	CAGR Revenue	CAGR Productivity		CAGR Revenue	CAGR Productivity
Firm E	8.1%	13.8%	Firm C	19.4%	11.0%
Firm F	9.9%	13.5%	Firm G	10.5%	21.1%
Firm H	3.1%	12.6%	Firm L	17.9%	13.6%
Firm J	9.2%	11.8%	Firm Q	13.7%	12.6%
Firm K	8.6%	11.7%			
				CAGR Productivity mean: 10.85%	
Firm B	5.5%	10.5%			
Firm D	7.9%	7.3%	Firm A	11.7%	7.8%
Firm I	6.5%	9.1%	Firm P	15.3%	4.2%
Firm M	9.4%	6.8%	Firm R	12.4%	5.0%
Firm N	9.2%	9.5%			
Firm O	5.2%	7.8%			
Quadrant III			**Quadrant II**	

this quadrant had expanded their employment rolls over the five-year period. Companies in Quadrant III had not demonstrated substantial growth for either of the two measures. Four of six firms here had eliminated jobs during the five years. Finally, the firms in Quadrant IV had grown more slowly than average but had achieved above-average productivity gains through restructuring and downsizing. All of the firms in this quadrant had eliminated jobs over the five-year period.

Managers may find this approach revealing for their own industries. Recall the powerful relationships we discussed in Chapter 6 between corporate growth rate and market-value growth rate as well as between productivity growth rate and market-value growth rate for the Fortune 500 and for the new economy sector. Managers would naturally want to position their firms in Quadrant I. Executives whose firms are not in this attractive position, however, might use the information on the graph in their goal-setting processes to attempt to move their organizations toward more-promising competitive positions on these measures, with the ultimate aim of creating value for their shareholders.

We will focus on one of the firms in the industry, Firm R, to illustrate the importance of productivity improvement to a firm's financial health and its potential to create value for the shareholders. We know that Firm R was the smallest firm in the industry based on revenues, ranked fifth in corporate growth rate, and ranked seventeenth of eighteen in productivity growth rate. Firm R is in Quadrant II on the two-way performance map, with above-average revenue growth and below-average productivity growth.

The table in Exhibit 7.4 shows actual performance data for Firm R over the five-year period examined. We see that Firm R's revenues grew from $1.7 billion in year 1 to $2.7 billion in year 5, and its employees grew from approximately 14,500 to 19,000 during the same period. We know from the performance map that Firm R's productivity growth rate was less

E X H I B I T   7.4

Firm R actual performance history.

Performance Measure	Year 1	Year 2	Year 3	Year 4	Year 5	5-Year CAGR
Revenue ($M)	1,697	1,838	1,947	2,300	2,706	
Annual Revenue Growth		8.3%	5.9%	18.1%	17.7%	12.4%
Employees	14,490	14,780	16,472	17,200	19,000	
Revenue per Employee	$117,119	124,359	118,214	133,728	142,430	
Annual Productivity Growth		6.2%	−4.9%	13.1%	6.5%	5%

than half the industry-average value. We would like to examine the effect this lower-than-average rate had on Firm R's earnings, as well as the potential effect it might have had on Firm R's stock price.

To begin with, we will examine how Firm R's employment levels would have looked had the organization improved its labor productivity at the industry-average rate. We assume that revenues followed their actual pattern of growth. Exhibit 7.5 reveals the results. Notice that the revenues used in the projection are the actual revenues shown earlier in Exhibit 7.4. The actual numbers of employees are shown for comparison purposes. In year 1, the actual labor productivity figure of revenues per employee of $117,119 is shown. This value, then, is grown at a rate of 10.85 percent per year, the industry average, to arrive at productivity figures for each of the remaining four years. Using these projected productivity figures and the actual revenues, we have calculated the expected number of employees Firm R would have had if it had grown its productivity at the industry average rate of 10.85 percent per year. Projected employees equal revenues divided by the projected productivity level. The cumulative effect is rather startling, with the difference in employment accounting for nearly one-fifth of the firm's employment by year 5.

An identical analysis was performed to determine how Firm R's employment levels would have looked had the company improved its labor productivity at a rate equal to the average rate of the firms in Quadrant I of our two-way performance map. Exhibit 7.6 reveals these results. As one would expect, the results would be even more dramatic. Had Firm R grown its productivity at 14.57 percent per year, it would have had nearly 30 percent fewer employees by year 5.

E X H I B I T   7.5

Projected productivity and employment levels based on competitor analysis (b).

Scenario 1:
Industry comparison starting in Year 1 and forecasting forward
Grow productivity at industry-average growth rate

	Year 1	Year 2	Year 3	Year 4	Year 5
Firm R's Revenue ($M)	1,697	1,838	1,947	2,300	2,706
Firm R's Actual Employees	14,490	14,780	16,472	17,200	19,000
Revenue per Employee Growth by 10.85%	$117,119*	129,827	143,913	159,528	176,836
Projected Employees	14,490*	14,168	13,531	14,418	15,303
Differences in Employees		622	2,941	2,782	3,697
Difference as % of Actual		4.2%	17.9%	16.2%	19.5%

*Actual

EXHIBIT 7.6

Projected productivity and employment levels based on competitor analysis.

Scenario 2:
Industry comparison starting in Year 1 and forecasting forward
Grow productivity at average growth rate of Quadrant I firms

	Year 1	Year 2	Year 3	Year 4	Year 5
Firm R's Revenue ($M)	1,697	1,838	1,947	2,300	2,706
Firm R's Actual Employees	14,490	14,780	16,472	17,200	19,000
Revenue per Employee Growth by 14.57%	$117,119*	134,184	153,734	176,133	201,796
Projected Employees	14,490*	13,698	12,666	13,059	13,410
Difference in Employees		1,082	3,806	4,141	5,590
Difference as % of Actual		7.3%	23.1%	24.1%	29.4%

*Actual

Continuing on, we examine the potential effects these different productivity growth rates would have had on Firm R's earnings. Exhibit 7.7 provides the details of one analysis of this question. A number of relevant pieces of information and assumptions are shown at the top of the figure. A conservative estimate of $40,000 pre-tax expense per employee was employed in the analysis. As we discussed in Chapter 5, this value should include all direct employment expenses. For both of the scenarios examined, the financial effects are shown for year 5 only, when the employment differences are the greatest. Scenario 1 reveals the potential differences that might have occurred had Firm R improved its productivity over the five-year horizon at the industry-average rate. Scenario 2 presents the same information for improvement at the average rate of the firms in Quadrant I.

Exhibit 7.7 begins the analysis by reporting the number of employees that Firm R would not have had on its employment rolls in year 5 had it improved its productivity at the two identified rates. These values—3,697 and 5,590—were previously calculated in Exhibits 7.5 and 7.6, respectively. These differences in employment were then multiplied by the assumed expense of $40,000 per employee to arrive at the total pre-tax savings that would have resulted from the reduced number of employees. The pre-tax savings were then converted to after-tax values using the assumed tax rate of 39 percent. We can see that these potential after-tax savings would have been quite substantial: $90 million for Scenario 1 and $136 million for Scenario 2.

It is interesting to examine the potential effects of these earnings differentials on the firm's stock price. The after-tax savings must first be converted to per-share values by dividing by the number of shares outstanding.

E X H I B I T   7.7

Potential impact of productivity growth rate on net income and stock price.

Assumptions		
Estimated expense per employee	$40,000	
Assumed tax rate	39%	
Firm R's shares outstanding (current)	90,021,489	
Firm R's share price (current)	$24.43	
Firm R's P/E multiple (current)	15	
Industry average P/E multiple (current)	23	
	Scenario 1	**Scenario 2**
Year 5 difference in employees	3,697	5,590
Pre-tax payroll savings	$147,880,000	$223,600,000
After-tax savings	$90,206,800	$136,396,000
Savings/incremental earnings per share	$1.00	$1.52
Potential stock price increase = P/E multiple × incremental earnings per share		
Potential stock price increase at Firm R's P/E multiple	$15.03	$22.73
Potential stock price increase at industry average P/E multiple	$23.05	$34.85

*Actual

In doing this, we find that $1 per share in after-tax earnings could have been generated or saved in year 5 under Scenario 1 and $1.52 per share under Scenario 2. We are able to translate these incremental earnings per share into potential or hypothetical stock price increases by multiplying them by Firm R's price-earnings multiple. Using the P/E multiple of 15 noted in the assumptions, we find that Firm R's stock price might have increased by as much as $15 under Scenario 1 and nearly $23 under Scenario 2. Because Firm R traded at a below-average multiple, the effects of the incremental earnings were less than they might have been for a firm trading at the industry average. To demonstrate the average effect such incremental earnings might have had on a firm's stock price, we multiplied the earnings by the industry-average P/E multiple of 23 (which is over 50 percent higher than Firm R's multiple). This resulted in values of $23.05 increase per share for Scenario 1 and $34.85 per share for Scenario 2.

The potential impact of the incremental earnings on Firm R's stock price is extraordinary, based on the analysis of Exhibit 7.7. Following the steps of the analysis, which we recognize as hypothetical and assume changes only in the earnings, we see that Firm R's stock price might have doubled from what it actually was in year 5 had the organization maintained a rate of productivity growth equal to the industry average. The increase might have been 150 percent with a productivity growth rate equal to the average of the firms in Quadrant I of the two-way performance map.

Such dramatic results do not arise from a one-time slowdown in productivity improvement. They are the result of an ongoing pattern of performance that creates a widening gap between a below-average firm and the top performers over time. In the case of Firm R, we saw that a substantial gap was created between the firm and even the average performer. We saw in Exhibit 7.4 that Firm R's productivity improved at an above-average rate (over 10.85 percent) only once in the five years examined. Furthermore, from year 2 to year 3, Firm R's productivity actually declined 4.9 percent, putting the firm at a significant disadvantage when compared to the average 10.85 percent improvement. An average cost per employee of $40,000 multiplies rapidly into considerable forgone earnings when a firm does not keep a tight rein on its headcount. Moreover, this figure is conservative for many organizations, making it all the more imperative for managers to manage their organizations' productivity closely.

We should recognize that Firm R would not have had to cut employment over the five years to have achieved the industry-average productivity growth rate of 10.85 percent. Rather, the firm could have added jobs, but obviously it should have added considerably fewer than it actually did. On the other hand, Firm R would have had to eliminate jobs to achieve the average productivity growth of the Quadrant I firms. Growth creates an environment in which organizations are able to increase employment while simultaneously improving productivity. Without growth, productivity improvements come only through job elimination. As a general rule, a firm's productivity growth equals its revenue growth when employment remains constant.

SUMMARY

Earlier chapters established the strategic importance of managing costs and the generic strategy of being the low-cost producer, which was defined as the producer that could ensure that no competitor could deliver an equivalent product or service at a lower cost. "Managing people" is the key to being the low-cost producer, because most other factor costs are similar for the majority of competitors. Most raw-material costs, direct wage rates, capital equipment costs, and computing software costs are approximately the same for a set of competitors or are at least available to all competitors at comparable rates. The firm that manages its employees best in its quest for positive productivity differentials will have a head start toward being the low-cost producer. Obviously, the converse is true: The firm that is at a disadvantage with regard to employee costs will find it difficult to become or remain the low-cost producer.

The problems and opportunities for the choice and refinement of the three generic strategies occur mostly within the operating divisions of a diversified, decentralized corporation. The corporate or parent company's strategic issues mainly consist of financing the company, choosing the businesses in which to compete, and the constant need to restructure the company through acquisitions and divestitures.

1. What is the practical importance of competitive analysis?
2. What natural instincts lead managers to resist detailed comparisons with competitors?
3. How do the economies-of-scale relationships among competitors assist strategic planning?
4. Similarly, how does the analysis of prevailing growth economies assist the strategic planning process?
5. How can two-way performance mapping assist a manager in understanding the competitive structure of his or her industry?

PART THREE

ANALYTICAL TOOLS FOR THE STRATEGIST

CHAPTER 8

Residual Income, Corporate Capital Charges, and EVA

INTRODUCTION

Parent companies measure a division's return on investment (ROI), a ratio of profit to investment, to determine the efficiency with which the division's assets are deployed to generate profits. An alternative set of approaches evaluates division performance based on variations of residual income (RI) measures, which include the recently popular Economic Value Added (EVA). Residual income and ROI measures both evaluate the performance of an autonomous division or profit center with the aim of relating the earnings of a division to the investment required to generate those earnings. RI and its derivative, EVA, are measured in dollars, however, rather than as a ratio.

In 1993, *Fortune* magazine's cover story, entitled "The Real Key to Creating Wealth," announced the arrival of EVA as the performance measure of the 1990s.[1] EVA is described in the literature as the "residual income" that remains after subtracting the cost of all capital (debt and equity) from after-tax operating profits. Since 1993, EVA has gained strong attention among managers of many U.S. companies. *CFO* magazine polled senior executives in November 1996 and reported that 30 percent had some form of EVA program in place and another 10 percent were currently evaluating this performance measure.[2]

The concept of EVA generated a surge of consulting activities, with numerous firms promoting their latest versions of effective performance measures. Cash flow return on investment (CFROI), total business return

---

1. "The Real Key to Creating Wealth," *Fortune*, September 30, 1993, 38.
2. "All About EVA" *CFO* (November 1996), 13.

(TBR), and shareholder value added (SVA) are just a few examples of the acronyms for various versions of the RI/EVA concept that became widely used in U.S. businesses. An appendix to this chapter contains additional information on some of these measures.

Is EVA really "residual income" repackaged for the 1990s? A practice leader at a leading compensation consulting firm seems to believe it is: "The fact is, EVA, CFROI, and all the others were premised on fundamental economics that 20 years ago was called residual income."[3] To simplify this discussion, we will refer to these various methods with the generic title residual income, or RI.

DEFINITION OF RESIDUAL INCOME

Residual income is a divisional profitability indicator that represents the "profit" remaining after the suppliers of all the resources required to generate revenues have been fairly compensated, including the supplier of the capital, the parent corporation. It is determined by assessing a capital charge, which is subtracted from division income, to arrive at division RI. The capital charge encourages judicious asset management at the division level because it assesses the division for the cost of the investment funds provided by the corporation. The capital charge is calculated by multiplying the investment base by a prescribed rate, which reflects the required return to the suppliers of capital.

For example, suppose a division had a year-end pre-tax profit of $20,000 on an investment (net assets) of $50,000, and suppose the company's cost of capital was 10 percent. The 10 percent would be applied to the investment base to determine a capital charge of $5000. The capital charge would then be deducted from the division profit of $20,000, to yield an RI of $15,000. The $5000 capital charge reflects the opportunity cost to the parent corporation of the division's investment base. The RI of $15,000 represents profit over and above the minimum division net income required to justify continued investment in the division.

RESIDUAL INCOME VERSUS RETURN ON INVESTMENT

The primary objective of a division manager is to sustain a consistently outstanding return on invested capital while meeting the corporate expectations for cash flow and growth, as described in Chapters 1 and 2.

Advantages of ROI Measures

The following are advantages of ROI measures:

---

3. "Metric Wars," *CFO* (October 1996), A1.

1. They measure the efficiency with which a division uses its assets, regardless of the size of the investment base.
2. They are familiar concepts in widespread use. The investment community commonly employs percentage rates of return to evaluate the performance of a company. Shareholders, security analysts, and business periodicals use ROI to compare the performances of industries, companies, and product lines.
3. They are directly comparable to the company's cost of capital. An ROI of 15 percent can be readily related to a 10 percent cost of capital.

One Major Disadvantage of ROI Measures

Under certain circumstances, a division manager may improve his or her ROI by not investing in, or even by divesting, lines of business that offer attractive returns. Any line of business that yields a return below the current average ROI (for all other lines of business in the division) reduces the overall ROI. The example below illustrates this incentive to disinvest or divest. Assume that the parent company of the XYZ Division has a cost of capital of 10 percent.

XYZ Division

| | Total | Products | | | |
		A	B	C	D
ROI, %	20	15	20	27	25
Cost of Capital = 10%					

Given the relative profitability of the product lines together with a bonus system that would handsomely reward the achievement of a high ROI, the division manager would conclude that Product A should be phased out.

In the above example, the division ROI was increased from 20 percent to 22 percent by liquidating product line A. The ROI for product line A, however, was 15 percent, well above the division's 10 percent cost of capital. But division performance, as measured by ROI, was improved by divesting this successful product line. This example shows how actions designed to maximize ROI could result in a reduction in the long-term performance of the firm—a distinct disadvantage of ROI measures.

The Advantages of RI Measures

The advantages of RI measures include the following:

1. They encourage division managers to invest in opportunities that generate a return above the cost of capital, because any such investment increases RI.

2. They allow for different rate-of-return objectives for different assets. Management may feel that inventories, which could be financed by short-term credit, should be charged a higher rate than fixed assets, which would be more likely to be financed by a combination of long-term debt and equity.

3. They allow for different return objectives for different divisions, which facilitates structuring division performance objectives and incentive compensation programs to be consistent with industry norms and overall corporate strategy.

The use of RI for performance evaluation would encourage further investment in each product line in the example cited above, because each would provide positive RI.

The Major Disadvantage of RI Measures

The use of RI measures may cause motivational problems, because the capital charge rate the parent corporation employs may seem arbitrary, complicate planning, frustrate managers, and thus reduce the incentives to control the investment base. This is especially true when the capital charge rate changes frequently, or if the capital charge results in a positive net income becoming a loss at the RI line.

COMPONENTS OF RI

Arbitrarily allocated costs, revenues, assets, or liabilities should not negatively impact the accurate assessment of division performance. Methods for valuing each component of RI are discussed below.

The Investment Base

The three most commonly used investment bases are total assets, net assets (total assets less current liabilities), and corporate equity (total assets less total liabilities).

Total Assets
The use of total assets as the investment base focuses on the capital employed by a division without regard to how the assets are financed. The inclusion of a specific balance-sheet account in the investment base depends upon the degree of control division management exercises over the level of the account. Cash should be included in the total asset base in the amount necessary for ongoing operations. Any excess cash, above the minimum cash balance required for division operations, would be carried in a corporate account.

Accounts receivable and inventory are usually under the control of a division and vary with the level of business activity and management policies; thus they are included in the total asset base. If corporate policy affects the level of these assets, then appropriate adjustments should be made to approximate the levels these asset accounts would take without corporate interference.

Fixed assets are included in the total asset base, but in the case of more than one division sharing the use of an asset, the value of the asset should be allocated among the divisions. The allocation of jointly used assets, such as a shared office facility, is frequently based on each division's proportional usage.

Idle assets, which do not contribute to profits, should be included in the investment base only if the division management has the option of disposing of the idle assets. Division management can then trade off the potential future benefit of keeping the assets versus reduced division performance in the near term. If the corporation requires that the idle assets be retained by the division, then these assets should be excluded from the division's investment base.

The use of total assets to determine the investment base is flawed in most situations because it overestimates the corporate investment in the division. Assets are financed by a combination if equity, debt, and current liabilities. The evaluation of division performance based on total assets ignores the impact division management can have on the level of accounts payable and other current liabilities. Accounts payable can contribute significantly to the financing of the division's assets. To exclude them in calculating the investment base does not provide division management with the proper incentives, nor does it reward the division's contribution to reducing the parent corporation's cash requirements.

Net Assets

Net assets are defined as total assets less current liabilities. Total assets should be determined as described in the previous section, including the discussion of idle assets. The appropriate current liabilities to deduct from total assets to determine the division's investment base are accounts payable, which are normally under the control of division management. Credit terms are frequently negotiable and can impact upon the ultimate price of purchased materials. The selection of vendors and the negotiating power and skill of the division management determines credit terms and can significantly alter the parent corporation's investment in a division. Any other short-term debt should be carried by the parent corporation, as well as any interest expense associated with the debt.

The use of net assets to determine the investment base provides the best measure of the investment demands that the division places on the parent corporation. It also provides the proper incentives to division management to minimize the investment required from the parent corporation.

Corporate Equity

Equating the division's investment base with corporate equity is equivalent to using a net-asset investment base, unless the division has long-term debt on its balance sheet. A more accurate evaluation of division operating performance would be achieved by eliminating all division debt from the investment base and all interest expense from the division's income statement. The end result would be that corporate equity and net assets are identical measures of the division's investment base.

Valuation of Assets

In general, the assets and liabilities included in determining the investment base for a division should be valued at their book value in the division's accounts. The alternatives available for fixed asset valuation are net book value, gross book value, and replacement cost. Net book value is the most common method of valuing assets, but it may reduce the management's incentive to invest in new equipment, especially if the equipment to be replaced has been heavily depreciated. Division management may attempt to improve performance by exploiting (and not replacing) the existing depreciated fixed asset base.

The use of gross book value in the investment base would keep the fixed asset values constant over time and eliminate the automatic improvement in returns that would result from using the lower, new book value. Valuing fixed assets at gross book value would fail to account for the declining profitability of older assets as a result of reduced productivity, increased maintenance expense, and increased downtime.

The use of replacement costs as a basis for fixed asset valuation would be intended to compensate for the long-term effects of inflation. Income based on current prices is often related to an investment base that includes a high proportion of older fixed assets, carried on the books at low historical costs. Return measures calculated on this base might indicate inflated returns compared, say, to a competitor with new assets purchased at more current prices. Implementing replacement-cost valuation methods, however, would require extensive effort and much subjective judgment, and it might not be possible because of imperfect markets, specialized equipment, or changes in technology. The replacement-cost approach is prohibitively difficult to implement, from a practical standpoint.

Inventory valuation is also affected by inflation. The use of LIFO (last in, first out) inventory accounting methods versus FIFO (first in, first out) could result in different asset valuations for the same physical inventory during periods of inflation. The Internal Revenue Service rules for inventory accounting usually result in a specified approach to these issues that are not greatly manageable by either a parent company or its divisions. The inventory values carried in the accounting records are generally preferable because they are objectively determined and readily available.

The Capital Charge Rate

The capital charge rate is used for the purpose of calculating RI and it is also the hurdle rate for new investment opportunities. A division manager

evaluated on the basis of RI would normally accept any investment proposal that promised a return greater than the capital charge rate. There are
two philosophies on how to set the capital charge rate: the weighted average of the cost of debt and the cost of equity, often referred to as the *cost of
capital*, or the cost of debt. These two approaches to setting the capital charge
rate define a range within which the capital charge rate would usually fall.
At a minimum, a division must return the cost of the debt that could be
eliminated if the division were liquidated. The most any division should be
required to contribute to a parent company would be its full share of the
corporation's cost of funds, which would be the corporation's weighted
average cost of capital (WACC). Lenders who supply funds contract for a
fixed return, while equity holders invest with the expectation of a return
commensurate with that of other investments of similar risk.

The Weighted-Average Cost of Debt and Equity

There are practical problems with assessing a capital charge equal to the
weighted-average cost of debt and equity:

1. Calculation of the cost of capital involves estimating the cost of
   equity. The cost of equity is the subject of considerable debate
   and depends on subjective estimates.
2. The corporation's risk profile may differ considerably from a division's risk profile. Adjusting the corporation's cost of capital to
   account for a division with a different risk level is subjective. Not
   adjusting for different risk levels among divisions might be unfair,
   penalizing low-risk divisions and benefiting high-risk divisions.

The Cost of Debt

Alternatively, a corporation could consider its equity investment fixed and
its basic objective to maximize profit for its shareholders. A division earning a return higher than the cost of borrowed funds would add to shareholder value, representing the effective use of financial leverage. The alternative to maintaining the investment in a division would be to divest the
division, recover the invested funds, and reduce the outstanding corporate
debt. Concomitantly, profits would be improved by divesting any division
that earned a return less than the interest rate on the corporation's debt. If
the parent corporation were debt-free, the operative capital charge rate
would equal the return that the corporation could earn on excess cash bal-
ances. The use of a capital-charge rate based upon the cost of debt would
be more appropriate for smaller divisions than those that make up a substantial part of the corporation, which might have funding needs large
enough to require additional equity.

The following are advantages of a capital charge rate based upon the
cost of debt:

1. It is a minimum figure that allows positive RI to be earned by a
   business that is struggling to improve and that has performance

approaching adequate levels. This positive RI will provide positive reinforcement for motivational purposes.

2. The capital charge assessed against a division would be accepted, because the interest rate on corporate debt would be understood and accepted by division managers.

The motivational benefits of a lower capital charge rate may be offset by the incentive to invest in marginal projects that return only slightly
more than the cost of debt. Accepting these marginal projects would increase
RI, but cash requirements would also grow. The growing cash needs would
have to be financed with higher-cost debt (with an increasing debt-to-
equity ratio) or with high-cost equity. Thus, the capital charge rate would
need to be equal to or greater than the interest rate on corporate debt but
less than or equal to the cost of capital.

Net Income

Division net income should normally reflect only those revenues and costs
that are the direct result of division efforts and decisions; they should include
no corporate cost allocations. Otherwise, substantial effort may be expend-
ed by division managers to alter the allocation of corporate expenses to
their divisions, diverting effort from the primary task of improving the division's contribution to corporate performance. The best measure of the contribution of a division to corporate profit is income before any corporate
allocations and before tax. This measure determines the amount each division has contributed to the parent, from which administrative expenses,
interest expenses, taxes, and dividends must be paid.

The allocation of corporate expenses to the divisions is controllable,
and therefore proper, when the divisions request the use of corporate
resources and are charged for the quantity consumed—for example, when
a division requests design assistance from the corporate engineering staff.
The division should be charged for the value of the services rendered by
the engineering staff just as if it had contracted with an outside consultant.
This would provide an accurate measure of the profitability of the division as a stand-alone economic entity.

Generally, taxes should be excluded from the calculation of RI, because
the amount of tax liability incurred by the corporation is a function of overall corporate profitability, past corporate performance, corporate tax-account-
ing policies, and tax rates. The exception to excluding tax effects from divisional performance evaluation applies to industries that qualify for special tax
incentives, such as mining or oil exploration. To compare the performance of
a division in the extractive industries to another division on a before-tax basis,
without accounting for the special tax treatment, would be misleading.

SUMMARY

RI is an effective management control tool because it reinforces the primary objective of a division manager, which is to sustain a consistently outstanding return on invested capital. Both ROI and RI measures encourage the efficient use of assets, but RI measures have the added advantage of encouraging profitable growth. The division's income and investment base should reflect only the impact of division management's actions and should exclude all corporate allocations. The capital charge rate should represent the opportunity cost to the parent corporation of the funds invested in the division.

We should emphasize that RI measures have their maximum effect when divisions have excessive assets in place, as might result from an absence of proper control. The implementation of an RI system in such a situation, combined with strong incentives based on the division's ROI, have been observed to lead to rapid and significant improvement in asset utilization. After asset levels reach more optimal levels, the continued use of the RI measures have a less-pronounced effect.

This discussion has focused on ways to motivate division management to maximize their returns on investment through performance measures that bring congruence to corporate-level and division-level goals and objectives. We move on in Chapter 9 to discuss the complex interrelationships among cash flow, growth, and ROI goals.

Review Questions

1. What are the basic differences between performance measures based on *return on investment* and those based on *residual income*?

2. What are the advantages and disadvantages of each method of performance measurement?

3. What factors should be considered in estimating the various parameters required for the calculation of RI?

4. Is RI an effective long-run management tool, or is it most effective when changes need to be induced?

Appendix 8A: Additional Information on value Added Measures

Economic Value Added (EVA)

Description: The residual income that remains after subtracting the cost of all capital (debt and equity) from after-tax operating profits.

$$EVA = (r - c) \times capital$$

Where r = rate of return on capital
    c = WACC
  Capital = capital employed at *beginning* of year

Therefore, a firm with

   A rate of return of 15 percent
   A cost of capital of 10 percent
   A capital base of $10 billion

Would have an EVA of $500 million:

$$EVA = (r - c) \times capital$$
$$\$500 \text{ million} = (15\% - 10\%) \times \$10 \text{ billion}$$

How Can EVA Be Increased?

EVA can be increased if the following occur:

1. If the return earned on the capital already employed is improved (i.e., if there are more profits without additional investments in capital).
2. If additional capital is invested in projects or strategies that generate earnings in excess of the cost of capital.
3. If capital is withdrawn from activities that produce inadequate returns.

Market Value Added (MVA)

Description: The difference between the cash that both debt and equity investors have contributed to a company and the value of the cash that they expect to get out of it over time.

Calculation: MVA = market value – capital

Therefore, a firm that has

   Current market value of $15 billion
   Raised directly from investors and retained from earnings $10 billion in capital

Would have an MVA of $5 billion:

$$MVA = \text{market value} - \text{capital}$$
$$\$5 \text{ billion} = \$15 \text{ billion} - \$10 \text{ billion}$$

CHAPTER 9

Analytical Relationships Among Cash Flow, Growth, and Investment Goals

INTRODUCTION

A corporate manager should attempt to achieve a pattern of improving operating results that are predictable from year to year. As we have seen, a number of different criteria are used to measure management or organizational performance and to assess its improvement. These measures include the levels of profit or cash flow and the growth rate of sales, assets, or profits of a given operating unit. Further, as noted in Chapter 8, some firms use more complex measures that involve various versions of profit or cash flow (i.e., before or after taxes) compared with the investment employed to generate the returns. The investment may be total assets or net assets (total assets less current liabilities). Plant, property, and equipment may be current book value or the constantly rising replacement cost. Some firms subtract all current liabilities to calculate net assets, while others subtract only accounts payable.

This chapter develops analytical relationships among these various growth, profit, and investment parameters. These relationships provide tools that assist in the strategic process of developing feasible, self-reinforcing sets of operating goals and in making efficient trade-offs among conflicting objectives. The computing technology available today makes the generation of pro forma financial statements a straightforward exercise. For the purpose of strategic planning, however, utilization of the quantitative relationships often helps to provide rapid estimates of the likely consequences of various strategic alternatives. These quantitative relationships also provide a means to examine trade-offs among strategic alternatives via the use of optimization techniques. Let us investigate some of these analytical relationships among the most common corporate goals.

THE RELATIONSHIP BETWEEN CASH FLOW AND GROWTH FOR A CORPORATION

In a familiar planning situation, the firm with the following financial results is approaching the end of an operating period and is planning for the next period.

Expected Balance Sheet at End of the Period

Cash	$25	Accounts payable	$ 50
Accounts receivable	75	Accrued taxes	50
Inventories	75	Current liabilities	$100
Current assets	$175		
Net fixed assets	200	Debt	$150
Other assets	25	Equity	150
Total assets	$400	Total liabilities	$400
		+ owners' equity (OE)	

Expected Income Statement for the Period

Sales	$500
Cost of goods sold	400
Gross margin	$100
General and administrative (G&A) expense	20
Interest expense	20
Profit before tax	$ 60
Tax	30
Profit after tax	$ 30
Dividends paid	$ 5

Other data needed are as follows:

Depreciation rate	=	10% of beginning fixed assets
Dividend-payout ratio	=	16.67%
Tax rate	=	50%

Using this example company, we will develop the options available for cash flow and growth based on the following assumptions:

1. The firm maintains a constant debt-to-equity ratio.
2. The firm maintains a constant dividend-payout percentage.
3. Profit before tax, current assets, current liabilities, fixed assets, and other assets change with the growth rate in sales.

4. Depreciation is reinvested in fixed assets.

Assume that the example firm grew at an actual positive growth rate, G, in the next period, where G is the combination of real growth and inflation. The general form of the cash flow would be as follows:

Cash-Flow Statement

Profit after tax	+
Depreciation	+
Change in cash	−
Change in accounts receivable	−
Change in inventories	−
Fixed-asset additions	−
Change in other assets	−
Change in accounts payable	+
Change in accrued taxes	+
Dividends paid	−
Additional debt	+
Cash flow	Total

where   + = a source of cash
          − = a use of cash.

With this cash-flow statement, we can develop a general expression for cash flow as a function of the growth rate, G:

$$
\begin{aligned}
\text{Cash flow} = \ & (\text{EBIT} - I)(1 + G)(1 - t)(1 - \text{DPO}\%) + \text{Depr} - \text{Depr} \\
- \ & [(\text{FA}_o)(1 + G) - \text{FA}_o] - [(C_o)(1 + G) - C_o] \\
- \ & [(\text{AR}_o)(1 + G) - \text{AR}_o] - [(\text{INV}_o)(1 + G) - \text{INV}_o] \\
- \ & [(\text{OA}_o)(1 + G) - \text{OA}_o] + [(\text{AP}_o)(1 + G) - \text{AP}_o] \\
+ \ & [(\text{AT}_o)(1 + G) - \text{AT}_o] + \text{Additional debt}
\end{aligned}
$$

where:

o = Beginning-of-period value
EBIT = Earnings before interest and taxes (current period)
Depr = Depreciation (next period)
G = Actual growth rate
I = Interest expense on beginning debt
t = Tax rate
DPO% = Dividend-payout percentage; $1 - \text{DPO}\% = P = \%$ of profit retained
FA = Fixed assets
C = Cash
AR = Accounts receivable
INV = Inventories
OA = Other assets

$$AP = \text{Accounts payable}$$
$$AT = \text{Accrued taxes}$$

Additional

$$\text{debt} = (\text{Debt-to-equity ratio, } D/E)(EBIT - I)(1 + G)(1 - t)$$
$$(1 - DPO\%)$$

Note that the o indicates the value of a variable at the beginning of the period. Multiplying the beginning-of-the period value by $1 + G$ provides the end-of-the-period value for that variable. Subtracting the beginning-of-the-period value from the end-of-the-period value gives the change in the variable during the period.

If we separate the terms, including G, and collect them, we have

$$\begin{aligned}
\text{Cash flow} = {} & (EBIT - I)(1 + G)(1 - t)(1 - DPO\%) + (D/E)(EBIT - I)(1 + G) \\
& (1 - t)(1 - DPO\%) + Depr - Depr + (AP_o)(1 + G) \\
& + (AT_o)(1 + G) \\
& - (FA_o)(1 + G) - (C_o)(1 + G) - (AR_o)(1 + G) \\
& - (INV_o)(1 + G) - (OA_o)(1 + G) + FA_o + C_o + AR_o \\
& + INV_o + OA_o - AP_o - AT_o
\end{aligned}$$

This will reduce to Equation 1:

$$\text{Cash flow} = (EBIT - I)(1 - t)(1 - DPO\%)(1 + G)(1 + D/E) - (NA_o)(G)$$

where

$$NA = \text{Net assets (total assets - current liabilities)}$$
$$D/E = \text{Debt-to-equity ratio}$$

Let us return to our example and substitute the values listed in the balance sheet and income statement to determine the equation relating cash flow to growth. The following equation is obtained:

$$\begin{aligned}
\text{Cash flow} &= (80 - 20)(0.5)(0.833)(1 + G)(1 + 1) - 300G \\
&= 50(1 + G) - 300G \\
&= 50 - 250G
\end{aligned}$$

This equation provides for the direct calculation of cash flow for any anticipated growth rate. Suppose we are interested in the cash-balancing growth rate (i.e., the rate at which the cash generated would just equal the additional cash needed to finance the expanded operations). Setting cash flow equal to zero, we have

$$\begin{aligned}
0 &= 50 - 250G \\
G &= 0.20
\end{aligned}$$

Thus, for our example firm, the cash-balancing growth rate is 20 percent.

Given the negative, linear relationship between cash flow and growth, we can graph a schedule for the firm:

Growth rate	−0.10	0	0.10	0.20	0.30	0.40	0.50
Cash flow	75	50	25	0	−25	−50	−75

These values are plotted in Exhibit 9.1. It follows that if market conditions don't permit growth at the rate of 20 percent per year, or if management chooses to grow more slowly, positive cash flows will result. At a 10 percent growth rate, a positive cash flow of 25 would be produced. Conversely, a 40 percent growth rate would require an external cash injection of 50. Therein lies the problem for fast-growing, start-up businesses.

THE EFFECTS OF BUSINESS GROWTH, INFLATION, AND CAPACITY/DEMAND RELATIONSHIPS

Recall the general cash-flow equation developed earlier (Equation 1):

Cash flow $= (EBIT - I)(1 - t)(1 - DPO\%)(1 + G)(1 + D/E) - (NA_o)(G)$

The growth rate, G, is recognized to be the composite of real growth in unit sales (e.g., board feet, tons) and inflation or deflation (i.e., price changes). Thus, in algebraic terms,

$$G = [(1 + G_p)(1 + G_v) - 1]$$

where

$$G_p = \text{growth in prices}$$
$$G_v = \text{growth in units}$$

Continuing, we redefine NA_o as follows:

$$NA_o = FA_o + WC_o$$

Where

$$FA_o = \text{Beginning fixed assets}$$
$$WC_o = \text{Beginning working capital}$$

E X H I B I T   9.1

Relationship between cash flow and growth.

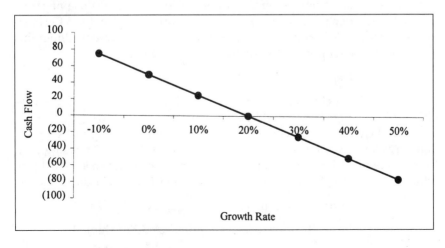

Substituting these terms in Equation 1 gives

Cash flow = $(EBIT - I)(1 - t)(1 + G)(1 - DPO\%)(1 + D/E) - FA_o(G) - WC_o(G)$

In many businesses, the growth rate of working capital equals the growth in sales, which we defined above to be $[(1 + G_p)(1 + G_v) - 1]$. In the short run, however, this assumption is not realistic for fixed assets. Fixed assets tend to increase in discrete increments as capacity is expanded, not smoothly as sales increase. Thus it is necessary to adjust the cash-flow equation to account for this circumstance if more exact cash flows are to be calculated in short-run situations.

If a capital plan exists for the company, either to expand capacity in large discrete increments or to rebuild its technological base, then the cash flow associated with the change in fixed assets, $FA_o G$, will equal depreciation (Depr) less planned capital expenditures (PCE). When a capital expenditure plan exists, the general cash-flow equation then becomes Equation 2.

$$Cash\ flow\ =\ (EBIT - I)(1 - t)(1 + G_p)(1 + G_v)(1 - DPO\%)(1 + D/E)$$
$$+\ Depr - PCE - WC_o[(1 + G_p)(1 + G_v) - 1]$$

Equation 2 presents a general expression for cash flow, particularly useful for firms seeking to rebuild their asset bases. Equation 2 can be altered to reflect the varying capacity/demand relationships faced by different businesses. The income portion of the equation would remain unchanged. The term $+ Depr - PCE - WC_o[(1 + G_p)(1 + G_v) - 1]$, however, would vary, depending on the asset strategy of the business.

The asset portion of Equation 2 would become $NA_o[(1 + G_p)(1 + G_v) - 1]$ in the case of a rapidly growing business in which the firm is operating at capacity and the fixed assets must be expanded in proportion to sales growth. This is known as a growth strategy for assets, and it might apply to a firm in a business such as computers.

In the case of an unprofitable business facing severe competition, excess capacity in its industry, and/or mature (slow-growth) markets, the firm might choose not to reinvest depreciation and might use negative growth rates (declining sales) to extract the working capital from the business; this strategy is known as "harvesting," or disinvestment. Under this scenario, the asset portion of Equation 2 would become

$$+ Depr - WC_o[(1 + G_p)(1 + G_v) - 1]$$

Note that a composite negative growth rate would result in working-capital changes that would generate positive cash flows.

In the case of an effective cash producer with a strong market position in a slow-growth market, the firm might use a "holding" strategy, reinvesting depreciation to maintain its competitive position as a low-cost producer. In this case, the asset portion of Equation 2 would become

$$+ Depr - Depr\ reinvested - WC_o[(1 + G_p)(1 + G_v) - 1]$$

The results for the four cases are summarized in Exhibit 9.2.

E X H I B I T   9.2

Expressions for Different Asset Strategies.

Strategy	Cash Flow from Asset Changes
Growth	$- NA_o[(1 + G_p)(1 + G_v) - 1]$
Disinvestment	$+ Depr - WC_o[(1 + G_p)(1 + G_v) - 1]$
Holding	$+ Depr - Depr\ reinvested$
	$- WC_o[(1 + G_p)(1 + G_v) - 1]$
Rebuild and general case	$+ Depr - PCE - WC_o[(1 + G_p)(1 + G_v) - 1]$

ADAPTING THE RELATIONSHIPS FOR A DIVISION OF A DECENTRALIZED COMPANY

The foregoing discussion has focused on the goal trade-offs for a corporation. Similar methods can be used to determine the cash-balancing growth rate for a division of a corporation. Recall Equation 1, where

$$\text{Cash flow} = (EBIT - I)(1 - t)(1 - DPO\%)(1 + G)(1 + D/E) - (NA_o)(G)$$

To apply this equation to the typical capital structure of an operating division of a company, we assume that all financing for the division is provided by the corporate parent. In most corporate structures, divisions have no debt or equity and pay no interest expense or dividends. For a division then, the cash-balancing growth rate becomes a function of the profit after tax (PAT) and the net assets (Equation 3):

$$\text{Cash flow} = (PAT_o)(1 + G) - NA_o G$$

Recall that this equation was developed based on the assumption that all balance-sheet items would grow at the same rate as sales. The asset section of the equation must therefore be adjusted if cash flows are to be calculated in the short run for different market situations and capacity/demand relationships. For the division situation, the asset portion of Equation 3 must be adjusted in the same way as the corporate adjustments for strategic situations of growth, harvest, hold, or rebuild.

SUMMARY

The algebraic relationships developed in this chapter assist the strategist in understanding the natural combinations of ROI, cash flow, and growth that are feasible with the organization's existing capital structure. These relationships apply in the same way to corporations, to divisions, or to product lines within divisions. The appendix to this chapter indicates that the formulation derived above is algebraically equivalent to the well-known finance formula for the sustainable growth rate for the special case of a company operating at capacity and growing rapidly. There are two advantages available from the approach developed here. The formulas developed in this chapter provide a means to calculate expected cash flows attendant to a given growth rate, as well as the cash-balancing growth rate for a company or a division of a company. The formulas derived here also allow for the analysis of cash flow and growth relationships for businesses with "hold," "harvest," and "rebuild" strategies, in addition to the "invest" strategy addressed by the standard finance formula.

The next chapter addresses the various methods used by strategists to value acquisitions and divestitures.

Review Questions

1. What is the basic form of the relationship between cash flow and growth for a company or a division of a larger company?
2. What are the basic asset strategies related to growth?
3. How do the equations presented above relate to the standard finance formula for a firm's cash-balancing growth rate?

Appendix 9A: The Long-Term Cash-Balancing Growth Rate of a Company

Equation 1, the formula for the cash-balancing growth rate in the next planning period, can be further modified to reflect longer term trends based on historical rates of return and interest rates.

$$\text{Cash flow} = (\text{EBIT} - I)(1 - t)(1 - \text{DPO\%})(1 + G)(1 + D/E) - (NA_0)(G)$$

Various algebraic manipulations show that Equation 1 is equivalent to the following (Equation 4):

$$G^* = D/E(r - i)P + rP$$

where

$$
\begin{aligned}
G^* &= \text{the long-term cash-balancing rate of growth} \\
D/E &= \text{debt/equity ratio} \\
P &= \text{\% of profits retained} \\
r &= \text{after-tax, before-interest return on beginning net assets} \\
i &= \text{after-tax cost of debt (on beginning debt)}
\end{aligned}
$$

Equation 4 is the well-known finance formula for the long-term maximum sustainable growth rate of a firm, given the previously stipulated assumptions about the relationships among sales, profits, and asset levels, and the following limitations. This formulation is based on the assumption that the fixed assets must grow at the rate of growth of sales, and thus it treats only the case of a rapidly growing business operating at capacity. This formulation also assumes that the firm has a return on beginning equity of less than 100 percent [or a return on net assets (NA) of less than $100\%/(1 + D/E)$]. A firm that is able to achieve a higher return will be able to finance any rate of growth through the use of internally generated funds. For such a firm, each dollar increase in assets results in at least a dollar increase in funds available. It is well known that the long-term cash-balancing growth rate is also equal to the return on equity times the percentage of profit retained, or the "rate of retained earnings to equity."

CHAPTER 10

The Valuation of
Acquisitions and
Divestitures

INTRODUCTION

Many companies are involved in a continuous strategic process involving acquisitions and divestitures. They are seeking to improve their strategic positioning by acquiring competitors or companies that extend product lines, or by improving the focus of their perceived "core businesses" through the divestiture of nonessential product lines, plants, or entire businesses. Business today is a worldwide, very complex, compete-or-perish environment. A firm may be active in the pursuit of acquisitions only to find that it has become a target of another predator company. This dilemma is so pervasive among publicly traded companies that a variety of "poison pills" have been devised to assist in warding off unwanted suitors. Privately held companies are immune to such hostile takeover attempts because there is no way "raiders" can force shareholders to consider the raiders' offers. Public companies, on the other hand, are always subject to offers to buy their shares, which the shareholders, as a group, are free to accept or reject.

Within this environment acquirers and divesters must mutually try to estimate the fair market value of a business. In fact, there is little likelihood of a deal being consummated unless both sides of the negotiation perceive the estimated value as "fair." This chapter discusses some of the methods that are widely used in efforts to derive this much-sought-after fair market value. Because the primary emphasis of this book is corporate strategy, not finance, these methods will not be developed in great detail. But recognize that strategists would be wise to understand the basic premises of these methods and their relevance to valuing acquisitions and divestitures. Also, they should understand the value of the current organization, which would assist them in arranging appropriate corporate financing and in properly analyzing such additional strategic options as continuing to operate the business, spinning off one or more businesses, or buying back the company's shares. These options are examined in more detail in Chapter 13.

This chapter also analyzes the significant difficulties that impede attempts to estimate fair market values for the ebusiness, high-technology, and communications sectors of the U.S. economy, herein referred to as "the new economy." As stated in Chapter 3, many of these businesses require extensive capital investment, may go for years in the development stage with little or no revenues, and may have trouble projecting far enough into the future to forecast any profits. Yet, capital is being raised, the R&D work is going forward, new products and services are being developed and perfected, and customers are eagerly waiting for the results. And the technology now available allows successful developments to be propagated through the economy at breathtaking speed. Many of the new-economy firms have public market valuations in the tens of billions of dollars, and certainly some methods must assist investors in the valuation process. This chapter shows some approaches that have been put forward to assist in the derivation of these elusive values.

TWO BASIC HISTORICAL APPROACHES TO THE VALUATION OF BUSINESSES

For more than a hundred years, two basic approaches have been used to determine the market value of a business. These determinations are based on two factors: (1) the value of the assets of the business, or (2) the actual or perceived earning power of the business. Even if a business is losing money in its operations, the business is usually worth at least the fair market value of its assets. This value might be the one remaining on the books after the write-downs for depreciation. It could be the replacement value or the amount of cash that would be required to replace the assets, if they are in good working order. The value of the assets usually places a floor on the fair market value of a business.

The ability to generate earnings elevates the value of a business beyond the value of the assets. A buyer of a business should be willing to pay a price such that the earnings of the firm represent a reasonable return on the buyer's investment. Thus, businesses that have a high degree of demonstrated earning power should command a higher fair market value. We discuss next the two basic methods for converting a business's earning power into a market price.

The Net Present Value Method

The first method of valuing a business based on its earnings performance is referred to as the net present value (NPV) method, or the discounted cash flow (DCF) method. This approach commences with a forecast of the future cash flows likely to accrue over some finite time horizon. In recent years, this so-called planning horizon has been getting shorter and shorter, as investors have become risk-averse in a time of rapid and precipitous change. The next step in this process is to discount the cash flows to derive the present value of the discounted cash flows (DCFS). The final step is to compare or net out the price to be paid with the present value of future cash flows, which leads to the NPV of the investment. It is also customary to calculate the internal rate of return (IRR) of the investment, which is the return the purchaser would receive on the investment given the forecast cash flows. The IRR also represents the discount rate at which the investment literally equals the discounted future cash flows. Exhibit 10.1 gives an example of the DCF/NPV analysis of the valuation of the Riviera Corporation, one of the divisions of the Pelican Corporation presented later in this book following Chapter 11. In this case, an acquisition of the target company at the indicated price of $30 million would provide the purchasers a substantial return on their investment. The strategic questions for Pelican are whether the best option is to sell the business, and secondarily, whether $30 million is a fair price.

The Multiples Method

The second basic method of valuing businesses employs multiples or constant multipliers of the firm's current, known performance measures, which are derived from the prevailing market values of similar or comparable businesses. In this approach, the usual measures of corporate performance, revenues, assets, net income, and cash flow (often EBITDA, earnings before interest, taxes, depreciation, and amortization) are compared to the market prices of recent transactions in which businesses were bought and sold. These comparisons produce ratios of the market prices of concluded deals to the various performance measures for the firms involved. The averages of these actual ratios of market price to performance measures, such as 10 times net income or 5 times EBITDA, provide a reasonable method of estimating the value of any comparable business. If a business in which we are interested has an EBITDA of $10 million, and the prevailing multiple (ratio) of fair market price to EBITDA is 5, then the business would be estimated to have a fair market value of $50 million.

This method avoids the obvious risk inherent in attempting to estimate the future cash flows of a business changing managements. We are obviously left with estimating each of the two parameters necessary to make the calculation of the value. First, the two parties to the negotiation must agree on a value of EBITDA to be used in the calculation. If the business is in a state of flux, there might be debate as to the use of the last completed year's EBITDA value; the trailing, most recent 12-month value; or some realistic estimate of the current year's likely value. If the financial attributes of the

E x h i b i t   10.1

NPV model for Riviera Corporation.

Bidding Price		$30,000				
Initial Equity Investment		$5,000				
Required Debt Amount		$25,000				
Interest Rate on Debt		10%				
Discount Rate (R)		15%				
Terminal Growth Rate (g)		0%				

	2001	2002	2003	2004	2005	2006
Sales	$29,550	$32,769	$33,753	$34,765	$35,808	$36,882
COGS		(21,031)	(21,325)	(21,617)	(22,201)	(22,867)
Gross Margin		11,738	12,428	13,148	13,607	14,015
SG&A		(6,789)	(6,992)	(7,202)	(7,418)	(7,641)
Misc. Income (Expense)		(297)	(306)	(315)	(325)	(334)
Corporate Overhead		(655)	(675)	(695)	(716)	(738)
EBIT		3,997	4,454	4,936	5,148	5,303
Interest Expense		(2,371)	(2,252)	(2,091)	(1,906)	(1,697)
Income Before Tax		1,626	2,203	2,844	3,242	3,605
Income Tax		(569)	(771)	(996)	(1,135)	(1,262)
Amortization of Goodwill		(2,185)	(2,185)	(2,185)	(2,185)	(2,185)
Net Income		(1,128)	(753)	(336)	(78)	158
Add: Depreciation		338	307	316	326	335
Add: Amortization of Goodwill		2,185	2,185	2,185	2,185	2,185
Less: Increase in NWC		(201)	(109)	(113)	(116)	(120)
Less: CAPEX		95	(435)	(448)	(461)	(475)
Free Cash Flow		$1,289	$1,194	$1,604	$1,856	$2,084

	2001	2002	2003	2004	2005	2006
Initial Equity Investment	$(5,000)					
Free Cash Flow		$1,289	$1,194	$1,604	$1,856	$2,084
Terminal Value (TV)						13,893
Total Cash Flow	$(5,000)	$1,289	$1,194	$1,604	$1,856	$15,977

Initial Equity Investment	$(5,000)
PV of Free Cash Flow	5,176
PV of Terminal Value	6,907
NPV of Cash Flow	$7,083
Internal Rate of Return (IRR)	39%
Payback Period	3.49 year(s)

business are stable, then there is little difficulty in agreeing on the appropriate value. The greater the recent volatility of results, the more likely there is to be difficulty in agreeing on the value. The second factor used in the process, the multiple, is also subject to the judgment of the parties to the transaction and to negotiation. The multiple may represent the average of a dozen transactions. Complicating the issue is whether the target company is average, or below average, or whether it should command a premium price because of its products, market share, or other positive attributes. In the end, the parties to the transaction must agree on these parameters sufficiently to close a deal.

One highly successful investor who has bought and sold many companies described his approach to valuing and purchasing businesses using multiples in the following way. First and foremost, he felt that an advantageous purchase had to begin with a fair price, because no amount of operational skill and competence could overcome the handicap created by having paid a disadvantageous price. To assess potential deals, then, he used three filters. He considered the fair market value of the assets of the business, along with a value of four-fifths (80 percent) of the revenues, and, finally, a value five times the EBITDA. His rule was that the price he would pay had to be on the better side of two of the three measures. That is, if the assets of a business were estimated to be worth $70 million, and 80 percent of the revenues were $80 million, and an EBITDA of $15 million produced the multiple value of $75 million, then he would pay no more than $75 million for the business. He felt that the deals he had passed on because of his filters would have been mistakes at higher prices, and in fact, his worst disasters had occurred when he had ignored his rules out of an eargerness to do the deals.

Valuations and the Old Economy

These methods, at various levels of complexity, have been the standard approaches for valuing businesses in the old economy. The United States is the envy of the other countries of the world in terms of the requirements for disclosure by, and the amount of detailed information available about, public companies and the readiness with which this information may be accessed. Such data create relatively efficient markets for the acquisition and divestiture of traditional businesses. Next, the problems inherent in trying to value businesses in the Internet, high-technology, telecommunications segment of the U.S. economy will be discussed. This segment is many times more volatile than the old economy.

VALUATION OF NEW-ECONOMY BUSINESSES

Some analysts had forecast the rapid growth of the new economy, but no one could have envisioned the proliferation of the Internet and its applications in such a short period of time. Similarly, the unprecedented increases in the market capitalization of Internet firms were unexpected by both analysts and investors. Is the Internet really the great business opportunity everyone makes it out to be? Did these firms, most with no earnings, justify these improbable valuations? How would one go about determining the "excellent" firms in the Internet sector that will be the industry leaders and provide consistent, long-term increases in shareholder value?

One of the biggest impediments to valuing new-economy firms is that the so-called experts—the Wall Street analysts—have such differing views on this issue. Not uncommonly, well-respected analysts have widely differing opinions about the target price of a firm or even about their recommendations or ratings of a particular firm as an investment opportunity. Yet rarely, if ever, has the difference of opinions been so disparate as it is within the new-economy sector. For example, within a one-week period, a well-known Internet firm found itself facing 12-month price targets published by reputable analysts that differed by $350 per share.

Such differences of opinion cause chaos and embarrassment in the quasi-scientific world of equity analysis, where time-tested valuation techniques and established principles are normally used to derive equity valuations. The problem is that few techniques exist to value publicly traded firms that have little or no earnings. Analysts formerly treated these firms as if they were privately traded, early-stage firms. Thus, underlying assumptions and logical conclusions varied greatly.

These dichotomies have spawned a search for credible valuation techniques for Internet firms. An Internet firm's stock can—and often does—experience daily or weekly price swings totaling 30 to 50 percent of the share price. Thus, there is a fervent search for valuation models that can deal effectively with the early-stage, new-economy firms that may have gone public before reaching profitability. Two of these approaches are presented below.

Harmon's WEBDEX Model

Steve Harmon, an on-line investment analyst, has proposed a valuation approach based on the ratio of the number of users each firm has (e.g., visits to the site, purchases) to the average value per user the market awards the company, calculated by dividing the firm's market capitalization by the number of unique users. Much as a television cable company is valued by establishing an estimated monetary value for each subscriber, this methodology values Internet firms on a per-user basis. The problem is that firms define "users" in different ways and, without standards to ensure that data are reported accurately, this method remains risky.[1]

---

1. Steve Harmon, The Internet Report, http://www.internetnews.com (February 1999).

The I-Quant Model

Andy Kessler of Velocity Capital has devised an approach to measuring the potential of Internet stocks that he named the "I-Quant model." This procedure measures the effectiveness with which marketing dollars are spent by Internet firms to attract new customers, by measuring whether firms are generating a dollar in incremental sales for each marketing dollar spent. The basic premise is that if a firm is generating a dollar more in incremental revenue than it is spending on advertising, then the money is well spent.[2] This may be a rational approach if market leadership is the only goal.

The Effect of New-Economy Valuations

Internet firms are puzzling to even the most savvy of analysts, because those that are traded publicly have been listed for such a short period of time (one to three years) that systematic patterns of stock price fluctuations cannot be determined. Numerous Internet firms operate as private firms, adding even more uncertainty to valuation attempts in this sector. An additional factor that affects the value of Internet shares is the relatively small float of these shares available to the publc. When a typical Internet firm goes public, few shares are made available to investors. In order for investors to purchase shares in Internet firms, high turnover rates must occur for the small number of shares. When demand exceeds supply in these situations, then share prices will rise, sometimes dramatically.

A number of additional factors contributed, individually or together, to the high valuations new-economy firms have experienced. These include the following:

- Irrational exuberance
- Many investors' having never witnessed a bear market
- A booming economy, which provided investors with more risk capital
- A true supply-and-demand problem—where few Internet shares existed in comparison to demand
- A new genre of investors known as day traders, who created wild volatility in the market
- An increase in the number of people possessing online investment accounts, which increased volatility

---

2. Andy Kessler, "Time for Net Stocks to Put Up or Shut Up,"
   http://www.TheStreet.com (January 1999).

- Extremely low interest rates, which provided investors with few alternatives for safe-haven investments such as U.S. Treasuries and bonds

- High technology's status as a mania

Each of these factors has contributed to the rapid advancement of share prices of new-economy firms.

VALUATIONS AND THE RAPIDLY CHANGING BUSINESS ENVIRONMENT

As described earlier, the two basic methods of valuing businesses for strategic purposes of acquisitions and divestitures have evolved over many decades. The accuracy and timeliness of the data available have continuously improved so that both sides of a possible transaction have access to credible information. These data are available both from subscription services which are designed for ease of use (sometimes described as customer-friendly) and are free on the Internet. The process of due diligence allows both sides of a potential transaction to understand other factors of the business that are not required to be made public. All of these methods and approaches are well systematized in regards to firms in the old economy.

It is a far different situation in the new economy. At a Berkshire Hathaway shareholder meeting, Warren Buffett was asked what he would do if he taught business students today. "For the final exam, I would take an Internet company and say, 'How much is this worth?' And anybody that gave me an answer, they would flunk."[3]

The new economy currently defies the long-standing fundamental logic for valuing businesses. With conventional valuation logic inoperable with regard to these firms, new methodologies have had to be created to assist in the valuation process. A relatively small number of proposed valuation techniques have been discussed, yet even the originators of these models realize their frailty. Transactions continue to be consummated, however, with old-economy firms acquiring new-economy firms, new-economy firms acquiring one another, and even new-economy firms acquiring old-economy firms. And so the strategic planning process will continue as buyers and sellers maneuver to create strategic advantages in a rapidly changing business environment.

The most pertinent recent development in the evolution of valuation techniques has been the tendency for analysts and investors to apply the mature valuation methods from the old economy to firms in the new economy. This means that these new-economy firms will increasingly be held to standards of performance in regard to cash flow, growth, and ROI similar

---

3. James Glassman, "At a Loss in Valuing Internet's Darlings," *The Washington Post* (July 12, 1998).

to firms in the old economy. This tendency is best illustrated by the corrections that have occurred to the NASDAQ Composite Index, which resulted from the restructured valuations of new-economy firms, more in cadence with established investor and analyst preferences. We might say that the dot-com mania is reaching its denouement with the financial community and with investors.

THE IMPORTANCE OF VALUATIONS FOR THE STRATEGIST

Most strategic issues are intertwined with the notion of the value of the firm, status quo. How would the CEO assess an offer to buy the firm from the perspective of the shareholders, or how would negotiations with a lending institution proceed without an understanding of the inherent value of the firm? How would we know the value of an acquisition or divestiture or its strategic potential to add shareholder value? All require an understanding of valuation.

The strategist must also be able to see value not apparent to others, as might result from a different use of an acquisition's assets or a different view of the value of such intangible assets as licenses, patents, or franchise rights. Valuation sets the bar for apparent or not-so-obvious synergies (most often meaning incremental improvements in costs or revenues). Although every deal represents a buyer and a seller agreeing on a fair price, there are few strategic options for the buyer who has paid too much. The results are generally devastating. One of the more risky aspects of acquisitions is the tendency to base the price on expected synergies when, in fact, synergies are often elusive or impossible to realize. This brings us back to the premise, explained in detail in Chapter 13, that buying back a firm's shares may be a superior strategy to the pursuit of acquisitions.

Thus, in today's environment of commonplace restructurings, valuation is a critical tool for executives and strategists alike. Both must have facility with the company's valuation to reasonably assess the strategic options available for a firm. Furthermore, strategists must be aware of the risks and uncertainties encompassed by the methods of valuation they employ. An attractively valued strategic acquisition or divestiture has the potential to create substantial shareholder value, just as a poorly valued change in the corporate portfolio has the potential to destroy it.

SUMMARY

This chapter has described how the continuous process of strategic acquisitions and divestitures creates a need for appropriate means of setting reasonable values for these business transactions. These values must be considered "fair" by both parties to a transaction if a deal is to be consummated. The valuation process is complicated by the differences between the large number of old-economy, mature firms for which a great deal of data and history are available, and the fast-growing high-technology firms of the new economy, which have no similar base of available data.

There are two basic approaches to valuing businesses: the value of the assets of the business and the actual or perceived earning power of the business. Even a business that is losing money is worth at least the fair market value of the assets. The ability of a business to generate earnings can create a value for the business beyond the value of the assets. Businesses that have extensive earning power command higher fair market values than lower-earning businesses.

There are also two basic approaches to estimating the value of a business based on its earning power, one based on historical performance and the other based on forecasts of future performance. The most widely used method, the multiples method, determines the fair market value of a business by relating one or more measures of operating results to the fair market value arrived at in recent transactions in which similar or comparable businesses were traded. The other method, the net present value method, involves forecasting the likely future cash flows of the business over some time horizon, often five years, and then discounting the cash flows arithmetically to produce a "net present value" of the cash flows, and thus the business. These two methods are often used to cross-check the range of feasible values during a negotiation.

Finally, the very difficult problem of valuing the volatile, high-technology firms of the new economy was also addressed. The financial community appears now to be applying the same methods of valuation to new-economy firms that have been used historically to value old-economy firms. Perhaps the time has come to abandon the distinction between old- and new-economy firms, especially in regard to valuing businesses.

Review Questions

1. Why are the methods for valuing a business so important to the strategist?
2. What are the two basic approaches to valuing a business? When is one or the other most appropriate for the strategist to use?
3. What special problems arise in attempts to value new-economy firms?
4. What factors have contributed to the expansive valuations enjoyed by new-economy firms?
5. What is the current posture of professional analysts in regard to valuing new-economy firms?

PART FOUR

STRATEGIC ISSUES AT THE CORPORATE LEVEL

CHAPTER 11

Strategic Issues for the Corporate Parent

INTRODUCTION

Parent companies, often referred to as holding companies, play an important role in the U.S. economy. Most domestic public companies operate through a decentralized organizational structure to compete effectively in diversified markets. Decades ago, as business organizations grew larger, and as their product offerings grew more diverse, it became more and more difficult for the CEO to understand all of the details of numerous market and product nuances. The operational answer, which began in a few pioneering companies and gradually spread though most of U.S. industry, was to decentralize operations. By this means, a management team was assembled to manage each unique business with the closest regard for its peculiar competitive product, marketing, and pricing environment. It was axiomatic that parent-company management would thereafter have less intimate knowledge of the details regarding operations at the decentralized units. These operating segments may be referred to as operating units, divisions, subsidiaries, businesses, corporations, or simply as companies.

The overriding objective for the parent or holding company is to earn a favorable return on investment for its shareholders. It is so whether the company is a public company, operating with a lot of public scrutiny, or a private company, with less disclosure of performance details. In either case, what is deemed a favorable return is determined by the community of investors. Whether they are venture capitalists, individual investors, or large institutional investors, their notion of a favorable ROI is shaped by the known pattern of returns available from alternative investments. Their natural proclivity for the highest possible returns will lead them to support successful managers by continuing to invest with them while limiting their investments with less successful managements.

CORPORATE STRATEGIC TASKS

We are concerned here with the strategic concepts and tasks that these parent or holding company managements must face. We will review the strategic tasks from corporate and divisional perspectives. We saw earlier that divisions concentrate on product and marketing issues and seek to dominate the competitive scenes they face. Corporate offices, on the other hand, have distinctly different strategic tasks. They must concentrate on earning an outstanding return on their investors' capital, the potential for which is largely determined by the businesses in which they are engaged. For instance, if all of the businesses are in slow-growing, mature industries, it will be very difficult for the corporation to grow rapidly. Additionally, the ROI and the generation of cash flow will be dependent on the basic characteristics of the industries in which the divisions compete.

Professional financial analysts largely determine the price of the shares of public companies by assessing the risks a company faces and the returns likely from that company in the future. Analysts seek firms that have outstanding and consistent returns. They will then favor growth over stagnation and positive cash flows over needs for additional capital. The CEO of a diversified, decentralized corporation must balance these desires for ROI, growth, and cash flow. These performance measures are interrelated, as we saw in Chapter 9. The cash-balancing growth rate was seen to be the rate of retained earnings to equity. The high-return corporation is thus rewarded by being able to internally finance a more rapid rate of growth. Growth at a rate slower than the cash-balancing rate of the firm would allow cash to accumulate that could be used to finance acquisitions or for other purposes.

The CEO of a diversified, decentralized company is thus at the mercy of the performance potential of the several operating divisions. The corporate ROI will be a weighted average of the returns of the divisions. Similarly, the growth rate of sales and profits and the cash flow will be the collective results achieved by the divisions. The CEO is responsible for all financial, legal, and regulatory policies and represents the corporation to the public, as well as the corporation's investors, customers, suppliers, and employees. The relative levels of debt and equity in the corporation's financing are ultimately decided by the CEO and the board of directors.

A CORPORATE CASE STUDY: PELICAN CORPORATION

The concepts in this chapter are illustrated by a case study describing, in some detail, a diversified, decentralized corporation. In this case study, the Pelican Corporation is described in terms of its set of operating divisions.

This case examines a diversified, decentralized corporation made up of 10 operating divisions. We are told the corporate breakdown of debt and equity, the interest rate on debt, and the level of corporate overhead expenses. This detail allows the reader to convert the financial statements resulting from division summaries into complete corporate financial statements. Additional details are provided for each division, giving the reader at least some opportunity to form an opinion as to the relative attractiveness of each division. Individual plans (including forecasts) submitted by each division allow the reader to understand the efficacy of the division planning processes.

Finally, the Pelican case allows the reader to bring together the financial situation at the corporate level with the operating realities at the division level to derive the most effective strategic plan for the company as a whole. The best solution necessarily involves the divestiture of at least some of the divisions.

Now, let's move on to the corporate and divisional case studies.

Review Questions

1. What is the primary objective of a corporation, whether it is a public or a private company?
2. How does a parent company determine the performance potential of its portfolio of businesses?
3. What criteria do financial analysts use to determine the share prices of public companies?
4. What business functions are normally handled at the corporate level in diversified, decentralized companies?

C A S E   11A

PELICAN CORPORATION

INTRODUCTION

The new CEO of the Pelican Corporation, a diversified company, needed to assess its problems and develop a plan to reinvigorate the ailing firm. In less than a year, Pelican's banks would be calling in $400 million in emergency loans. There would have to be quick action; the board of directors had requested an initial assessment at the end of the week. Should Pelican accept an outside consultant's conclusions regarding the Pelican divisions? How could Pelican's resources be used better to generate needed earnings? How could the current capital structure be molded to meet the expectations of investors?

THE EARLY YEARS

Years ago, an aggressive entrepreneur, combining his savings with funds from a few wealthy friends and some outside investors, purchased a company that had been languishing under poor management. The company was renamed Pelican Corporation, and an experienced manager was recruited to be CEO. His management skills helped turn Pelican into a success almost immediately, doubling revenues to $42 million after the first two years of operation. With the company running smoothly, the CEO eagerly sought opportunities to repeat his success and fuel Pelican's further growth. He established an aggressive acquisition strategy to meet his goals. Under his plan, Pelican purchased a number of moderately performing companies, then streamlined operations to improve performance and the companies' value to Pelican's investors. This strategy met with great success for a number of years, and Pelican eventually became a publicly held, highly diversified company with 10 divisions spanning a wide range of industries. The company had recently seen its fourth straight year of record increases in revenues and profits.

   Though Pelican had experienced debt-to-total-capital levels as high as 85 percent during some periods, the company strove to return the ratio to 35 percent as quickly as possible, to retain shareholder confidence and ensure Pelican's eligibility for a AA bond rating. The company's shareholders saw their investment increase substantially under this acquisition strategy. In 1997, the market had valued Pelican's 18.1 million shares at $42.80 each. This valuation represented an average multiple of 8 times net income (earnings) per share.

THE COLLAPSE

When Pelican's debt reached $650 million, the economy took a turn for the worse. Because several of Pelican's most profitable divisions competed, for the most part, in cyclical industries, the company found itself highly exposed as a result of an economic slowdown. The company struggled for the next two years. For the year 2001, it appeared that only 2 of the 10 divisions would reach their sales targets. Furthermore, the downturn in the business cycle eliminated any possible need for the excess capacity existing in most of Pelican's competitive environments.

The economic slowdown, as well as internal factors, seriously hampered Pelican's ability to generate funds needed to pay down the debt. In an effort to raise cash quickly and improve efficiencies, Pelican attempted to reduce inventories and tried to pressure vendors for better terms. Although these efforts yielded some small operating improvements, the debt-servicing costs, 12 percent, and inordinately high corporate overhead expenses also continued to put strong pressure on earnings. Revenues and profits continued to plummet. A 22 percent decline in revenues and 386 percent drop in profits left Pelican with its first net loss year on record at the end of 2000.

The company's banks, nervous about Pelican's high debt levels, began to press for repayment. Investors also became concerned about Pelican's future. By the middle of 2001, Pelican's stock had dropped to $9.55 per share and appeared likely to drop even further (see Exhibit 11.1). Pelican, at one time a highly successful and fast-growing company, now found itself on the verge of bankruptcy. The board took drastic action to save the corporation. The CEO and chairman of the board stepped down. The board began a search for a new CEO and ordered an immediate outside assessment of the 10 divisions.

Pelican's banks agreed to help. Many of the company's banks were located in towns where Pelican either owned plants or operated major offices. Although the banks were not optimistic about Pelican's prospects, they found the cost of a one-year waiver on the terms of Pelican's debt to be far less than the litigation expenses and the losses of local business the banks would incur in the event of bankruptcy proceedings. Together the banks agreed to a one-year restructuring of $400 million of Pelican's debt at a 15 percent interest rate. Pelican's recent personnel changes at the executive levels provided the board with additional leverage in the negotiations. At the announcement of the debt restructuring, the stock price dropped to $4.80 per share.

E X H I B I T   11.1

Pelican Corporation stock price, 1996–2001.

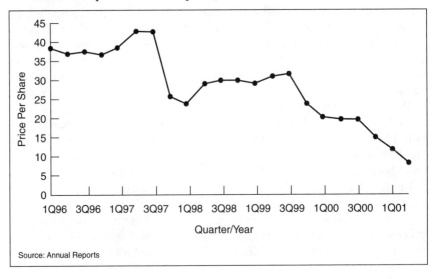

Source: Annual Reports

NEW LEADERSHIP

In August 2001, the board selected a new CEO for the Pelican Corporation. The board felt that the new CEO's aggressive style and established credibility in the industry would reinvigorate Pelican. The board also hoped this action would send a strong signal of change to restore further the confidence of employees and creditors. The new CEO arrived at Pelican with eight months remaining on the one-year phase of the debt-restructuring agreement. Finding a way to pay down the $400 million callable portion of the debt was the highest priority. In the short term, a cohesive corporate strategy would need to be determined. The company would need to return to profitability; downsize a bloated corporate office; restore the confidence of investors, creditors, and employees; and reverse the decline in the stock price. Furthermore, these goals would have to be established under the burden of a slight recession in Pelican's markets, which seemed to drag on, as well as 30 percent excess capacity in the industries of most operating units. Finally, the most favorable long-term scenario involved providing sufficient cash flow to allow stronger units to expand as much as possible, including through acquisitions. It seemed a truly daunting set of tasks. The independent assessment of the divisions, commissioned by the board two months earlier, had been delivered via overnight mail the evening prior to the new CEO's first day at Pelican. There was little time to spare; the board would be expecting an initial analysis at the end of the week.

THE DIVISIONS

Recently prepared (August 2001) division forecasts and corporate totals for 2002, are shown in Exhibit 11.2. The status of the divisions, based on the report, are summarized below.

Riviera Corporation

Riviera designed and manufactured specialty devices for industrial, commercial, and residential consumers. This division had demonstrated consistently high profits and was first in its industry in return on assets. With sales of only $33 million, however, Riviera's size made the division too small to fit into Pelican's current strategic goals and also placed it at a competitive disadvantage as far as economies of scale were concerned, because many of its competitors were significantly larger.

Foxbrook Corporation

Foxbrook was considered a growth company with revenues for 2002 forecast to be $105 million. Pelican's corporate office had encouraged the division to strive for growth as high as 10 percent per year. Foxbrook sold specialized polymer products to medical and other end users. With the best distribution network in the industry, the division was recognized as the North American market leader in the specialized polymer industry, and distributors rarely, if ever, handled competitive products. The critical nature of this business required that the division's products and production facilities conform to strict quality standards, and Foxbrook's plant had been certified to standards of the International Organization for Standardization (ISO), specifically ISO 9001 standards.

Rugby Corporation

Rugby was a midsized division of Pelican, with 2002 revenues forecast to be $53 million. Rugby's revenue growth rate was expected to be stagnant, similar to the industry average. The division would be fortunate to break even from a profit perspective, given the extreme competitive situation in the industry. Rugby Corporation manufactured precision instruments and specialized components for a number of different industries. Because the customers recognized the division as the technical leader, the engineers who developed these products were often considered industry experts. Unfortunately, foreign competitors, most with financial support from their governments, created a very difficult competitive situation for Rugby.

E X H I B I T 11.2

2002 financial projections ($ in millions).

Assumption	Concord	Eastwood	Foxbrook	Grove	Highfield	Lewis	Monument	Raintree	Riviera	Rugby	Pelican	Total
Sales Growth	5.7%	(7.1%)	6.2%	3.3%	8.5%	11.1%	(3.9%)	27.0%		10.9%	6.2%	7.7%
COGS, % Sales	77.0%	87.7%	53.6%	59.3%	73.6%	78.6%	71.5%	77.1%		65.2%	89.5%	73.2%
SG&A, % Sales	15.9%	10.5%	12.9%	21.1%	24.2%	14.9%	19.2%	9.2%		20.7%	12.9%	15.9%
Income Statement												
Sales	$133.5	$28.5	$105.1	$39.3	$114.0	$113.3	$172.8	$174.4		$32.8	$53.4	$967.1
COGS	(102.8)	(25.0)	(56.3)	(23.3)	(83.9)	(89.1)	(123.6)	(134.5)		(21.4)	(47.8)	(707.7)
Gross Margin	30.7	3.5	48.8	16.0	30.1	24.2	49.2	39.9		11.4	5.6	259.4
SG&A	(21.3)	(3.0)	(13.6)	(8.3)	(27.6)	(16.9)	(33.2)	(16.0)		(6.8)	(6.9)	(153.5)
NOPAT[a]	$6.1	$1.6	$21.6	$5.1	$4.3	$4.3	$8.6	$15.1		$2.8	$(1.5)	$68.1
Cash Flow												
NOPAT	$6.1	$1.6	$21.6	$5.1	$4.3	$4.3	$8.6	$15.1		$2.8	$(1.5)	$68.1
Depreciation	0.7	0.6	1.1	0.3	2.9	2.4	2.6	2.1		0.3	0.7	13.7
Change in NWC	12.8	1.7	1.3	(0.1)	13.5	1.7	4.3	(8.3)		(0.3)	0.9	27.6
CAPEX[b]	(0.2)	1.6	(2.7)	(2.0)	(12.6)	(2.7)	(5.4)	(1.6)		0.1	(1.9)	(27.4)
Cash Flow	$19.4	$5.5	$21.3	$3.3	$8.1	$5.7	$10.1	$7.3		$2.9	$(1.8)	$81.9
Balance Sheet												
Current Assets	$38.4	$13.7	$17.7	$7.0	$129.7	$40.3	$41.3	$39.4		$8.5	$12.6	$348.6
Fixed & Other Assets	1.6	8.5	8.0	2.0	25.1	13.1	23.9	11.2		4.3	5.7	103.4
Total Assets	40.0	22.2	25.7	9.0	154.8	53.4	65.2	50.6		12.8	18.3	452.0
Current Liabilities	14.5	4.8	17.0	8.5	38.1	13.4	14.9	25.3		4.8	12.1	153.4
Net Assets	$25.5	$17.4	$8.7	$0.5	$116.7	$40.0	$50.3	$25.3		$8.0	$6.2	$298.6

(a) Net of miscellaneous expenses and income and taxes at 35 percent.
(b) CAPEX stands for planned capital expenditures.

Raintree Corporation

Raintree's forecast of $174 million in sales made it the company's largest division in terms of expected 2002 revenues. The division supplied highly specialized equipment, parts, and service to the industrial-maintenance markets, and a lean cost structure helped make Raintree the top performer in its industry. Raintree's very optimistic forecast of 27 percent growth for 2002 far surpassed the average growth rate in the industry and indicated Raintree's intention to expand its industry leadership. Because Raintree clearly constituted one of the company's stellar divisions, the consultants classified Raintree as a growth division and recommended Pelican channel even more resources to this division, in the hopes of expanding market share during the next few years.

Grove Corporation

Grove, though ranked seventh in terms of sales, was Pelican's fifth-largest contributor of net income. As a manufacturer of high-technology specialty consumer products, Grove constituted one of two Pelican divisions that produced primarily consumer goods rather than industrial products. Grove boasted very strong performance in both profitability and ROA, but its $39 million sales volume was less than ideal for Pelican. Grove's low 3 percent projected annual growth rate further exacerbated the size problem.

Eastwood Corporation

Eastwood, Pelican's smallest division with 2002 projected revenues of only $28.5 million, seemed destined to hold that position. Eastwood manufactured high-quality electrical switching components for aerospace, defense, telecommunications, and industrial applications. The company was one of only two divisions to forecast a negative growth rate for the coming year. Eastwood's projected 7 percent decline seemed particularly severe when compared to its industry's recent average 11 percent positive growth. Eastwood also performed near the bottom of its industry in most financial measures.

Highfield Corporation

Highfield, with forecast 2002 sales of $114 million, had also been placed in the category to divest. Highfield manufactured a variety of products for the industrial construction industry and anticipated a strong 8 percent sales increase for 2002, almost double the industry average. This growth would not translate to a desirable level of earnings, however, because the division competed with one of the highest cost structures in the industry. In addition, retooling the division would require additional sizable capital expenditures.

Lewis Corporation

Lewis designed, manufactured, and installed systems using filters and separators in a variety of commercial and industrial applications. The division forecast 2002 sales of $113 million, and its aggressive 11 percent growth forecast for 2002 would exceed the expected industry average of 9 percent and signaled the division's optimism about its future. The division was currently among the high-cost producers for its industry, however, and had high working capital needs (up to 33 percent of sales) that made Lewis a heavy user of cash. Lewis also had retooling requirements that would call for additional capital expenditures.

Monument Corporation

Monument, with forecast 2002 sales of $173 million, represented one of Pelican's largest sources of revenue and income. Monument manufactured high-technology communication systems for commercial customers and needed cash for acquisitions in its mushrooming markets. Monument's competitors in the commercial high-technology communications sector averaged growth projections of 10 percent, with the top performer projecting a growth rate as high as 32 percent. In spite of its gloomy growth forecasts, the analysts had ranked Monument as one of Pelican's top growth divisions and recommended that Pelican try to grow this division by as much as 20 percent in the coming year, probably through acquisitions.

Concord Corporation

Concord specialized in the design, production, installation, and maintenance of industrial, commercial, and residential alarm systems. Concord tended to rank near the middle or bottom of its crowded industry on most financial measures and had forecast another year of substandard growth. Concord had forecast only 6 percent annual growth, less than half of the 13 percent industry average. In spite of its poor performance, this labor-intensive division made the fourth-largest profit contribution to the corporation and required few fixed assets.

ISSUES AND ALTERNATIVES

The CEO studied the summary chart showing each division's ranking on certain financial criteria (see Exhibit 11.3) and also considered the information shown in Exhibit 11.4, which showed the outside analysts' placement of each Pelican division on a widely used strategic-analysis matrix. How could all of this information be used to balance the corporation's performance and meet both Pelican's short-term cash requirements and longer-term earnings goals? If sales could be increased significantly, Pelican could generate some of the necessary cash. Indeed, a few of the divisions had submitted quite aggressive forecasts, but could growth alone produce the cash Pelican needed to satisfy its creditors and stockholders?

An attempt could also be made to generate needed cash by squeezing performance improvements in productivity, gross margin, or sales, general, and administrative (SG&A) expenses from some of the key divisions. Benefits from this type of initiative, however, seemed unlikely to materialize in the short time available, particularly on the scale that would be needed to satisfy the banks. As a last resort, one or more of the divisions would have to be divested in order to raise some of the needed funds, but which ones? The report also advocated growth for some of the better-performing divisions at levels that seemed possible only through acquisitions. This recommendation would require still more cash, but how would the cash be raised?

EXTERNAL FINANCING ISSUES

Aside from short-term creditor requirements, the CEO had to consider longer-term concerns of outside investors, creditors, and analysts. Pelican's current ratio of debt to total capital was clearly unacceptable to the current stockholders and a far cry from Pelican's average in healthier times. How

E X H I B I T   11.3

2002 division business and corporate rankings.

Corporate Divisions	Sales	Rank	Net Income	Rank	Cash Flow	Rank	ROS	Rank	RONA	Rank	Sum of Ranks	Total Rank
Foxbrook	$105.1	6	$21.6	1	$21.2	1	20.5%	1	246.7%	2	11	1
Raintree	174.4	1	15.1	2	7.2	5	8.7%	3	59.6%	3	14	2
Monument	172.8	2	8.6	3	10.1	3	5.0%	6	17.1%	6	20	3
Concord	133.5	3	6.1	4	19.6	2	4.6%	7	24.2%	5	21	4
Grove	39.3	8	5.1	5	3.3	8	12.9%	2	1142.9%	1	24	5
Lewis	113.3	5	4.3	6	5.7	6	3.9%	8	11.0%	7	32	6
Highfield	114.0	4	4.3	7	8.1	4	3.8%	9	3.7%	9	33	7
Riviera	32.8	9	2.8	8	2.9	9	8.65%	4	35.5%	4	34	8
Eastwood	28.5	10	1.6	9	5.5	7	5.5%	5	9.1%	8	39	9
Rugby	53.4	7	(1.5)	10	(1.8)	10	(2.9%)	10	(24.2%)	10	47	10
Total	$967.1		$68.1		$81.9		7.0%		22.8%			

E X H I B I T   11.4

Strategic analysis matrix.

		Industry Attractiveness		
		High	Medium	Low
Business Strength	High	I FOXBROOK	I RAINTREE GROVE RIVIERA	S
	Medium	I	S LEWIS MONUMENT	H HIGHFIELD
	Low	S CONCORD	H EASTWOOD	H RUGBY

Key:
I = Invest/Grow
S = Selectively Invest/Manage for Earnings
H = Harvest Profits/Divest Division

could Pelican's capital structure be adjusted to make it more attractive? The consultants' report had excluded interest charges and a bloated corporate overhead from division performance measurement, yet at a corporate level, debt service was clearly an issue. How much debt could be afforded? How much would the investors tolerate? The company's present 15 percent interest rate on the debt indicated the market's wariness of Pelican's current capital structure. Should an attempt be made to raise additional equity? The banks were looking for a stable, long-term capital structure to replace the current emergency plan.

ASSUMPTIONS FOR 2002 PRO FORMA ESTIMATES

The following assumptions would provide a basis for Pelican's eventual emergence from the brink of bankruptcy. The debt level of $650 million carried a stiff interest rate of 15 percent. It was assumed that the interest rates would gradually adjust to a more reasonable 10 percent if Pelican reached a debt-to-capital ratio of 35 percent. As Pelican returned to profitability, the company would benefit from a tax loss carryforward of $270 million, a legacy from the recent collapse. This provision in the tax law would shield an equal amount of future profits from corporate income taxes.

For the purpose of creating a corporate income statement and balance sheet from the division summary given in Exhibit 11.2, it would be necessary to separate the net assets from the division summary into debt and equity. Corporate interest expense would have to be deducted to calculate corporate profit before tax. Corporate overhead, which was currently a bloated 5 percent of revenues, would also have to be addressed. Pelican would have to move rapidly to reduce the corporate office to a more realistic 1.5 percent of revenues, consistent with well-managed corporations. By setting the examples at the corporate level, Pelican could encourage its operating units to achieve improvements in gross margin and SG&A of 1 percent of sales per year, until they reached a level of outstanding performance (equal to, or above the top quartile on each variable) relative to their competition. The fourth quarter of 2001 provided a window of opportunity for Pelican to go into 2002 with a drastically improved corporate structure. The achievement of that result would require decisive action on a number of issues.

Now let us consider the individual division situations in the cases that follow. These materials have been extracted from the detailed strategic plans submitted to the corporate office by each division. The placement of each division on the strategic analysis matrix in the case studies was decided by the new CEO. Some differ from the recommendations of the outside consultants shown earlier in Exhibit 11.4.

C A S E   11A-1

RIVIERA CORPORATION

INTRODUCTION

The general manager (GM) of Riviera Corporation was reviewing the comments from the parent company, Pelican Corporation, regarding Riviera's original business plan for 2002 (see Exhibit 11.5). The plan had been submitted to the parent company a month earlier. The comments revealed significant changes in Pelican's expectations for the division and established ambitious performance targets for Riviera for the upcoming year. The parent's response also called on the division GM to submit detailed proposals for achieving these enhanced goals.

E X H I B I T   11.5

2002 Projection-business plan for Riviera Corporation, submitted August 2001 ($ in millions).

Income Statement	2001	% of Sales	2002	% of Sales
Sales	$29.6		$32.8	
Sales Growth		N/A		10.9
COGS	19.4	65.5	21.4	65.2
Gross Margin	10.2	34.5	11.4	34.8
SG&A	6.1	20.6	6.8	20.7
Misc. Expenses & Income	(1.8)	(6.1)	(0.3)	(0.9)
Profit Before Tax	2.3	7.8	4.3	13.1
Taxes (35%)	0.8		1.5	
Net Income	$1.5		$2.8	

Cash Flow				% of Fixed Assets (FA)
Net Income			$2.8	
Depreciation			0.3	7.2
Change in Working Capital			(0.3)	
Change in Fixed & Other Assets			_____	0.1
Cash Flow			$2.9	

Assets	2001	% of Sales	2002	% of Sales
Current Assets	$7.4	25.0	$8.5	25.9
Current Liabilities	4.0	13.5	4.8	14.6
Fixed & Other Assets	4.7	15.9	4.3	13.1
Net Assets	$8.1		$8.0	
Return on Net Assets	18.3%		35.5%	

Although he believed that the original plan was a fair estimate of Riviera Corporation's performance capabilities for the upcoming year, the GM was guardedly optimistic that his management team would be able to achieve the more challenging goals set by corporate headquarters. Productivity would have to be improved, but how? By downsizing the labor force? Increasing sales? Moving production offshore?

As he prepared to reread the business plan, the GM reflected on the significance of the challenge confronting him. If Riviera could attain or exceed Pelican Corporation's new goals, his future with the corporation would be secure. On the other hand, if he was unable to meet these expectations, his tenure with the corporation could be in doubt. Determining the steps that Riviera would take to achieve the new performance targets would be one of the most important activities of his professional life.

RIVIERA CORPORATION'S PRODUCTS, MARKETS, AND PERFORMANCE

Riviera Corporation was established to produce and sell specialty devices for industrial, commercial, and residential consumers. From the outset, Riviera established a corporate goal of manufacturing quality products with the tightest tolerances possible. Over time, adherence to this goal enabled Riviera to develop a strong brand name, which became synonymous with exceptional quality, value, and reliability. Riviera Corporation operated manufacturing facilities in the United States and Mexico to manufacture products for four primary business sectors: consumer, industrial, scientific, and commercial. Revenues for the division in 2001 were distributed across the business segments as follows:

Consumer	59%
Industrial	21%
Scientific	6%
Commercial	14%
Total	100%

The company's past success was based on a strong distribution channel through traditional retail hardware stores. This channel had been effective in distributing Riviera's products to the company's present consumers. To grow its market base, the company was cultivating new business through nontraditional channels such as supermarkets. This action was a response to the significant changes that were occurring in the consumer market. The continued growth and success of national retail chains and the increasing presence of home-improvement superstores provided intense competition for traditional houseware and hardware retailers. Riviera Corporation's reliance on traditional retail outlets posed a significant problem for the company in the current consumer market.

Sales of Riviera's products to the nonconsumer sectors were made through a variety of channels. Industrial sales were made primarily through regional distributors, industrial original equipment manufacturers (OEMs), and industrial-equipment exporters. Scientific sales were achieved through specialty supply houses serving educational and industrial laboratories. Commercial sales were made through specialized distributors serving a wide variety of commercial end users.

A study of Riviera Corporation's performance for the previous five-year period compared key operating results to those of a representative set of comparable companies with the same industry classification. The calculation of relative scale economies revealed that Riviera was operating inefficiently and had not achieved the prevailing industry-average pro-ductivity levels. With an annual sales volume of about $30 million, Riviera operated with a productivity level of 13.5 employees per $1 million of sales; the industry average was closer to 6.5 employees. Despite the below-average productivity performance of the division during the past five years, the company's longer-term productivity trend was positive. The compound annual growth rate of Riviera's productivity during the previous five years had been almost 10 percent.

Among the division's strengths were its strong brand name, its dom-inant position in traditional consumer-hardware distribution channels, its expanding distribution network in nontraditional channels, and its world-class injection-molding capabilities at its Mexican facility. Counterbalancing the perceived strengths of the division were several weaknesses. Riviera did not have an in-house digital measuring capability, forcing the division to rely on outside expertise in this area of product development and research. Riviera, to its disadvantage in regard to working capital requirements, maintained an expansive product line, especially in the industrial sector [over 800 stock keeping units (SKUs)], even though many of these products had low sales volumes and small market shares. And finally, the information systems used to support such functions as order entry, inventory man-agement, shipping, and billing, were obsolete.

PELICAN CORPORATION'S EXPECTATIONS FOR RIVIERA

Pelican's financial and operational expectations for the Riviera division were detailed in the corporation's comments on the division's original business plan. The new performance targets were an indication that Pelican Corporation expected better results than were initially projected by the GM and his management team. Riviera Corporation's new goals called for at least 1 percent (of sales) improvements in the division's projected sales growth rate, gross margin, and SG&A expenses. To assess the impact that such improvements would have on the division's cash flow and net income, a sensitivity analysis was performed on these variables. It was found that attainment of these goals would increase the division's net income by about $460,000 and its cash flow by about $380,000.

The GM knew that Pelican was experiencing financial difficulties and that corporate management was conducting a review of the viability and attractiveness of each of the 10 operating units. Although he wasn't sure which methods of analysis were being used by the corporation to assess the business strength and industry attractiveness of each operating unit, he was aware of the existence of a corporate strategic-analysis matrix, which considered several factors in performing such as assessment. The location of a company within this matrix was useful in determining whether investments should be made in a division and whether that division should be grown, managed for earnings, harvested for cash, or divested. He wondered how corporate management would evaluate Riviera using this strategic analysis tool.

The corporation's decision regarding the strategic value of the division would likely determine the fate of the Riviera Corporation. To provide himself with an assessment of the division's current estimated market value, the GM collected industry data on completed transactions involving the sales of a set of comparable companies. Performing a multiples analysis based on this information, he arrived at an estimated value for the division of approximately $17 million.

IMPROVEMENT OPPORTUNITIES

The GM was aware that there were many opportunities for improving the performance of his division, with the low productivity levels being the most urgently in need of improvement. He considered several alternatives for addressing the division's productivity problem:

- **Automate the production facilities.** This step would require a significant capital investment by Riviera Corporation. Given the recent financial performance of the parent company, the division would need to demonstrate the necessity and long-term profitability of such a capital-intensive proposal.
- **Consolidate all production at the Mexican plant.** Although not fully automated, the Mexican plant had significantly lower labor costs than the U.S. facility. Additionally, goods produced at this plant already represented more than 65 percent of the total divisional sales revenues. With greater access to the U.S. market for Mexican products following the passage of the North American Free Trade Agreement (NAFTA), and an expanding domestic market, the attractiveness of shifting production operations to Mexico was greatly enhanced.
- **Reduce the number of SKUs produced by the company.** The excessive number of product variations offered by Riviera required additional skilled laborers in the manufacturing process, inflating the division's labor force and driving down individual productivity. By trimming the product lines and

standardizing product designs across applications, Riviera would be able to reduce its labor and inventory costs and would free capacity to produce its more-profitable items.

- **Develop a research and design capability for manufacturing processes.** Little manufacturing redesign had taken place in recent years, and the GM believed that developing in-house process design capabilities would help to manage the improvement of production costs and enhance division productivity.

Another idea for improving productivity and reducing costs at the production facilities was to implement team-building and quality assurance programs at the sites. The team-building program, under consideration for implementation at both manufacturing facilities, would be structured to locate all members of each manufacturing team on the production floor. The idea would be to have the production control, engineering, and manufacturing supervisors on the factory floor with the production group. This interaction was expected to improve department communication, shorten production cycle time, reduce scrap, and raise employee morale, all of which should result in higher productivity and lower costs. The quality assurance program, on the other hand, was only being considered for implementation at the U.S. plant. This program would set quality standards for saleable products. This program was expected to minimize customer rejections, reduce scrap, and free capacity in the plant to undertake more precise molding.

In addition to these manufacturing considerations, the division was also considering implementing an enhanced customer service information system at a cost of $525,500. This system would enable Riviera Corporation to do the following:

- **Electronically receive customer orders into the system.** The manual entry of an average of 20 customer orders per day would be eliminated. Order accuracy also would be enhanced, with an estimated decrease in data entry error. Data element standardization would provide significant information control and would allow purchase order information to be captured and used in package labeling.
- **Electronically send customer invoices and purchase orders.** Electronic invoicing had become a core business requirement of several of the large retail customers. The use of electronic purchase orders would dramatically shorten the supply chain cycle, lowering the division's inventory carrying costs and increasing inventory turns.
- **Manage customer-specific unit pricing and promotion information.** Customer service would be enhanced because customers' account information would be up-to-date, complete, and readily accessible by customer-service agents and account

representatives. The result would be higher customer-service productivity levels and increased customer satisfaction.

- **Manage customer credit accounts.** Information regarding purchases, returns, and account credit would be up-to-date and accurate.

STRATEGIC SUMMARY

The GM was confident that his division could meet the corporation's expectations, but he needed to identify specifically how the company would increase market penetration and lower operational costs. He knew that he had to consider the cash flow–growth equation shown in Exhibit 11.6 as he developed his improved strategy.

E X H I B I T   11.6

2002 Cash-flow calculation for Riviera Corporation.

	2002
Sales[a]	$32.8
Sales Growth 10.9%	
2001Sales = $29.6	
COGS	21.4
Gross Margin	11.4
SG&A[b]	6.8
Misc. Expenses & Income	(0.3)
Profit Before Tax	4.3
Taxes	(1.5)
Net Income	$2.8
Net Income	$2.8
Depreciation[c]	0.3
Change in Working Capital	(0.3)
Change in Fixed & Other Assets	0.1
Cash Flow	$2.9

Cash Flow = Net Income + Depreciation – Change in Working Capital – Change in
                       Fixed & Other Assets

(a) 2001 Sales * (1 + growth)
(b) Total expense – debt service
(c) Based on a ratio of beginning fixed assets and other assets

STRATEGIC ANALYSIS: STRENGTHS AND WEAKNESSES

Strengths

- Strong brand name
- Dominant position in consumer market
- Strong distribution through traditional hardware stores
  - Growing presence in nontraditional distribution channels
- Cultivation of new business with national retail chains and home improvement superstores
- World-class injection-molding facilities in Mexico
  - Highly but not fully automated
  - Low labor costs
- Production in Mexico already at 65 percent of sales
- Productivity growth of almost 10 percent was double the rate predicted for Riviera's current sales growth rate, although it was only marginally above average for the entire industry
- SG&A expense ratio well below industry average of 35.9 percent
  - 2001: 20.6 percent, projected 2002: 20.7 percent
- ROS improving to above industry average of 5.8 percent
  - 2001: 5.0 percent, projected 2002: 8.6 percent
- RONA three times industry average of 6.0 percent
  - 2001: 18.3 percent, projected 2002: 35.5 percent

Weaknesses

- Reliance on traditional distribution channels in consumer segment
- Growth of nontraditional channels such as national retail chains and home improvement superstores, putting pressure on existing hardware store channels
- Larger and more sophisticated retailers demanding electronic data interchange
- Productivity well below industry average of 7.5 people per $1 million in sales
  - Currently 13.5 people per $1 million in sales
  - Productivity growth of 10 percent was comparable to industry average of 9.2 percent
  - The productivity gap was not shrinking
- Lack of an in-house R&D capability
- Slow product development

- Long production cycles
- Increasing production costs
- Extremely broad product line (800 SKUs)
- Unprofitable products using valuable production resources
- High inventory carrying costs; increased labor costs
- Manufacturing that was labor intensive
- Capacity constraints on more automated equipment
- High cost structure and/or low profitability
- Lack of adequate information technology to meet customer needs
- Industrial/scientific and commercial customers who were demanding enhanced customer service
  - Electronic data interchange
  - Automated pricing and promotion information
  - Gross margins well below the industry average of 47.2 percent
  - 2001: 34.3 percent, projected 2002: 34.8 percent
  - Growth rates that lagged the industry average of 11.8 percent
  - 2001: 4.6 percent, projected 2002: 10.9 percent

Industry Characteristics

- Fragmented industry, dominated by small- to medium-sized firms
- Diseconomies of scale that penalized firms above approximately $40 million
- Intense competition in distribution channels of consumer segment
- A market growing at 11.8 percent on average since 1997
- Relatively modest profit potential
  - Industry RONA: Five-year average 6.0 percent; high 13.8, percent in 1997; low, –5.5 percent in 1999

STRATEGIC SUMMARY

Business Strengths

Riviera Corporation held a dominant position in a relatively small market. It had strong brand recognition and a leading presence in the traditional distribution channels of the consumer segment. The firm coexisted with a myriad of small- to medium-sized firms. Riviera had a world-class production facility in Mexico and had high returns over the past several years. ROS had improved from 5.0 percent, to just below the industry average of 5.8 percent, and was projected to be 50 percent higher than the average in 2002. RONA had remained three to six times the industry average of 6.0 percent.

Several critical weaknesses detracted from these strengths. Poor productivity had led to gross margins 30 percent below the industry average. Additionally, productivity growth had been even with the industry, indicating that Riviera was not closing the productivity gap. SG&A ratios well below the industry average had made up for low gross margins and currently supported the attractive returns. However, SG&A levels this far below industry average were indicative of deeper and longer-term problems. Most critically, a lack of investment in the resources required to compete in its changing markets had not equipped the company to handle the challenges being presented by nontraditional distribution channels in the consumer market. Riviera's lack of information systems and advanced customer-service capabilities reflected this situation and did not bode well for the future.

Overall business strength: Medium.

Industry Attractiveness

The specialty device industry had exhibited moderate growth of approximately 11.8 percent over the five years. Profit levels had been moderate and relatively stable. Over the same time period, RONA had averaged 6.0 percent, with a low of minus 5.5 percent and a high of 13.8 percent. The industry was fragmented and dominated by smaller firms with sales of approximately $25 million to $45 million. Significant diseconomies of scale occurred for firms larger than this size and helped to explain the absence of large and dominant competitors.

Changing dynamics in the distribution channels of the consumer segment represented a severe challenge to firms in this industry. The rise of nontraditional retail channels, such as national retail chains and home improvement superstores, was putting pressure on the industry's bread-and-butter channel, the traditional hardware store. In addition, technological change was driving the need for greater investment in information technology, both for enhanced customer service and for more efficient supplier-buyer data exchange.

Overall industry attractiveness: Medium to Low.

RECOMMENDATIONS

The relatively small size at which firms in the industry were optimally efficient seemed to limit the potential returns to a level that was incompatible with the strategic and financial goals of Pelican Corporation. Pelican should divest Riviera and reinvest proceeds in stronger businesses and more attractive industries with similar returns and greater absolute profit potential.

If Retained, What Should Riviera Do?

- Improve productivity in both the United States and Mexico
- Automate production facilities in the United States
- Implement a team-based manufacturing strategy
- Improve communications among production control, engineering, and manufacturing
- Evaluate the viability of shifting all production to the Mexican plant
- Eliminate production bottlenecks at the United States plant
- Trim the highly proliferated product line
- Implement quality programs to reduce rejects, rework, and scrap
- Defend leadership position in the consumer segment
- Extend into nontraditional channels
- Invest in necessary resources to compete in changing distribution system
- Develop in-house R&D capacity
- Redesign manufacturing process to reduce costs and improve productivity
- Reduce development time for new products
- Modernize information systems
- Develop electronic data interchange capability
- Enhance customer-specific pricing and promotions
- Provide up-to-date customer account information

If Divested, What Sales Price Could Be Expected?

The average of 11 completed transactions (sales) of comparable companies provided prevailing multiples of sales price to revenue, total assets, net assets, and earnings before interest and taxes (EBIT). These multiples provided a wide range of estimates for the market value of Riviera Corporation. Asset multiples provided low-end values of approximately $9 to $10 million and did not reflect the potential value of continued operations of the firm. A revenue multiple provided a high-end value of approximately $22 million and assumed future performance consistent with historical levels. Because very few data points were available for the calculation of the EBIT multiple because of outliers, the EBIT multiple was not used to estimate a market value for Riviera. The average of the two estimates cited above provided an estimated value of $17 million for Riviera Corporation.

C A S E   11A–2

FOXBROOK CORPORATION

INTRODUCTION

Foxbrook sold specialized polymer products to medical and other end users. With the best distribution network in the industry, the division was recognized as the North American market leader in the precision medical instruments industry, and distributors rarely, if ever, handled any competitive products. Because markets for medical products recognized the division as the technical leader, the engineers who developed these products were often considered industry experts. Frequently, the company's engineers and product managers served in leadership capacities on the committees setting standards for the industry.

FOXBROOK CORPORATION'S PRODUCTS, MARKETS, AND PERFORMANCE

The critical nature of this business required that the division's products and production facilities conform to strict quality standards. Foxbrook's plant had been certified to ISO 9001 standards. Despite the technical excellence and high quality of existing product lines, the division had been unable to develop a steady stream of new products or product improvements. The information systems department had recently converted the division's computer systems to an integrated computer networking system that managed production, transaction, and logistics information for each of the division's product lines. In addition, electronic data interchange links, which would connect Foxbrook's distributors into the information system, were close to completion. The new system had made considerable progress in reducing the division's overdue backlog; however, accurate inventory control remained a problem.

In general, the division maintained better operational efficiencies than most of its competitors in the industry. A study of operating performance for the most recent five-year period compared key operating results to those of a representative set of comparable companies in the same Standard Industrial Classification (SIC) code. The calculation of or relative economies of scale revealed that Foxbrook had achieved levels of productivity similar to the best economies of scale achieved by any comparable companies. Further, an industry analysis relating productivity growth to sales growth for the most recent five-year period revealed that the rate of productivity growth for Foxbrook was slightly greater than the 8 percent average achieved by its competitors. This indicated that the division was in a strong position to retain its leadership role in the industry.

PELICAN'S EXPECTATIONS FOR FOXBROOK

Pelican's financial and operational expectations for the division were detailed in the corporation's comments on the division's original business plan. The original plan is shown in Exhibit 11.7. The GM was moderately surprised by these new expectations, because he believed that the division's original plan contained realistic performance targets based on the previous year's results. The parent company apparently felt that the division was capable of better performance. First, the corporate management expected the medical division to capitalize on its market-leadership position by growing more aggressively, by at least 10 percent per year. Second,

E X H I B I T   11.7

2002 Projection-business plan for Foxbrook Corporation, submitted August 2001 ($ in millions).

Income Statement	2001	% of Sales	2002	% of Sales
Sales	$99.0		$105.1	
Sales Growth		N/A		6.2
COGS	53.7	54.2	56.3	53.6
Gross Margin	45.3	45.7	48.8	46.4
SG&A	13.8	13.9	13.6	12.9
Misc. Expenses & Income	(0.6)	(0.6)	(2.0)	(1.9)
Profit Before Tax	30.9	31.1	33.2	31.6
Taxes (35%)	10.8		11.6	
Net Income	$20.1		$21.6	
Cash Flow				**% of FA**
Net Income			$21.6	
Depreciation			1.1	16.6%
Change in Working Capital			1.3	
Change in Fixed & Other Assets			(2.7)	
Cash Flow			$21.3	
Assets	**2001**	**% of Sales**	**2002**	**% of Sales**
Current Assets	$17.7	17.9	$17.7	16.8
Current Liabilities	15.7	15.9	17.0	16.2
Fixed & Other Assets	6.4	6.5	8.0	7.6
Net Assets	$8.4		$8.7	
Return on Net Assets	239.0%		247.0%	

they called for at least 1 percent of sales improvements in the division's gross margin and SG&A projections. To assess the impact that such improvements would have on the division's cash flow and net income, a sensitivity analysis was conducted on these variables. It was found that attainment of these goals would increase the division's net income and cash flow by more than $2 million each.

The GM knew that the corporate staff was conducting a review of the viability and attractiveness of each of the 10 operating units. Although he wasn't sure which methods of analysis were being used by the corporation to assess the business strength and industry attractiveness of each of the operating units, he was aware of the existence of a corporate strategic-analysis matrix that considered several factors in performing such an assessment. He thought it would be prudent to consider how Foxbrook would be characterized using such a tool.

MEDICAL PRODUCTS

The division maintained a 38 percent market share in its medical products niche. Its two strongest competitors were making significant advances, however, holding market shares of 28 percent and 12 percent, respectively. The medical products business, which produced specialized polymer products, had been very successful in North America. Given the important medical applications for these products, there was a constant drive within the industry for product regulations and standardization.

To meet its new short-term sales goals, the division would need to meet the established industry requirements for deliveries. Additionally, it would need to offer unique product features that would enable the division to command premium prices. As competition in the industry was expected to increase, it was critical to have a stream of new products and feature improvements to differentiate the division's offerings from those of its competition.

OPPORTUNITIES

New marketing programs were designed to include such items as increased marketing efforts in underserved markets in the Pacific Rim and Europe, new promotional campaigns, and the competitive conversion of existing products. To achieve these sales objectives, the GM considered the following opportunities in the medical products markets. The cycle time for new-product development would need to be decreased. Although the division had adopted a new-product development process based on cross-functional teams, the division still was unable to get new products to market rapidly. Because new-product offerings were vital to future sales growth, the GM knew that Foxbrook would have to make further process improvements in this area if the division was going to meet its 2002 projections.

Many of the division's existing products were older designs that were reaching the end of their effective product life cycles. This situation presented an opportunity for the division to replace existing products with new product designs. The challenge was to maintain customer loyalty and satisfaction while new products were being developed and brought to market. Foxbrook would also need to capitalize on international marketing opportunities for the medical segment product lines. Although these products enjoyed a strong domestic market, international sales lagged. To spur international sales growth, the division sought a joint venture partner in China, planned for expansion in Eastern Europe from its base in the Czech Republic, and worked to develop a partnership with a Brazilian partner to expand its market presence in South America.

STRATEGIC QUESTIONS

The GM reflected on the likelihood of achieving the new performance targets. Were there enough market opportunities to achieve the sales-growth target established by Pelican? Were there ways to accelerate new-product launches? And would Pelican provide financial support to Foxbrook to make such sales growth possible? The GM knew that he had to find the answers to these and other questions before he met again with Pelican's executive committee. It was going to be a long month.

STRATEGIC ANALYSIS: STRENGTHS AND WEAKNESSES

Strengths

- Leading market position, 38 percent share, competitors at 28 percent and 12 percent
- Best distribution in the medical products industry
  - Exclusive agreements with distributors
- Well known for technical excellence
  - Highly regarded engineers and product managers
  - Outstanding reputation for quality
  - ISO 9001 certified
- Having state-of-the-art information systems
  - Nearing completion of electronic data interchange (EDI) system
- Productivity well above average in the industry for the corporation's relative size
  - 6.25 employees per $1 million in sales vs. industry average of 8.25
- Gross margins above industry average of 29 percent

- ROS 5 to 6 times the industry five-year average of 3.5 percent
- RONA 45 times the industry five-year average of 5.13 percent

Weaknesses

- Inventory-control accuracy below expectations
- Very few weaknesses in this very profitable operation

Industry Characteristics

- Slow growth in the industry
- High returns that may attract new competitors but may also provide entry barrier
- Significant opportunity for international expansion
- Slight diseconomies of scale above $275 million in sales
- Significant economies of growth

STRATEGIC SUMMARY

Business Strengths

Foxbrook was the leader in its market segments. The division had earned superior returns over the past several years and was well positioned to continue to do so. The division held a commanding market share of 38 percent. It was highly regarded for its distribution network and was recognized as the technical leader. The division had a strong reputation for superior quality. It could suffer from an aging product line, however, if it did not continue to develop new products.

The division's greatest weakness was its new-product development process. This was more than offset by the strengths listed above. Additional strengths included a level of productivity well above the industry average for firms of a similar size and a state-of-the-art information system that would allow continued emphasis on cost containment and customer service. Gross margins had exceeded the average for the industry and made possible expansive returns.

Overall business strength: High

Industry Attractiveness

The medical products industry had consistently produced high returns. The increasing demand for innovative products and higher levels of customer service was putting pressure on the current market leaders to adapt their strategies or face limited future success. High returns had led to increasing competitive intensity, as the industry had seen the rapid growth of the second- and third-largest firms and faced the prospect of increased competition, which could result in lower future returns. The medical products industry offered the opportunity for international expansion. The industry was expected to continue to experience new real growth as attractive new products were introduced.

Overall industry attractiveness: High

RECOMMENDATIONS

Pelican should invest in and grow the powerhouse Foxbrook division. The division should concentrate on improving the processes for new product innovation. That should be the key to future growth and profitability.

If Retained, What Should Foxbrook Do?

- Reduce cycle time for new product development and introduction
- Improve the effectiveness of cross-functional product development teams
- Upgrade existing products while maintaining the loyalty of existing customers
- Capitalize on international marketing opportunities
  - Implement joint venture in China
  - Expand in Eastern Europe
  - Establish a Brazilian partnership as a base for South American expansion
- Continue the impressive level of performance of recent years

If Divested, What Sales Price Could Be Expected?

A list of completed transactions involving the sale of comparable companies in the last 10 years was prepared. The average sales prices of 18 transactions in the medical products industry provided average multiples of the sales price related to revenue, total assets, net assets, and EBIT. The most likely market value for Foxbrook was a multiple of approximately 17 times EBIT, for an estimated market value of $355 million.

C A S E   11A–3

RUGBY CORPORATION

INTRODUCTION

The GM of Rugby Corporation was wondering how to achieve the tough expectations for future performance established by the management of Pelican Corporation. As a result, Rugby would need to reduce its sales in 2002 by at least 3 percent. (See Exhibit 11.8 for the original plan.) In addition, the division would need to find a way to decrease its SG&A expense

E X H I B I T   11.8

2002 Projection-business plan for Rugby Corporation, submitted August 2001 ($ in millions).

Income Statement	2001	% of Sales	2002	% of Sales
Sales	$50.3		$53.4	
Sales Growth		N/A		6.2
COGS	45.7	90.8	47.8	89.5
Gross Margin	4.6	9.2	5.6	10.5
SG&A	7.0	13.9	6.9	12.9
Misc. Expenses & Income	(0.3)	(0.6)	(1.0)	(1.9)
Profit Before Tax	(2.7)	(5.4)	(2.3)	(4.3)
Taxes (35%)	0.9		0.8	
Net Income	($1.8)		($1.5)	
Cash Flow				**% of FA**
Net Income			($1.5)	
Depreciation			0.7	16.6
Change in Working Capital			0.9	
Change in Fixed & Other Assets			(1.9)	
Cash Flow			($1.8)	
Assets	**2001**	**% of Sales**	**2002**	**% of Sales**
Current Assets	$12.6	25.0	$12.6	23.6
Current Liabilities	11.2	22.3	12.1	22.6
Fixed & Other Assets	4.5	8.9	5.7	10.7
Net Assets	$5.9		$6.2	
Return on Net Assets	(29.0%)		(24.2%)	

and increase its gross margin by 1 percent of sales to conform to Pelican's aggressive performance goals. These drastic and aggressive improvement goals were necessitated by the division's continued operating losses.

The GM was responsible for the development and implementation of a revised business plan that would satisfy the corporation's performance expectations for the division. He knew that Pelican Corporation's board of directors was intent on quickly improving the corporation's financial and operational performance, and he viewed the current situation as an opportunity to further enhance his career with Pelican Corporation. Meeting the corporation's aggressive operational targets represented the strongest challenge he had faced since coming to Rugby.

RUGBY CORPORATION'S PRODUCTS, MARKETS, AND PERFORMANCE

The Rugby division provided high-technology manufacturers with a line of precision instruments and specialized components. Because the precision products markets recognized the division as the technical leader, the engineers who developed these products were often considered industry experts. The critical nature of this business from a safety standpoint required that both the products and the production facilities conform to strict quality standards. The division's plant had been certified to both Boeing Advanced Quality System (AQS) D1-9000 and ISO 9001 standards. Despite the technical excellence and high quality level of Rugby's existing product lines, the division had been unable to develop a steady stream of new products or product improvements. Although Rugby's products were considered good, solid, and reliable, they generally were not considered innovative or technologically progressive. This lack of new product development prevented the division from achieving a reputation as a leader in innovation. Furthermore, the failure of Rugby to maintain product differentiation threatened to cast the company as a supplier of commodity products. Such a characterization would force Rugby to compete solely on price and would put even more downward pressure on division margins.

In general, the division experienced better operational efficiencies than most of its competitors in the industry. A study of Rugby's performance for the most recent five-year period compared key operating results to those of a representative set of comparable companies in the same SIC code. The calculation of relative economies of scale revealed that the division had achieved levels of productivity similar to the best economies of scale achieved by comparable companies. Further, an industry analysis relating productivity growth to sales growth revealed that while the industry-average level of productivity growth was slightly less than 8 percent, the actual figure realized by the division was closer to 3 percent, a troublesome trend.

PELICAN CORPORATION'S EXPECTATIONS FOR RUGBY

Pelican Corporation's financial and operational expectations for the Rugby division were detailed in the corporation's comments on the division's original business plan. The GM was moderately surprised by these new expectations, because he believed that the division's original plan contained realistic performance targets based on the previous year's results. Although he wasn't sure which methods of analysis were being used by the corporation to assess the business strength and industry attractiveness of each of the 10 operating units, he was aware of the existence of a corporate strategic-analysis matrix that considered several factors in performing such an assessment. The location of a company within this matrix was useful in determining whether a division should be invested in and grown, managed for earnings, or divested or harvested for cash. He thought it would be prudent to consider how Rugby would be characterized using such a tool.

PRECISION PRODUCTS

In its precision-products niche, the division commanded a 53 percent share of the world market, and high-technology manufacturers recognized its name as the premium supplier of precision components. The global precision products industry was struggling, however, under the economic pressures caused by severe competition. Over the next three to five years, further consolidation was expected of high-technology manufacturers and distributors. These factors led many of the division's customers to demand multiyear price freezes and improved customer service. In addition, to control their own inventory carrying costs, many customers were expecting their suppliers either to provide consigned inventories or to adopt just-in-time (JIT) practices. Although the division was believed to be capable of meeting these more stringent customer requirements, it was saddled with a reputation of not meeting customer-specified delivery dates.

OPPORTUNITIES

The GM of Rugby believed sales of precision components could be improved in several areas. First, the company could market aggressively to original equipment manufacturers (OEMs), because further industry consolidation was expected to strengthen the surviving OEMs. Thus, by aggressively marketing to these firms now, the division would ensure customer loyalty and dedication in future years. Second, Rugby would need to develop new-product technologies. Several products representing advanced technological designs had recently passed product testing and would be ready for market introduction in the near future. These items represented the first major breakthroughs in the specialized precision product line in the past 10 years. Third, the division would need to penetrate underserved service markets in repair work, retrofit programs, and factory-refurbished parts. The service of existing parts and components had traditionally been an important source of revenue in the specialized precision products industry, but Rugby had never aggressively capitalized on this aspect of the business. Finally, Rugby could offer leasing programs to the large OEMs for big-ticket items. Such a program was already being examined for implementation. This would increase division profitability through the avoidance of negotiated OEM purchase agreements.

STRATEGIC QUESTIONS

The GM reflected on the likelihood of achieving the new performance targets. Was the organization disciplined enough to achieve the target for sales established by Pelican?

STRATEGIC ANALYSIS: STRENGTHS AND WEAKNESSES

Strengths

- Leading market position in precision components niche
- 53 percent share in precision products
- Strong brand name in the precision products industry
- Well known for technical excellence
    - Highly regarded engineers and product managers
- An outstanding reputation for quality
    - ISO 9001 and AQS D1-9000 (Boeing standard) certified
- Productivity well above average for size
    - 6.25 employees per $1 million sales vs. industry average of 8.25
- SG&A expense ratio below industry average of 15.5 percent
    - 2001: 14 percent, projected 2002: 13 percent

Weaknesses

- Precision products business unit was losing money.
- In 2000, the division lost $1.4 million on sales of $56.3 million.
- Since then, sales had been flat and earnings negative.
- Product lines were aging.
- Unable to rapidly introduce new products or upgrades.
- Differentiation of products was increasingly difficult.
- The division had a poor reputation for innovation.

- Productivity growth rate in 2001 was well below predicted level of 8 percent.
- Inventory control accuracy was still below expectations.
- The precision products division was unable to meet customer delivery dates.

Industry Characteristics

- Slow growth, averaging just 0.6 percent
- Poor global industry dynamics
- Increased competition, leading to further consolidation
- Focus on cost reduction (e.g., JIT sourcing), because of margin pressure
- Increased competitive intensity
- Critical quality and technical factors
- Increasingly important innovative product features
- Industry returns that appear to have topped out

STRATEGIC SUMMARY

Business Strengths

Rugby was the global leader in its industry, with a 53 percent share. It had a widely recognized brand name and was also well known for its technical expertise. The company's reputation for quality was tremendous, and the division was certified to ISO 9001 as well as AQS D1-9001 standards. Its presence in international markets was strong, with distributors serving Europe and the Pacific Rim. Its product line was aging, although several new products were nearing market introduction. The division had been unprofitable in recent years.

Overall, Rugby's most troublesome weakness was its new product development processes. Its strengths included a level of productivity well above the industry average for firms of similar size, and a state-of-the-art information system that would allow continued emphasis on cost containment and customer service. Gross margins had been squeezed by the industry's severe level of competition.

Overall business strength: Medium.

Industry Attractiveness

Increasing demand for innovative products and the need for higher levels of customer service were putting pressure on current market leaders to adapt their strategies or face limited future success. Additionally, the pre-

cision products industry was currently suffering from the intense competition in the global industry that it supplied. As this industry absorbed the
bulk of the division's sales, continued consolidation within the industry
would likely make any early turnaround for precision products a questionable proposition. Precision products at least offered an opportunity for
international expansion. Growth, which had been stagnant, was likely to
continue to be minimal.

Overall industry attractiveness: Low.

RECOMMENDATIONS

Pelican should divest Rugby. In markets noted for their reliance on product innovation, the division's overall weakness in this area was a source of
concern.

If Retained, What Should Rugby Do?

- Emphasize its ability to find profitable segments within its diffi-
  cult industry
- Improve its cost structure as a means of returning to profitability
- Aggressively target specialty precision OEMs
- Build a base for future success marketing to this rapidly consoli-
  dating industry
- Evaluate leasing as a means of profitability improvement
- Develop new product technologies
  - Existing product lines were approaching the end of the prod-
    uct life cycle
- Aggressively grow the service business
  - Service business was an important source of revenue within
    the industry
  - Rugby had not traditionally capitalized on the service oppor-
    tunities

If Divested, What Valuation Could Be Expected?

A list was developed of nine transactions involving the sale of precision
products companies in the past five years. Averages of the completed transaction provided estimates of the multiples between market prices and revenues, total assets, net assets, and EBIT. These multiples provided a wide
range of estimates for the market value of Rugby Corporation. The division
was expected to be valued by the market at approximately $56 million,
based on these transactions involving comparable businesses.

C A S E   1 1 A – 4

RAINTREE CORPORATION

INTRODUCTION

The GM of Raintree Corporation had just received the response by the parent company, the Pelican Corporation, to the division's business plan for 2002 (See Exhibit 11.9). The Pelican Corporation's expectations for the division had been raised significantly, and the GM was unsure as to whether Raintree was capable of achieving these ambitious performance targets. Raintree's parent company expected the division to improve upon its sales growth, gross margin, and SG&A projections by at least 1 percent (of sales) over the division's previously submitted plan.

E X H I B I T   11.9

2002 Projection-business plan for Raintree Corporation, submitted August 2001 ($ in millions).

Income Statement	2001	% of Sales	2002	% of Sales
Sales	$137.3		$174.4	
Sales Growth		N/A		27.0
COGS	113.7	82.8	134.5	77.1
Gross Margin	23.6	17.2	39.9	22.9
SG&A	12.0	8.7	16.0	9.2
Misc. Expenses & Income	13.5	9.8	(0.7)	(0.4)
Profit Before Tax	25.1	18.3	23.2	13.3
Taxes (35%)	8.8		8.1	
Net Income	$16.3		$15.1	

Cash Flow				% of FA
Net Income			$15.1	
Depreciation			2.1	17.6%
Change in Working Capital			(8.3)	
Change in Fixed & Other Assets			(1.6)	
Cash Flow			$7.3	

Assets	2001	% of Sales	2002	% of Sale
Current Assets	$31.3	22.8	$39.4	22.6
Current Liabilities	25.5	18.6	25.3	14.5
Fixed & Other Assets	11.7	8.5	11.2	6.4
Net Assets	$17.5		$25.3	
Return on Net Assets	93.4%		59.6%	

Raintree faced several immediate challenges. The GM had to determine whether the corporate targets were feasible. If they were, then his management team would need to determine a plan of action for achieving the goals. If they were considered unattainable, however, he would need to be prepared to negotiate new division goals. No matter how much progress the division made, it seemed that he was never free of corporate intervention.

RAINTREE CORPORATION'S PRODUCTS, MARKETS, AND PERFORMANCE

The division was a worldwide supplier of highly specialized equipment, parts and service to the industrial maintenance markets. Raintree had more than a hundred domestic and more than fifty international sales and service locations to support its goal to achieve and maintain a profitable competitive position in the global market. To attain this position, the division utilized its competitive advantages: an educated and motivated work force and state-of-the-art technology.

The division's markets had been experiencing rapid growth in sales over the previous four years. This industry growth had been accompanied by increasing competitiveness, however, as new domestic and international companies entered the market. Competition in both categories was based primarily on price and, to a lesser degree, on the quality of customer service. Customers were extremely price sensitive, and sales contracts would be lost if company prices were not in line with industry expectations. Product liability had become a major cost driver in the industry, however, making product quality and safety important issues. Raintree benefited from this emphasis because the company maintained a reputation for manufacturing high quality products.

Within the standard industrial maintenance markets, the division had two main product lines: Product A and Product B. Raintree's market share for Product A had increased from 13 percent in 1996 to 14 percent in 1998. Although Raintree expected a further increase in its market share, Product A's overall market size was predicted to shrink by an average of 8 percent per year over the following three years. Therefore, all of Raintree's growth in the Product A market would have to come at the expense of its competitors. In the Product B segment, Raintree's market share had increased even more dramatically, growing from 3 percent in 1996 to 8 percent in 1998. By 2001, Raintree expected to achieve a 15 percent share of this market. Product B's market was expected to grow, however, by an average of 8 percent over the next three years.

Raintree also manufactured products for the specialized emergency equipment market. This market was expected to grow at a steady 3 to 4 percent per year for the foreseeable future. Raintree's market share had averaged close to 19 percent in recent years. Although growth in this industry was limited, the division's steady introduction of product innovations was expected to allow Raintree to continue as the market leader.

One additional factor affecting the cost of Raintree's products, as well as attainment of the division's new performance targets, was the company's level of productivity. A study of Raintree's productivity performance for the most recent five-year period compared key operating results to those of a representative set of comparable companies in the same SIC code. The calculation of relative economies of scale revealed that Raintree had achieved a slightly better productivity level based on economies of scale than were achieved by comparable companies. In addition, the analysis showed that the division had achieved the industry's expected productivity growth rate, given its current rate of sales growth. These data indicated that there was a good chance the division could maintain its position as the industry leader.

PELICAN'S EXPECTATIONS FOR RAINTREE

Pelican's financial and operational expectations for the Raintree division were detailed in the corporation's comments on the division's business plan. The GM was moderately surprised by these new goals because it was believed that the division's original plan contained realistic performance targets based on improvements over the previous year's performance. The corporation, however, apparently felt that Raintree was capable of better results. Pelican's new goals called for at least 1 percent (of sales) improvements in the division's projected sales growth rate, gross margin, and SG&A figures. To assess the impact that such improvements would have on the division's cash flow and net income, a sensitivity analysis was performed on these variables. It was found that attainment of these additional improvements would increase the division's net income by about $2.4 million and its cash flow by about $2.2 million.

The GM knew that corporate management was conducting a review of the viability and attractiveness of each of the 10 operating units. Although he wasn't sure which methods of analysis were being used by the Pelican Corporation to assess the business strengths and industry attractiveness of each of the ten operating units, he was aware of the existence of a corporate strategic-analysis matrix that considered several factors in performing such an assessment. He thought it would be prudent to consider how Raintree would be characterized using such a tool.

MARKETING OPPORTUNITIES

Given the modest growth in Raintree's primary markets, the GM believed the best way to increase sales revenues would be to expand the division's marketing efforts to capture a larger portion of the existing international and domestic markets. To achieve this market growth internationally, Raintree would need to pursue strategic alliances, acquisitions, or joint ventures that would promote profitable global expansion. Several alternatives were being considered, including expanding the current sales collaboration agreement (SCA) in effect with Raintree's Japanese partner. Expansion of this agreement would broaden the SCA to include marketing of the full line of Raintree products in Japan, as well as providing for limited technology transfer to the Japanese partner. By expanding the SCA to include technology transfer for two of Raintree's lesser-known products, the GM expected to improve relations with this marketing partner. The result could provide a projected increase in sales of close to 8 percent. Also, by offering to transfer the technology behind Raintree's second-tier products, the division hoped to avoid requests to transfer technology for its main product lines.

Raintree could also establish a relationship with a well-known Korean manufacturing and marketing company. Although such a relationship could result in increased sales revenues of up to 5 percent, the GM was cautious about pursuing such a strategy. He was aware that some Korean companies were seeking partnerships with established manufacturing firms for the purpose of acquiring advanced manufacturing technologies, which would then be used to compete with the former partner. His willingness to engage voluntarily in limited technology transfer with the Japanese firm was based on an existing relationship. No such history existed with the Korean firm.

He could also develop exclusive distribution networks in Taiwan, Indonesia, Singapore, Malaysia, Thailand, and the Philippines. Although these six Asian countries already had achieved moderate sales of Raintree's primary products, the division relied on nonexclusive product distributors to market its products. He believed Raintree should establish its own network of dealerships in each of these countries. He also expected to enter the Chinese and Vietnamese markets. By all accounts, these two socialized market economies had great potential for future market development and growth. With expected increases in infrastructure development in both countries, huge untapped demand could exist for Raintree's specialized industrial maintenance equipment. The challenge for the division's management team was to assess the political and economic risk associated with doing business in each economy and to determine what level of risk was acceptable to Raintree and to Pelican.

Finally, Raintree should enhance its European operations and market presence. Although the division already had a significant presence in Europe, it was seeking a new partner to handle distribution and manufacturing. Older dealers in several countries, including France, Spain, Austria, and Turkey, were not as aggressive in marketing Raintree's products as the division desired, and it was feared that market share would be eroded in these countries unless a new partnership was established.

In addition to these international marketing initiatives, the GM also considered several opportunities for improving domestic sales. The division could continue its successful advertising campaign, which focused on Raintree's claim to the lowest total cost of ownership (which included purchase, maintenance, and operating costs) as well as the highest resale value of its products. Another consideration was the development of its parts and service business, which currently accounted for only 8 percent of total company revenues but contributed 30 percent of profits. It was felt that providing 24-hour technical service and parts would lead to growth in the parts business.

COST REDUCTIONS AND PROFITABILITY IMPROVEMENTS

In addition to increased sales, the division could improve its financial performance and profitability by reducing its operating costs. The division's goal was to attain the lowest cost position in all of its market segments, using its manufacturing competencies to its competitive advantage. To be considered a success, however, these cost improvements would have to be attained without sacrificing Raintree's high product quality standards. Several potential areas for cost reductions were available, including the implementation of ISO 9001 quality standards.

Although Raintree's manufacturing processes were among the best in the industry, there was room for improvement. Raintree's quality program, though effective, had been developed in-house and was not as demanding as more formal, standardization programs. Thus, by adopting the ISO standards, Raintree would raise its level of quality, which in turn would lower its total costs by eliminating inefficiencies, reducing waste, and minimizing product returns. An added benefit of adopting the ISO standards would be increased sales, since many international customers required ISO certification for their suppliers.

Raintree also needed to evaluate product specifications against customer needs as a continuous process. The GM was concerned that Raintree's emphasis on technological leadership caused the company to engineer its products with tolerances and specifications that were unnecessarily stringent. Pursuing such high levels of technical excellence was costly, and unnecessarily so if the market did not consider such technological advancements as adding perceptible benefits for which customers would pay a premium price. By continually evaluating market demand for certain product qualities and capabilities, Raintree could better control production and design costs, making its products more competitive in the long run.

Raintree also could implement cross-functional teams across the entire division. Some of Raintree's manufacturing units already had work teams, but the GM was considering implementing the team concept throughout the firm. Though short-term costs would need to be incurred for program training and organizational restructuring, the GM believed that the long-term savings associated with adoption of the team concept would outweigh these costs.

Limited service guarantees should be offered on all Raintree products. None of Raintree's competitors currently offered service guarantees, which would make such an offer by Raintree unique, would differentiate its products, and help increase sales. It would also force Raintree to increase the quality of its products to keep the cost of the guarantee down. Building quality into the production process would also decrease production costs in the long run and improve margins.

There was a strong need to reduce product liability costs for Raintree products. The operation of specialized industrial maintenance equipment involved a significant amount of risk. The GM saw an opportunity for cost savings if Raintree could reduce this risk, which would, in turn, reduce the likelihood of product liability lawsuits. Several possible ways to reduce risk included providing interactive training videos to new customers and holding product liability seminars for Raintree dealers. If Raintree could explain the risk to its dealers, the dealers would be able to emphasize the importance of safety to their customers and hopefully reduce the number of potential accidents.

STRATEGIC QUESTIONS

As the GM reflected on the various alternatives for achieving Pelican's revised performance targets, many thoughts ran through his head. Which improvement opportunities were most likely to enable Raintree to achieve Pelican's optimistic performance goals? Were there any opportunities that he had not thought of? And lastly, how would the division's performance impact his professional career, whether the division was retained or sold?

STRATEGIC ANALYSIS: STRENGTHS AND WEAKNESSES

Strengths

- Strong reputation for quality
- Increased significance of quality leadership position because of product liability concerns
- State-of-the-art manufacturing technology
- Educated and motivated work force
- Strong position in several niches
- 19 percent share in specialized emergency equipment
- 14 percent share in two categories of standard industrial maintenance equipment
- Small but highly profitable parts and service business
  - 8 percent of revenue, but 30 percent of profit
- Established presence in international markets
  - Focus on Japan and Europe

- Productivity slightly better than industry average
  - 8.75 employees per $1 million sales vs. 9.25 employees per $1 million sales
- Growth well above industry average of negative 5.5 percent
  - 2001: 65.6 percent, projected 2002: 27 percent
- SG&A expense ratio well below industry average of 19.1 percent
  - 2001: 8.7 percent, projected 2002: 9.2 percent
- ROS 10 to 15 times the industry average of 0.6 percent
  - 2001: 5.5 percent (excluding extraordinary income), projected 2002: 8.7 percent
- RONA 15 to 20 times the industry average of 2.5 percent
  - 2001: 43.2 percent (excluding extraordinary income), projected 2002: 59.6 percent

Weaknesses

- Reliance on mature or declining segments
- Specialized emergency equipment segment flat for over 20 years
- Raintree Corporation products compete in two standard heavy construction equipment segments which should grow by only 1 percent annually for the next three years
- Nonstandard quality program
- Not currently ISO 9001 certified
- Limited international growth
- Overemphasis on product technology
- Overengineering of products, which raised costs
- Growing pains in international partnerships
  - Japanese partners looking for increased technology transfer
  - European partners not promoting Raintree's products aggressively enough
  - Nonexclusive distribution agreements in Taiwan, Indonesia, Singapore, Malaysia, Thailand, and the Philippines
- Gross margins below industry average of 25.3 percent
  - 2001: 17.2 percent, projected 2002: 22.9 percent

Industry Characteristics

- Large and mature domestic industry with several rapidly growing segments

- Many large and untapped international markets
- Dominated by large and powerful competitors
- Increased competitive intensity resulting from new domestic and international entrants
- Differentiation through service
- Minimal economies of scale but significant economies of growth
- Price sensitive customers
- Price competitiveness was essential
- Increasing liability concerns which raised importance of quality, safety, and service
- Low but relatively stable profit potential
- Industry RONA: five-year average 2.53 percent

STRATEGIC SUMMARY

Business Strengths

Raintree was well positioned to continue its extraordinary growth while maintaining superior profitability. An entrenched reputation for quality products played to customers' fears of increased liability exposure. State-of-the-art manufacturing facilities allowed Raintree to back up this reputation with a competitive cost position. These strengths, as well as an educated and motivated work force, were expected to give the division the resources to pursue continued growth, both domestically and internationally. In addition, a small but successful parts and service business offered the opportunity to differentiate itself profitably, through enhanced service offerings, in an increasingly commodity-like market. In recent years growth had far outstripped the general industry, which had seen a 5.5 percent decline since 1996. Returns during this period had improved dramatically, with ROS 10 to 15 times the industry average and RONA 15 to 20 times greater.

Although SG&A expenses of less than half the industry average had helped to support such superior returns, maintaining them at such low levels might be an uncertain proposition. Increased investments in marketing, needed to support further expansion and to combat increased competition, could cause SG&A expense to creep upward, putting pressure on profits. Gross margins, which had lagged the rest of the industry, had started to improve. Continued improvement would be imperative, should SG&A expenses rise. Other areas of concern included overreliance on mature or declining segments, the cost of improved quality programs, and the uncertainties inherent in international markets.

Overall business strength: High.

Industry Attractiveness

The industrial maintenance markets had experienced negative growth of 5.5 percent over the previous five years. Profit levels were low but relatively stable. Over the same time period, RONA had averaged 2.5 percent, with a low of minus 4.3 percent and a high of 5.75 percent. Growing and profitable niches had existed, with the specialized high-technology segment being one. Large and diversified domestic and international competitors dominated the industry, although economies of scale had only a minimal impact.

Competition in the industry took place primarily on the basis of price. Opportunities for differentiation existed through enhanced offerings and related lines of business, such as parts and service. Increased concerns about product liability had highlighted product quality in the minds of the industry and its customers. Safety and quality might prove to be increasingly important points of leverage as customers would tend to focus on total ownership costs, the reduction of liability exposure, and the cost savings associated with quality improvements.

Overall industry attractiveness: Medium to high.

RECOMMENDATIONS

Pelican should retain Raintree; invest in international expansion, increased domestic marketing, and quality improvement; and focus on growing the highly profitable parts and service business.

If Retained, What Should Raintree Do?

- Expand international presence through acquisitions/alliances/joint ventures
  - Establish presence in Chinese and Vietnamese markets
- Expand existing SCA with Japanese partner
- Work for exclusive distribution agreements in other Asian countries
- Reevaluate existing European manufacturing, distribution, and sales relationships
- Increase domestic marketing
- Focus on the lowest total cost of ownership
- Emphasize highest resale value
- Grow parts and service business
- Improve quality programs
- Implement ISO 9001 standards
- Increase the use of team-based organizational structures

- Build quality into the manufacturing process
- Differentiate Raintree with service enhancements
- Establish "guaranteed" service
  - 24-hour parts and service
- Reduce product liability costs
- Provide training to dealers and customers through videos and seminars

If Divested, What Market Price Could Be Expected by Pelican?

A list of completed transactions involving the sale of comparable businesses was prepared. Averages of the 10 completed transactions provided multiples of expected sales prices to revenues, total assets, net assets, and EBIT. These multiples provided a wide range of estimates for the market value of Raintree. Asset multiples provided low-end estimates of market values that did not reflect the potential value of continued operations of the firm, while revenue multiples provided midrange values. EBIT multiples provided the most realistic, high-end estimate of $405 million, assuming future performance consistent with recent levels.

C A S E   11A–5

GROVE CORPORATION

INTRODUCTION

The president and GM of Grove Corporation, a division of Pelican Corporation, had just received a fax from the corporate office. The fax was the result of a recent meeting with corporate executives, at which the GM had presented Grove's revenue and cash-flow forecasts for 2002. The fax presented a great challenge for him and all the employees at Grove. The message communicated a set of revised performance expectations for Grove. It

E X H I B I T   11.10

2002 Projection-business plan for Grove Corporation, submitted August 2001 ($ in millions).

Income Statement	2001	% of Sales	2002	% of Sales
Sales	$38.0		$39.3	
Sales Growth		N/A		3.3
COGS	21.7	57.1	23.3	59.3
Gross Margin	16.3	43.0	16.0	40.7
SG&A	7.7	20.2	8.3	21.1
Misc. Expenses & Income	0.2	0.5	0.1	0.2
Profit Before Tax	8.8	23.2	7.8	19.8
Taxes (35%)	3.1		(2.7)	
Net Income	$5.7		$5.1	
Cash Flow				**% of FA**
Net Income			$5.1	
Depreciation			0.3	98.6%
Change in Working Capital			(0.1)	
Change in Fixed & Other Assets			(2.0)	
Cash Flow			$3.3	
Assets	**2001**	**% of Sales**	**2002**	**% of Sales**
Current Assets	$6.1	16.1	$7.0	17.8
Current Liabilities	7.8	20.5	8.5	21.6
Fixed & Other Assets	0.3	0.8	2.0	5.1
Net Assets	($1.4)		$0.5	
Return on Net Assets	NA		1142.0%	

stated that the division should achieve a sales growth rate 1 percent (of sales) above the projected sales growth rate of 3.3 percent, contained in the division's original business plan (see Exhibit 11.10). The parent company also expected the division to improve upon its gross margin and SG&A figures by 1 percent of sales over the original business plan.

GROVE CORPORATION'S PRODUCTS, MARKETS, AND PERFORMANCE

Grove was one of the smaller divisions of Pelican. Its main line of business was the manufacture and sale of high-technology specialty consumer products. Grove's products were sold into niches of a total market that had grown at a real rate of 3 percent in recent years to a record $17.7 billion total market. During the same time period, Grove's specific market segments had grown at a compound rate of 5 percent per year, reflecting strong consumer interest in its high-technology specialty products. Grove also generated revenue by selling parts to repair the installed base of its products.

Within the United States, strong relationships with the channels of distribution were critical to succeeding in Grove's industry. Recognizing this and considering these relationships a priority, Grove used local distributors to sell its products in Canada, England, and France. Products sold in the Pacific Rim were distributed for Grove by an international exporting firm. Spare parts were distributed using the same channels as new products, both domestically and abroad. The division had been successful in supplying large developers of condominiums and apartments, a significant growth segment.

Manufacturing involved both parts fabrication and product assembly. Both the fabrication and assembly facilities were in need of refurbishing. According to the director of manufacturing, there had been a history of disinvestment in Grove. This problem manifested itself across the board from the building (the roof leaked) to the fabrication facility, where workers were forced to "cannibalize" machines for repairs.

Despite this lack of investment in physical assets, Grove was still able to achieve productivity rates that were consistently better than the industry average. A study of Grove's performance for the most recent five-year period compared key operating results to those of a representative set of comparable companies in the same SIC code. The calculation of relative economies of scale revealed that Grove had achieved a substantially better productivity level, based on scale economies, than was achieved by comparable companies. In addition, the analysis showed that the division far exceeded its expected productivity growth rate, given its current rate of sales growth.

PELICAN'S EXPECTATIONS FOR THE GROVE CORPORATION

Pelican's financial and operational expectations for the Grove division were detailed in the corporation's comments on the division's business plan. The GM was very surprised by these new goals, because he believed that the division's original plan contained realistic performance forecasts based on realistic improvements over the previous year's performance. The corporate staff, however, apparently felt that Grove was capable of even better results. Pelican's new goals called for increasing forecast sales growth by 1 percent and improving the division's gross margin and SG&A forecasts by 1 percent of sales. To assess the impact that such improvements would have on the division's cash flow and net income, the GM performed a sensitivity analysis on these variables. He found that attainment of these goals would increase both the division's net income and cash flow by approximately $600,000.

Although he wasn't sure which methods of analysis were being used by the parent company to assess the business strengths and industry attractiveness of each of the operating units, he was aware of the existence of a corporate strategic-analysis matrix that considered several factors in performing such an assessment. The location of a company within this matrix was useful in determining whether a division should be invested in and grown, managed for earnings, or divested or harvested for cash. He thought it would be prudent to consider how Grove would be characterized using such a tool.

PERSONAL CONSIDERATIONS

Before weighing his options, the GM thought about his, and Grove's, future. The executives at Pelican believed that economies of scale would be a disadvantage to a smaller division. Given Grove's position, would the parent company allow the GM to grow the business aggressively but naturally? He doubted it. Maybe Grove would be merged into another division. At first glance, that would appear to be bad news for all of Grove's employees. If such a move were made, the GM would report to an additional layer of management between him and Pelican's CEO. On the other hand, Grove was one of the most profitable divisions in the company. He decided that his best bet for the future was to continue to maximize the operating results of Grove and not to worry about matters he couldn't control.

MARKET OPPORTUNITIES AND CONCERNS

Grove's managers had several options available to improve sales growth. First, if they continued in their current markets with their current product lines, the growth would have to come from aggressive marketing. Grove had been modifying its product mix to maximize contribution. The division had been in a harvest mode with some of its product lines because of a lack of cash from Pelican. Now that Grove was being given the mandate to grow aggressively, maybe this harvesting process could be reversed. The option to grow aggressively could not be pursued, however, without a major investment in manufacturing capacity. Such an expansion could occur through the purchase of additional equipment for the existing facility or through the acquisition of a company with similar capabilities.

External expansion would be preferable if an acceptable acquisition could be found, and, after a brief search, two companies were identified as potential targets. One was a company in North Carolina, with sales of $19 million and a faltering product line that was too narrowly focused. Even though the company's business represented a fit with Grove, three aspects bothered the GM. First, it was too far away. In spite of Pelican's size, Grove was a small company based in Washington State. Second, although the materials and the fundamental processes were the same, the products of the two companies were quite different. This would complicate the integration of the two companies. Third, because of the more bureaucratic mentality in the other business, he feared that cultural differences would exacerbate the geographic obstacles to a smooth transition to one company.

The second potential target was a small appliance manufacturer located in California. Unlike Grove, this company outsourced virtually all of the component and subassembly manufacturing in the products it sold. It relied on a flexible assembly operation and good relationships with some of the larger companies interested in offering its products under a private label. With sales of $47 million, this company's acquisition would come close to positioning Grove as a legitimate stand-alone business. Sales at this target had increased moderately for the past three years. And although the family-controlled company would not be a bargain, it could be bought at the right price.

The GM had three primary concerns with the potential acquisition of this company. First, he was concerned that the company might be too large to be effectively incorporated into Grove. He was also concerned that more than doubling Grove's size by acquiring an assembler would make it very difficult to maintain the positive financial performance that had elevated Grove into its current strong competitive position. Finally, the GM wondered just how much such an acquisition would cost.

As with the prospect of acquisitions, internal expansion promised interesting challenges. Although the manufacturing organization had been complaining about the lack of commitment of funds from the corporation, the reality was that life in a company that was not expanding could become comfortable. The GM was afraid that if he tried to use his current staff to control twice the number of assets, they might not be up to the task. Another concern was financial: one reason Grove's financials looked strong was that its assets were almost fully depreciated. A plant expansion would change the company's balance sheet and make many of its ratios less favorable.

Other marketing options included more aggressively pursuing international markets and adding product lines to the company's current offering. Although Grove had made headway internationally, most sales were still generated in the United States. U.S. exports of Grove's products were, however, expected to expand as global trade barriers continued to decline.

STRATEGIC QUESTIONS

The GM knew he had to respond quickly to Pelican's request for a modified business plan. There were many ways in which Grove could potentially reach the revised sales goals presented by the corporation, and it was up to the GM to determine which path the company would follow.

STRATEGIC ANALYSIS: STRENGTHS AND WEAKNESSES

Strengths

- Strong international presence
  - Canada, England, France
  - Pacific Rim
- Strong relationships with distributors
- Fully depreciated assets, which remained productive
- Spectacular forecast RONA, over 200 times the industry five-year average of 4.3 percent
- Superior ROS, 25 to 30 times the industry five-year average of 0.5 percent
  - 2001: 15.1 percent, projected 2002: 12.9 percent
- Gross margins well above the industry five-year average of 32.2 percent
  - 2001: 43 percent, projected 2002: 40.7 percent
- SG&A expense ratio below industry average of 23.5 percent
  - 2001: 20.3 percent, projected 2002: 21.1 percent
- Productivity levels well above predicted level for size
  - 4.5 employees per $1 million of sales versus industry average level of 6.75 employees per $1 million of sales
  - Productivity improvements three times the expected level for the division's growth rate

Weaknesses

- A harvest mind-set
- Lack of growth orientation
- Inability of current staff to handle increased size and/or growth

- A size significantly smaller than average in the industry
- Existing capacity constraints that limited growth opportunities
- Aging manufacturing facilities in need of significant investment
  - Fabrication and assembly in general state of disrepair
- Growth below industry five-year average of 7.3 percent
  - 2001: 6.5 percent, projected 2002: 3.3 percent

Industry Characteristics

- Industry dominated by several very large firms
- Growth estimates were moderate to low, and they varied widely
  - Five-year average of 7.3 percent
  - Industry growth rate from 1996 to 2000, nominal 2.2 percent, real 1.5 percent
  - Industry growth rate from 1998 to 2001, nominal 2.1 percent, real 2.7 percent
- Tight ROS indicated high level of competitive intensity
  - Industry ROS: Five-year average 0.5 percent
- Both economies of scale and economies of growth exist but were not statistically significant
- Industry returns were unattractive
  - Industry RONA: Five-year average 4.3 percent

STRATEGIC SUMMARY

Business Strengths

Grove was a highly efficient producer of high-technology specialty consumer products. It had been operated in a harvest mode for several years and was suffering from aging facilities and limited capacity. Despite this, the company had generated almost $11 million in net income over the previous two years while tying up very little capital.

Grove had produced returns on sales and net assets that far outdistanced the rest of the industry. With fully depreciated facilities, its cost structure had put it in an advantageous position. In addition, it had a strong relationship with its distribution network and a presence in a variety of international markets. Offsetting these strengths were a number of weaknesses.

Grove was in need of major capital investments to update its manufacturing facilities and expand its capacity. Aging fabrication and assembly facilities were not adequate for future growth. A leaking roof and rampant cannibalization for spare parts were indicative of severe neglect. The harvest mind-set was a problem among the staff as well. It was doubtful whether existing staff could handle the increased volume that would be required to position Grove for continued success. Lastly, existing capacity constraints had limited growth to well below the levels achieved by comparable companies.

Overall business strength: Medium-to-high.

Industry Attractiveness

The specialty consumer products industry had experienced moderate real growth over the previous five years. In 2000, the larger industry grew at a real rate of 3 percent, while the Grove segments grew at 5 percent. In recent years, however, prices had not kept pace with inflation, as increased competitive pressures had weakened producers' ability to maintain margins.

Additional evidence of this competitive intensity could be seen in the ROS figures for the industry. The average five-year industry ROS was just over 0.5 percent. The continued stagnation of ROS figures supported the contention that price competition had had a negative impact on the industry. As a result, the industry was marked by modest returns that averaged only 4.3 percent over the past five years, and had exhibited a high degree of volatility.

Overall industry attractiveness: Low.

RECOMMENDATIONS

Pelican should divest Grove Corporation. Grove had generated impressive results over the past several years—and could probably be harvested for several more. To ensure long-term competitiveness, however, a significant influx of capital would be required. The small size of Grove limited the absolute profit potential to a level that made renewed investment in the company undesirable. The existence of a positive market opinion of Grove was expected to bring a favorable valuation.

IF RETAINED, WHAT SHOULD GROVE DO?

- Aggressively market existing products
- Evaluate expansion in international markets
- Explore development of new product lines
- Provide the capacity expansion required by more rapid growth
- Expand capacity internally
- Replace staff who had questionable ability to manage required expansion
- Refrain from adding new assets, as they would damage financial performance

- Seek acquisition candidates with compatible products and excess capacity
  - California Company, $47 million in sales—Too big to handle, negative impact on financial performance, potential to be too costly
  - North Carolina Company, $19 million in sales—Too far away, incompatible products, cultural and market differences

IF DIVESTED, WHAT VALUATION COULD BE EXPECTED?

The GM of Grove had prepared an estimate of the market value of the company using Grove's recent financial results and data on 11 completed transactions involving the sale of similar businesses. The result was an estimated valuation for Grove of approximately $75 million.

CASE 11A-6

EASTWOOD CORPORATION

INTRODUCTION

The GM of Eastwood knew that he had just been given the most difficult challenge of his career. Only hours earlier, he had met with the executive committee of Eastwood's parent, Pelican Corporation. He had been warned prior to his arrival that the corporation's expectations for its 10 operating divisions had been changed. He discovered that the original business plan for his division (see Exhibit 11.11), submitted a month earlier in August 2001, would need to be revised to account for the corporate change in

EXHIBIT 11.11

2002 Projection-business plan for Eastwood Corporation, submitted August 2001 ($ in millions).

Income Statement	2001	% of Sales	2002	% of Sales
Sales	$30.7		$28.5	
Sales Growth		N/A		(7.1)
COGS	30.9	100.7	25.0	87.7
Gross Margin	(0.2)	(0.7)	3.5	12.3
SG&A	4.9	16.0	3.0	10.5
Misc. Expenses & Income	1.8	5.9	1.9	6.6
Profit Before Tax	(3.3)	(10.7)	2.4	8.4
Taxes (35%)	(1.2)		0.8	
Net Income	($2.1)		$1.6	
Cash Flow				**% of FA**
Net Income			$1.6	
Depreciation			0.6	5.3
Change in Working Capital			1.7	
Change in Fixed & Other Assets			1.6	
Cash Flow			$5.5	
Assets	**2001**	**% of Sales**	**2002**	**% of Sales**
Current Assets	$14.9	48.5	$13.7	48.0
Current Liabilities	4.3	14.0	4.8	16.8
Fixed & Other Assets	10.7	34.9	8.5	29.8
Net Assets	$21.3		$17.4	
Return on Net Assets	(10.4%)		9.1%	

goals. Despite his requests for more reasonable expectations and more time, he had to accept what he considered to be very difficult improvement goals for his division. He now had two weeks to submit a revised business plan outlining a formal strategy for achieving or exceeding the new objectives.

EASTWOOD CORPORATION'S PRODUCTS, MARKETS, AND PERFORMANCE

Eastwood was a manufacturer of high quality electrical switching components for aerospace, defense, telecommunications, and industrial applications. From the division's founding, Eastwood was one of only a few suppliers to these niche markets. The lack of competition during those years had allowed Eastwood to enjoy high margins and a captive customer base. Unfortunately, Eastwood was unable to protect the niche markets that it had created and dominated.

Partly because of the success of Pelican and partly because of its own failures, Eastwood allowed inefficiencies to develop in its operations. To maintain the margins that the company had enjoyed for many years, Eastwood raised its prices rather than address the underlying cost drivers of its products. As prices climbed and quality deteriorated, competitors began entering the market. By 1994, Eastwood had lost most of its share of the telecommunications and aerospace markets as a result of high prices, late deliveries, and an indifference to customer needs and requests. Similarly, by the mid-1990s, Eastwood had witnessed the erosion of its market share in the defense and industrial applications markets.

In 2000, a new GM was appointed to lead Pelican's floundering Eastwood division. By that time, the division was plagued by high prices, declining profit margins, long-term contracts that obligated Eastwood to sell its products at a loss, large inventories, high fixed costs, late deliveries, and an indifference to its customers. The GM's first action was to implement several quality assurance programs designed to improve customer service, lower costs, and improve productivity.

A study of Eastwood's performance during the most recent five-year period compared key operating results to those of a representative set of comparable companies in the same SIC code. The calculation of relative economies of scale revealed just how inefficient the division was in comparison with its industry competitors. At its current sales volume, the company was only half as efficient as the industry average, requiring approximately 16 employees per $1 million in sales. The company, however, was improving. Eastwood had recently achieved annual productivity growth rates of 6 percent per year, which were higher than the industry average productivity growth rate.

Improvement efforts had been interrupted unexpectedly in 1998, when the corporation decided to relocate the division's operations from

Texas to North Carolina. Despite this setback, the GM still believed that the company could return to its status as a market leader within the next five years. Unfortunately, Pelian had given him no more than one year to turn things around.

PELICAN'S EXPECTATIONS FOR EASTWOOD

The GM was moderately surprised by the new division goals, because he believed that the division's original plan was aggressive and contained realistic performance targets. In 2001, Eastwood's cost of goods sold was expected to be 101 percent of revenues, and SG&A 16 percent of revenues. As a result, Eastwood would suffer a loss of $2.2 million during the year. Under Eastwood's original plan for 2002, cost of goods sold were expected to be 88 percent of sales and SG&A would be 10 percent of sales, which was expected to result in a profit of $1.6 million.

The parent company, however, believed that Eastwood was capable of even better results. Pelican's new expectations called for at least 1 percent (of sales) improvements in sales growth, gross margin, and SG&A expense, above the company's original business plan. To assess the impact that such improvements would have on the division's cash flow and net income, the GM asked his finance manager to perform a sensitivity analysis on these variables. The analysis showed that attainment of these new goals would increase the division's net income by about $390,000 and its cash flow by about $200,000.

The GM knew that corporate management was conducting a review of the viability and attractiveness of each of the 10 operating units. Although he wasn't sure which methods of analysis were being used by the corporation to assess the business strengths and industry attractiveness of each operating unit, he was aware of the existence of a corporate strategic-analysis matrix that considered several factors in performing such an assessment. He thought it would be prudent to consider how Eastwood would be characterized using such a tool.

The result of Pelican's strategic analysis of the division likely would determine Eastwood's fate within the corporation. To estimate the current value of his division, the GM collected data on Eastwood's recent financial performance as well as information on completed financial transactions involving comparable companies. His analysis yielded an estimated valuation for the company of nearly $31 million.

CHALLENGES FACING EASTWOOD

Any realistic strategic plan that the GM and his team developed had to account for the many problems that plagued the division as it approached 2002. In preparing Eastwood's original business plan several months earlier, the GM had asked his management team to list the critical problems confronting the division in the coming year. His staff identified key problem areas that Eastwood would have to address in 2002.

First, the prices of Eastwood's products were higher than those of competitors' products. Unlike earlier years when Eastwood was the sole producer in its markets, the current markets were saturated, and no one company could dictate the selling price of the products. Despite this competitive environment, however, Eastwood had continued to raise prices over the last few years to reflect higher overhead costs. The price increases were not accepted by the market, and Eastwood's customers began finding alternative sources to replace Eastwood's products.

Second, Eastwood had a reputation of being unable to meet delivery deadlines. A typical comment voiced by customers was, "Eastwood has a good product, if you can get it." Late deliveries, in conjunction with higher prices, led customers to second-source or drop Eastwood's products altogether.

Third, Pelican's financial difficulties had made many of Eastwood's suppliers and customers uneasy. Many existing customers had expressed their concerns about Pelican's financial stability and, in turn, the ability of Eastwood to satisfy its obligations to both customers and suppliers.

Fourth, the decision to move Eastwood's operations from Texas to North Carolina caused several important customers to find alternative suppliers. These customers were geographically closer to Texas and believed that the increased distance would lead to even higher prices and further delays in delivery. Eastwood lost key personnel as a result of the decision to move operations to North Carolina. When the decision to move Eastwood was announced, many of the division's seasoned engineers and other key personnel chose to remain in Texas. Several of these former employees either joined competitors or started their own companies to compete directly with Eastwood.

Last, the division no longer had original equipment manufacturer (OEM), aftermarket (replacement parts), or international representation. Until recently, Eastwood had relied on a very effective representative in these markets. The representative had unexpectedly announced three months previously that it would no longer represent third parties. Unfortunately, the division was a party to several long-term contracts that required Eastwood to deliver custom-made systems to major customers in the aerospace industry at a substantial loss. These contracts had been executed prior to the GM's arrival at Eastwood, and he was uncertain how difficult it would be to renegotiate them.

OPPORTUNITIES

In spite of the difficulties noted above, the GM felt that the division had weathered the storm. Eastwood was expected to produce a positive cash flow with minimum capital requirements for the foreseeable future. The

Eastwood brand, while experiencing some erosion, maintained excellent name recognition in the niche markets in which it operated. Additionally, over the last year, the division had greatly improved delivery performance, the quality of its products, and the attentiveness of its personnel to customer needs and complaints. It was believed that additional opportunities for improvement existed in each of Eastwood's functional departments, described below.

Sales and Marketing

The loss of the distributor was believed to be more of a benefit to Eastwood than a setback. The use of a third-party distributor had contributed to the decline in division responsiveness to customer needs and problems. With significant growth potential in the national and international OEM markets, the GM believed that direct marketing and sales efforts would reestablish Eastwood as the OEM market leader for switching systems.

Manufacturing

The sales and marketing efforts were dependent upon continued improvement by manufacturing. If production costs could be reduced further, sales and marketing could reduce prices and make their products more competitive. The following manufacturing objectives were thought to be achievable:

- **A reduction in rework in the fabrication area.** In 2001, the fabrication area had reduced rework from 16 percent to 4 percent. It was believed that another 2 percent decrease was possible in 2002.
- **A reduction in scrap.** In 2001, manufacturing had reduced scrap from 10 percent to less than 2 percent. In 2002, it was felt that a further reduction in scrap to 0.5 percent was attainable.
- **Productivity increases in fabrication and assembly.** For 2002, it was projected that productivity could be increased by 7 percent in fabrication and 5 percent in assembly.
- **Additional improvements in the Quality Improvement Department.** Improvements should result from the quality assurance programs implemented by the division several years earlier. The quality assurance programs would be upgraded by the addition of experienced personnel, implementation of statistical process control (SPC), and other statistical control programs. The adoption of a vendor qualification program, the development of an internal audit department, and the formation of a continuous training program would also improve quality.

Engineering

Because of the relocation from Texas to North Carolina, Eastwood lost many of its talented engineers to competitors. A successful turnaround would depend heavily on the division's ability to attract and retain qualified personnel. The restaffing efforts to date had been extremely successful. In addition to the personnel issue, several initiatives had been undertaken by the engineering department and were expected to be completed in 2002. These included the following:

- **The redesign of the switching systems currently marketed and sold to the aerospace industry.** Currently, the weight and size of the systems exceeded customer specifications and were higher than those offered by competitors. The new systems would be superior in quality to those of competitors.

- **A formalized program designed to increase coordination between the marketing and engineering departments, including increased visits to customers.** This initiative was aimed at decreasing total production costs and improving customer service.

- **A reduction in product lines within certain product families.** Fewer product offerings would decrease setup times and increase the capacity of each of the machines. The net result would be greater operational efficiencies and lower total costs.

STRATEGIC ANALYSIS: STRENGTHS AND WEAKNESSES

The GM understood the magnitude of the challenges facing his division. As he reviewed the problems and opportunities confronting him, he wondered what actions should be taken and what priorities should be assigned.

Strengths

- Strong brand equity despite recent slippage
- Productivity improvements two times the predicted level of 2.8 percent for Eastwood's growth rate
  - 2001: 6.2 percent, projected 2002: 5 to 7 percent
- Improved product quality
- Previously implemented quality assurance programs taking effect
- Rework in fabrication reduced from 16 percent in 2000 to 4 percent in 2001
- Scrap reduced from 10 percent in 2000 to 2 percent in 2001
- Improved delivery performance

- Increased customer focus
- Loss of distributor, beneficial in this respect
- Success in replacing personnel lost in move
- SG&A expense ratio below industry average of 24.8 percent
  - 2001: 16.0 percent, projected 2002: 10.5 percent

Weaknesses

- Small size—a disadvantage in an industry with significant economies of scale
- Poor productivity
  - 16 employees per $1 million sales—well above expected level of 11 employees
  - The most efficient firms employed 8 employees per $1 million of revenues and had revenues of approximately $200 million
- Critical engineering personnel lost in move to North Carolina
- Market share declines resulting from customer defections driven by the following eight factors, below
  - High prices
  - Poor delivery
  - Move from Dallas to North Carolina is inconvenient to some customer, suppliers, and employees
  - Customers have concerns about Pelican
  - Majority of market share lost in all segments
  - Locked into long-term loss-generating contracts in aerospace market
  - Lacking distribution in OEM, aftermarket, and international markets
  - Loss of distributor
- Must develop marketing and sales for segments previously serviced by distributor
- Growth projection well below industry five-year average of 10.9 percent
  - 2001: 11.8 percent, projected 2002: –7.1 percent
- Gross margins well below industry five-year average of 35.7 percent
  - 2001: –0.7 percent, projected 2002: 12.3 percent
- ROS well below industry five-year average of 6.2 percent
  - 2002: –6.8 percent, projected 2002: 5.5 percent
- RONA well below industry five-year average of 12.4 percent
  - 2001: –10.4 percent, projected 2002: 9.1 percent

Industry Characteristics

- Strong industry growth, five-year average of 10.9 percent
- Potential growth in OEM markets, both internationally and domestically
- Crowded industry with high level of competitive intensity
- Many large competitors
- Competition on the basis of price
- Pricing power controlled by buyers
- Economies of scale up to approximately $200 million, slight diseconomies above that
- Very large growth economies
- Attractive industry returns
- Industry RONA: Five-year average 12.4 percent; high 15.7 percent in 1999; low 6.3 percent in 1997

STRATEGIC SUMMARY

Business Strengths

Eastwood Products retained the strong brand recognition that it had always had, but little else. In 2000 it lost over $9 million on revenue of $27 million. Its losses narrowed considerably in 2001, when it generated revenue of $30.7 million and produced a loss of $3.3 million (pre-tax). In 2002, Eastwood was forecast to earn $2.4 million on revenue of $28.5 million. Based on these somewhat optimistic assumptions, the company would still trail the industry in gross margin, revenue per employee, return on sales, and return on net assets.

Recent efforts to improve the performance of the division had resulted in significant progress. Rework and scrap rates had fallen dramatically. Delivery performance had improved, and replacement efforts for personnel lost due to the move to North Carolina had gotten off to a good start. Additionally, plans to build a marketing and sales force portended improved customer service.

Despite these efforts to improve, Eastwood remained a small and inefficient firm in an industry dominated by larger and more efficient firms. In the industry, smaller firms had consistently lost money. Its size was an inherent disadvantage, which was compounded by its inefficiency. The negative growth forecast for 2002 didn't appear to offer any hope of rectifying the situation.

Overall business strength: Low.

Industry Attractiveness

The switching systems industry was a crowded one, which was dominated by large firms. It had exhibited strong growth over the past five years, averaging almost 11 percent. Returns on investment during this period had averaged over 12 percent and had never been negative. Opportunities in the OEM market would provide continued room for growth.

An increasing trend toward price competition had the potential to depress returns. The larger firms controlled pricing in the crowded industry. As a result of significant economies of scale, firms of approximately $200 million were the best positioned for efficient manufacturing. Smaller firms had traditionally seen lower returns in this industry than their larger competitors. In addition, economic cycles tended to exaggerate the swings in performance of smaller competitors in the switching systems industry.

Overall industry attractiveness: Medium.

RECOMMENDATIONS

Pelican Corporation should divest Eastwood. Although the switching systems industry was reasonably attractive, Eastwood was not well positioned to regain a leadership position. Improvements in performance such that the division could return to a stable and profitable position in the industry were unlikely. Even if such improvements were likely, they would lead to little more than marginal improvements, because the division's small size severely limited its potential in this scale-driven industry. Additionally, the modest size of the potential returns indicated that Pelican's attention and resources would be better spent on more competitive businesses.

If Retained, What Should Eastwood Do?

- Continue emphasis on improved operational efficiency
- Go for productivity improvement of 7 percent in fabrication and 5 percent in assembly, achievable in 2002
- Renegotiate money-losing long-term contracts in the aerospace market
- Continue emphasis on improved quality
- Scrap reduction from 2 percent to 0.5 percent, possible in 2002
- Rework reduction from 4 percent to 2 percent, possible in 2002
- Implement SPC, vendor qualification, internal auditing, continuous training, and improved scheduling and ordering system
- Begin product redesign program
- Redesign products for cost reduction and performance improvement

- Improve coordination between engineering and marketing by more frequent customer contact
- Prune product lines
- Free up capacity on constrained production lines
- Eliminate marginally profitable products

If Divested, What Price Could Be Expected?

The data on nine completed transactions involving the sale of comparable companies provided multiples for revenue, total assets, net assets, and EBIT. These multiples provided a wide range of estimates for the market value of Eastwood. Asset multiples provided high-end values of approximately $30 to $34 million but did not reflect the questionable value of the continued operations of the firm. An EBIT multiple supported these estimates and assumed future performance consistent with historical levels. A revenue multiple provided a low-end value of approximately $28.5 million. A grand average of all of these values provided an estimate of the market value of Eastwood of approximately $31 million.

C A S E   11A–7

HIGHFIELD CORPORATION

INTRODUCTION

The GM of Highfield was reviewing his division's financial projections on the return flight from the August 2001 strategy meeting with the parent company, Pelican Corporation. Instead of approving Highfield's original financial projection for 2002 (see Exhibit 11.12), management had requested that Highfield revise its plan to provide additional growth, net income, and cash flow. He considered the reasons for the requested changes in his

E X H I B I T   11.12

2002 Projection-business plan for Highfield Corporation, submitted August 2001 ($ in millions).

Income Statement	2001	% of Sales	2002	% of Sales
Sales	$105.1		$114.0	
Sales Growth		N/A		8.5
COGS	71.9	68.4	83.9	73.6
Gross Margin	33.2	31.6	30.1	26.4
SG&A	21.7	20.6	27.6	24.2
Misc. Expenses & Income	2.2	2.1	4.2	3.7
Profit Before Tax	9.3	8.9	6.7	5.9
Taxes (35%)	3.3		2.4	
Net Income	$6.0		$4.3	
Cash Flow				**% of FA**
Net Income			$4.3	
Depreciation			2.9	18.6
Change in Working Capital			13.5	
Change in Fixed & Other Assets			(12.6)	
Cash Flow			$8.1	
Assets	**2001**	**% of Sales**	**2002**	**% of Sales**
Current Assets	$140.3	133.5	$129.7	113.8
Current Liabilities	35.2	33.5	38.1	33.4
Fixed & Other Assets	15.4	14.7	25.1	22.0
Net Assets	$120.5		$116.7	
Return on Net Assets	5.0%		3.7%	

division's plan, which he thought had been reasonable in light of the situation in which Highfield found itself. He knew that the division was not one of Pelican's strongest performers. Did the corporate office feel that he was not managing the division effectively? He realized that the corporation might be trying to extract as much cash as possible from Highfield prior to selling the division.

HIGHFIELD CORPORATION'S PRODUCTS, MARKETS, AND PERFORMANCE

The division manufactured a variety of products for the industrial construction industry, and it operated a manufacturing plant and a network of branch offices that produced, sold, leased, and installed its products throughout the continental United States. Highfield's product lines were closely tied to the level of domestic industrial construction and, therefore, to fluctuations in the economy affecting the construction industry. Sales directly tracked the level of nonresidential construction spending. Highfield's products were not technologically complex. They were primarily "tried-and-true" designs that had not changed substantially in recent years, with no major design changes anticipated in the near future. Manufacturing technology, on the other hand, was changing as a result of a foreign firm's entry into the North American market. In addition, government regulations impacted both design and manufacture but were not expected to cause major product changes.

Highfield's largest competitor controlled 33 percent of the market. Highfield was the second largest, with an 11 percent market share. In addition to selling the products it manufactured, Highfield was heavily involved in leasing both new and used equipment. Although the leasing business had been profitable, it was also highly asset-intensive. In fact, in 2001, Highfield carried more than $75 million in rental-equipment inventory and receivables.

PELICAN'S EXPECTATIONS FOR HIGHFIELD

After reviewing the strategic planning matrix and his division's possible position within that matrix, the GM focused his attention on the financial details that the corporate office had requested of Highfield. Although Highfield's original plan had projected for 2002 an income of $4.3 million and a cash flow of $8.1 million, Pelican management had directed that Highfield improve its forecast of gross margin, SG&A, and sales by 1 percent (of sales). He performed a sensitivity analysis on these variables and found that the attainment of these goals would increase the division's net income by $1.5 million and increase the cash flow by $0.4 million. He was not convinced that any of these improvements were possible.

OPERATIONAL ASSESSMENT

Competitive Analysis

The GM was unsure of the criteria that corporate management would use to assess the performance of the divisions. He decided that if he first understood Highfield's performance with respect to its competitors, he might be able to understand what corporate management could reasonably expect from the division. He thus collected available financial data for 10 of the company's public competitors. He then calculated various ratios for these companies from which he could measure his own company's performance relative to the industry. He was disappointed to see that Highfield's productivity (as measured by number of employees per $1 million of sales) was considerably worse than average. He was further disappointed that Highfield's productivity growth was significantly lower than the industry's average, indicating future profitability problems if the company were unable to improve this measure.

Highfield had a strong reputation for quality products, technical expertise, and its vertical integration. Its designs were considered the best in terms of both strength and flexibility of configuration, and its quality continued to be the best in the industry. Customers regularly looked to Highfield's safety and engineering departments for advice on job design and equipment setup. Its branch managers and sales representatives were the best trained and most experienced in the industry. Turnover was so low that the division had not lost a branch manager or sales representative in the previous five years.

Highfield frequently experienced cash flow problems because most of its products were sold on account, and leasing also created a drain on cash. The single plant increased the costs of both manufacturing and distribution. Because a significant portion of the raw materials and components required for the manufacture of Highfield's products came from the midwest, the cost of freight was added to both the manufacturing and distribution costs. Highfield also outsourced many of the parts that went into making its products, increasing the division's manufacturing costs. Finally, the division's headquarters was located in a different city from the plant, making communication with the plant difficult.

Manufacturing

Highfield's major competitor had used its leading position and reputation for quality to increase its market share to 33 percent over the previous two years. This share growth had come at the expense of weaker firms, but continued growth might affect Highfield's share as well. Recently acquired by a foreign firm, the leading competitor had the capital and technology to continue to grow rapidly. It was currently expanding its plant and installing the latest technology for automatic materials handling and integrated process manufacturing. None of the other eight major manufacturers were known to have any current plans for expansion. All eight were privately owned and did not appear to have strong financial backing.

Business Risks

Construction spending was generally tied to the country's overall economic condition. This made a serious downturn in the economy the major risk to Highfield's business. This situation could lead to severe price cutting during economic downturns as competitors sought to maintain volume. On the other hand, during economic upswings, it provided the opportunity to increase prices at a greater rate than costs. The threat of large product liability lawsuits and worker's compensation claims was on the rise. As a nationally recognized company, Highfield was more likely than its smaller competitors to be the subject of lawsuits that sought "deep pocket" firms in hopes of winning large jury awards. The probability of new firms entering the U.S. market in either manufacturing or distribution was low. Start-up costs for either of these markets were high, providing a significant barrier to entry. Nevertheless, it was possible that foreign firms might seek to enter the U.S. market by acquiring an established firm, as had occurred with the market leader. Foreign firms were unlikely to seek to acquire a firm unless it had a proven track record of success. Labor disputes or the loss of key personnel were not anticipated at Highfield. A formal management succession plan was in place at company headquarters, while a branch-manager-in-training program assured smooth management at the branches.

Business Opportunities

Most of Highfield's recent growth had come at the expense of competitors' market shares. The best market opportunities thus lay in taking advantage of the relative weakness of several of the current competitors. Several branch offices of Highfield's competitors had recently closed or become independent distributors. This provided an opportunity for Highfield to acquire these branches if they were in areas not currently served by Highfield. If they were in areas covered by Highfield, their closure might allow rate increases as a result of decreased competition. There was also the possibility of acquiring ongoing independent businesses to add to the branch network. Another area of opportunity came from the impending expiration of several competitors' contracts with chemical plants and petroleum refineries. Some of these customers had expressed concerns that the competitor might be gouging them and had solicited bids from Highfield and other competitors.

Highfield's three branch offices in southern Texas were well situated to serve the northern Mexican market, in which Mexican competitors were eager to partner with U.S. firms. Highfield was currently involved in discussions with distributors in Mexico City, Tijuana, and Guadalajara.

STRATEGIC SUMMARY

The GM wanted to prepare an estimate of the division's market value because he suspected that corporate management planned to divest Highfield. He would be interested in the possibility of leading a leveraged buyout of the division by its management. He suspected that a fair market value for Highfield would be around $125 million.

STRATEGIC ANALYSIS: STRENGTHS AND WEAKNESSES

Strengths

- Established brand name
- Nationally known
- Name and logo considered a "selling point" by distributors
- Well-known reputation for quality
- Products recognized for "strength and flexibility"
- Material and manufacturing quality recognized as best in the industry
- Recognized for technical expertise
  - Safety and engineering departments respected across industry
  - Best-trained branch managers and sales representatives in the industry
- Loyal work force
  - Extremely low turnover
- One of only two competitors with manufacturing and distribution/leasing operations
- Strong distribution network, including 31 company-owned branches and 22 independent distributors
- Efficient and profitable leasing operations
  - Newest equipment available, automated systems
- Revenue growth well above industry average of 4.4 percent
  - 2001: 24.5 percent, projected 2002: 8.5 percent
- Gross margins above industry average of 26.3 percent
  - 2001: 31.6 percent, projected 2002: 26.4 percent
- ROS well above industry average of –0.3 percent
  - 2001: 5.8 percent, projected 2002: 3.8 percent

- RONA well above industry average of –1.42 percent
  - 2001: 5.0 percent, projected 2002: 3.7 percent

Weaknesses

- Distant number two market share position in both manufacturing/distribution and leasing
  - 11 percent share of manufacturing/distribution vs. 33 percent for leader
  - 5.5 percent share of leasing vs. 20 percent for leader
- Asset-intensive leasing business requiring continued investment to support projected growth
- Manufacturing market leader growing rapidly, 26 percent share to 33 percent in two years
  - Recent acquisition by foreign parent
  - Capital availability to expand and modernize
- Recent restructuring putting upward pressure on costs
  - Closing of New York and Ohio plants has increased raw material costs
- Increased outsourcing raising component costs
- Operational problems due to distance between headquarters and manufacturing facility
- Productivity much worse than industry average
  - 11 employees per $1 million vs. 7.8 employees per $1 million
- Productivity growth much worse than industry average
  - Negative 5 percent in 2001 vs. predicted 0.5 percent for 8 percent sales growth for 2002
- SG&A expense ratio above industry average of 21.5 percent
  - 2001: 20.6 percent, projected 2002: 24.2 percent

Industry Characteristics

- Highly cyclical industry dependent on nonresidential construction and vulnerable to fluctuations in commodity metal prices
- Mature domestic construction and industrial maintenance markets led to a high level of competitive intensity
- Manufacturing segment was dominated by large national competitors, while more than half of leasing/distribution segment was controlled by regional or local firms
- Consolidation potential was high, as smaller and less profitable firms withdrew from intensely competitive industry

- Productive technology was poised to change significantly
- Advances in manufacturing technology that resulted from a foreign acquisition of the largest manufacturer necessitated increased investment
- Customers not price-sensitive, although competition for market share had led to price wars in previous business downturns
- Increased environmental concerns and Environmental Protection Agency (EPA) oversight, raising the importance of quality and safety
- Minimal profit potential
  - Industry RONA: Five-year average – negative 1.42 percent; high, 3.5 percent in 1997; low, negative 6.9 percent in 2000

STRATEGIC SUMMARY

Business Strengths

Highfield Corporation had a tremendous brand franchise, a vibrant distribution network, and a deep relationship with customers. Supporting these strengths were a nationally recognized reputation for quality and a level of technical expertise upon which the industry had come to rely. A recent restructuring, and the closing of a manufacturing plant, had raised the cost of raw materials sourcing, and the increased outsourcing of components had exacerbated the problem.

Performance in 2001 reflected the strength of Highfield's market position. Projections for 2002 indicated sharply lower results, however. The division had experienced strong growth, although 2002 projections at 8.5 percent were well off the recent high of 24.5 percent. Gross margins that had historically been 20 percent above the industry average were projected to decline in 2002, putting Highfield in line with the industry at approximately 26 percent. While returns were projected to remain well above industry levels, 2002 projections showed steep drops in ROS and RONA, compared to recent results.

Overall business strength: Medium to high.

Industry Attractiveness

The two largest competitors together controlled almost 45 percent of the market and their share had been increasing. The distribution and leasing segment was much more fragmented, with regional and local firms controlling 55 percent of the market. Only Highfield and one other firm competed in both of these segments.

Product designs had remained relatively unchanged in recent years. The economics of the manufacturing process was such that higher volumes were necessary to generate the required economies of scale. Manufacturing technology had already begun to change, brought on by the entry of a foreign firm into the domestic market. The move toward greater automation and integrated design and manufacturing had necessitated increased investment to remain competitive.

Gross margins in the industry had declined by 11 percent since 1996, even as the industry had experienced modest growth, averaging 4.4 percent annually. Over the same time period, RONA had averaged –1.4 percent. All of the trends mentioned above indicated continued pressure on profit margins in the industry.

Overall industry attractiveness: Low

RECOMMENDATIONS

The Highfield division should be divested by Pelican. Despite a relatively advantageous position as the number two firm in its industry, the division could not currently provide the returns required by Pelican and its shareholders. Although the opportunity to compete for the number one market position existed, the added investment required to do so, as well as the low level of profit throughout the industry, made this an undesirable option. Highfield's positive market position and valuable brand franchise should provide the basis for an attractive market price.

If Retained, What Should Highfield Do?

- Grow through domestic acquisition
- Acquire branches closed by competitors, if they complement existing network
- Acquire new distributors to add to existing network
- Explore acquisition of leasing/distribution competitors that expressed an interest in selling all or part of their operations
- Grow through domestic expansion
  - Focus on areas where competitors had recently closed branch offices
- Increase size of independent distributor base
- Pursue entry into new market segments
  - Chemicals and petroleum were attractive industries and would put pressure on the market leader to defend its "home turf"
  - Grow through international expansion
  - Continue discussions with Mexican firms
- Improve management of current accounts so as to free cash for use in growing the profitable leasing business

- Continue to invest in successful leasing operations
- Reexamine manufacturing operations with the goal of improving cost position

If Divested, What Valuation Could Be Expected?

The averages of the 11 completed transactions involving sales of comparable companies in the last five years provided ratios of the sales prices to revenue, total assets, net assets, and EBIT. These multiples (ratios) provided a range of estimates for the value of Highfield Corporation. The average of these multiples leads to an estimated market value of $125 million for Highfield.

CASE   11A–8

LEWIS CORPORATION

INTRODUCTION

The GM of the Lewis Corporation took a hard look at the significantly more demanding expectations for 2002 he had just received from the Pelican corporate office. The more he read the revised goals, however, the more worried he became. He thought his original plan (see Exhibit 11.13) was ambitious, but Pelican expected Lewis to improve on its sales growth, gross margin, and SG&A estimates by at least an additional 1 percent of

EXHIBIT   11.13

2002 Projection-business plan for Lewis Corporation, submitted August 2001 ($ in millions).

Income Statement	2001	% of Sales	2002	% of Sales
Sales	$102.0		$113.3	
Sales Growth		N/A		11.1
COGS	84.2	82.6	89.1	78.6
Gross Margin	17.8	17.5	24.2	21.4
SG&A	15.2	14.9	16.9	14.9
Misc. Expenses & Income	(5.0)	5.0	(0.6)	(0.5)
Profit Before Tax	(2.4)	(2.3)	6.7	6.0
Taxes (35%)	(0.8)		2.4	
Net Income	($1.6)		$4.3	
Cash Flow				**% of FA**
Net Income			$4.3	
Depreciation			2.4	18.4
Change in Working Capital			1.7	
Change in Fixed & Other Assets			(2.7)	
Cash Flow			$5.7	
Assets	**2001**	**% of Sales**	**2002**	**% of Sales**
Current Assets	$38.7	37.9	$40.3	35.6
Current Liabilities	10.1	9.9	13.4	11.8
Fixed & Other Assets	12.8	12.5	13.1	11.6
Net Assets	$41.4		$40.0	
Return on Net Assets	(3.7%)		11.0%	

sales. It was August 2001, and the GM was starting to doubt his decision to take over as president of Lewis the previous January. He had left his partnership at a consulting firm in New York, where he had worked since receiving his MBA. His general-management MBA and operational expertise, combined with his West Point engineering degree and five years of experience managing soldiers in the U.S. Army infantry, had prepared him for his position at Lewis. He was excited to be running a major division for the Pelican Corporation, but he had just begun to realize, however, that "running your own show" meant feeling a lot more corporate pressure than he had previously thought. Prior to the upcoming corporate planning meeting, he and his staff would have to consider how they could achieve the revised goals.

LEWIS CORPORATION'S PRODUCTS, MARKETS, AND PERFORMANCE

Lewis designed, manufactured, and installed systems using filters and separators in a variety of commercial and industrial applications. These systems cleaned gases, air, and liquids by removing solids as they passed through a piping system. The products were sold to gas producers; gas gathering, transmission, and distribution companies; producers of industrial liquids for commercial use; chemical manufacturers; oil refiners; and manufacturers of nuclear equipment. Through the utilization of the latest-technology manufacturing equipment and processes, product innovation, and a focus on continuous improvement, Lewis sought to provide systems of the highest quality and performance to the global marketplace. Lewis was committed to delivering sustained sales and profitability growth by improvements in productivity, customer responsiveness, and the fostering of new ideas. Expectations were for the market to continue to grow rapidly for several years to come. Government environmental regulations and growing public concern for the environment were the primary drivers of demand for filtration systems in the United States.

The Lewis division was active in six major filtration product categories: gas and air filtration systems, petroleum filtration devices, chemical systems, highly specialized engineered systems, general applications, and nuclear filtration devices. Lewis's products held the number one or number two market share in every category, with the exception of petroleum filtration devices and nuclear filtration systems. Lewis's short-term goals included reaching its 2002 business plan, returning the division to profitability, and producing positive cash flow. The 2002 plan, submitted previously, had projected sales growth of 11.1 percent, gross margin of 21.4 percent, SG&A expense of 14.9 percent, and return on net assets of 11 percent, compared with industry averages of 9.4 percent, 33.2 percent, 14.9 percent, and 5.5 percent, respectively. Lewis's long-term goals were to produce $150 million in sales by 2006, sustain a minimum growth rate in sales of 10 percent, attain and maintain first or second market position in every product line, and consistently produce 30 percent gross margins.

One factor affecting Lewis's ability to achieve these performance targets was the company's level of productivity. A study of Lewis's performance for the most recent five-year period compared key operating results with data from a set of comparable companies in the same SIC code. The calculation of relative economies of scale revealed that Lewis had achieved levels of productivity slightly better than the average predicted economies of scale achieved by comparable companies. In addition, the analysis showed that at its current level of sales growth, Lewis should be able to achieve significantly higher productivity growth rates than previously.

PELICAN'S EXPECTATIONS FOR LEWIS

Pelican's financial and operational expectations for the Lewis division were detailed in the corporation's response to the division's 2002 business plan. The GM was moderately surprised by these new projections, because he believed that the division's original plan contained realistic performance targets. Pelican's new goals called for at least 1 percent (of sales) improvements in the division's projected sales growth rate, gross margin, and SG&A figures. To assess the impact that such improvements would have on the division's cash flow and net income, the GM performed a sensitivity analysis on these variables. He found that attainment of these goals would increase the division's net income by about $1.5 million and its cash flow by about $1.2 million.

Improved operational performance would also enhance Lewis's position in comparison with industry competitors. The 1 percent increase in sales growth would make Lewis fourth of 14 companies, up from twelfth in 2001. With a 1 percent increase in gross margin, Lewis would rank in twelfth position, but this represented an improvement over 2001's last-place finish. And a 1 percent decrease in SG&A expense would place Lewis first out of 14, up from second in 2001. The cumulative effect of these improvements would be an increase in return on net assets, boosting Lewis from twelfth to second position overall.

The GM knew that Pelican was conducting a review of the viability and attractiveness of each of the 10 operating units. Although he wasn't sure which methods of analysis were being used by the corporation to assess the business strength and industry attractiveness of each of the 10 operating units, he was aware of the existence of a corporate strategic-analysis matrix that considered several factors in performing such an assessment. He thought it would be useful to consider how Lewis would be characterized using this matrix.

CHALLENGES FACING LEWIS

The GM knew that any strategic business plan he and his management team implemented would have to address the problems that had plagued Lewis throughout 2001. These problems included the following areas:

- **Customer confidence in Lewis was rapidly eroding.** The primary cause of the loss in confidence was the extended shipment lead times for products in all lines. Lewis required three weeks to complete the order-to-delivery cycle for most systems, even though only 72 hours were required to deliver a system from finished goods inventory to anywhere in the continental United States. These results were far inferior to industry standards. Some competitors required two weeks lead time and others required only 48 hours. In the increasingly competitive filtration business, order-to-delivery time was becoming crucial.

- **Lewis's research and development lagged the industry.** Lewis had been a leader in filtration systems for so long that the company took its market leadership for granted. Lewis's competitors, meanwhile, had made significant strides in developing new technologies, pushing Lewis behind in such areas as nuclear filtration technology.

- **Strong price competition existed in all of Lewis's markets.** Competitive pressures in the early 1990s led industry competitors to cut prices dramatically. As the economy rebounded, however, industry prices remained stagnant because of intense competition. Real prices on filtration products had not increased during the previous several years.

- **Advertising and promotional expenditures lagged the competition.** Although Lewis's core product lines (gas and air, chemical, and engineered systems) maintained strong brand images, the nuclear and petroleum filtration product lines suffered from poor market positions and were in desperate need of increased market promotion.

- **Financial management information systems were inadequate and underdeveloped.** The lack of an adequate financial information system made it difficult for the division's management team to control expenses and probably contributed to Lewis's high cost of goods sold and SG&A expenses in the past. Although Lewis's controller had been working on updating the current system, there was concern that the necessary modifications might be too costly and too late.

OPPORTUNITIES

The GM felt that his team could attain or exceed Pelican's enhanced operational performance targets by capitalizing on several competitive conditions. Lewis's strengths included excellent brand recognition, powerful market-share positions in four of six product lines (with growth opportunities in the other two), and a strong management team. Lewis could undertake a number of initiatives to capitalize on the recovering filtration systems market. Among the opportunities for improvement were the following:

- **Emphasize a customer-focused approach to the business.** By encouraging more frequent interaction between company personnel and its customer base, Lewis would be better able to stem the erosion of customer confidence in the division. The company would better understand customer requirements and concerns and would be able to respond to these concerns in a more timely fashion. Improved customer relations would translate into a potential for higher sales growth in the future.

- **Improve the company's current distribution system.** Failure to meet the industry averages in order-to-delivery cycle time was a key hurdle in maintaining customer satisfaction, controlling costs, and ensuring future sales growth. It was believed that Lewis could lower its cycle time to achieve the industry-average delivery performance through improvements in the current warehouse stocking plan and distribution capabilities.

- **Offer innovative marketing alternatives.** Introducing new marketing concepts such as product "bundling" offered the company a way to differentiate itself and increase market share. In addition, such a tactic did not require large capital expenditures.

- **Improve product and process quality throughout the company.** Lewis had already undertaken several measures to improve organizational quality. These included the implementation of quality teams, the adoption of ISO 9002 standards (in an effort to gain certification), and the utilization of precision computer numerical control (CNC) machines in the manufacturing process.

STRATEGIC ISSUES

The GM was optimistic about Lewis's future and confident in his management team's ability to respond to the challenges confronting them. Lewis was operating in a diverse and growing industry. The company held a commanding market share in many of its market segments. Lewis's management felt that the division had the potential to achieve an exceptional return on net assets, if the division could meet or exceed the corporation's aggressive projections.

The GM would have to address several questions to achieve this success. What should Lewis do about its nuclear and petroleum filtration product lines? How could Lewis better control overhead costs? Where should Lewis look for future sales growth—in the international market, the domestic market, or both? Should additional growth be sought within existing or with new product lines? Finally, the GM wondered whether the corporation's decision to grow, maintain, or harvest the division would limit the alternatives available to him. All things considered, this would be an interesting month.

STRATEGIC ANALYSIS: STRENGTHS AND WEAKNESSES

Strengths

- Great brand equity in core lines of business
  - Gas and air, chemical, engineered systems, pre-engineered systems
- Leading position in four of six product lines
  - 27.3 percent share in chemical filtration
  - 25.6 percent share in engineered systems
  - 16.8 percent share in pre-engineered systems
  - 15.4 percent share in gas and air filtration
- Strong management team
- Overall market share of 13.4 percent
- Growth projection above industry five-year average of 9.4 percent
  - 2001: 5.4 percent, projected 2002: 11.1 percent
- SG&A expense ratio well below industry average of 28.2 percent
  - 2001: 14.9 percent, projected 2002: 14.9 percent
- ROS projection two times industry five-year average of 1.6 percent
  - 2001: –1.5 percent, projected 2002: 3.9 percent
- RONA projection well above industry five-year average of 5.6 percent
  - 2001: –3.7 percent, projected 2002: 11 percent

Weaknesses

- Extended order-to-delivery cycle: typically three weeks, compared to industry standard of between two weeks and 48 hours

- Declining level of service which was increasingly important to customers
- Growing erosion of customer confidence in Lewis Corporation
- Weak research and development effort which lagged the industry
- Declining once-strong position in product technology
- Nuclear product line suffering as a result of decline in position
- Insufficient marketing and sales expenditures
- Nuclear and petroleum product lines in need of support
- Inadequate and underdeveloped information systems infrastructure
- Inability to control expenditures and cut costs because of poor infrastructure
- High costs that resulted in high cost of goods sold and inefficient use of SG&A
- Productivity growth rate in 2001 well below average industry level of 3.5 percent
  - 2001 productivity declined by 0.5 percent from 2000
  - Future productivity increases questionable, even if revenue growth target of 11.1 percent should be achieved
- Gross margins below industry five-year average of 33.2 percent
  - 2001: 17.5 percent, projected 2002: 21.4 percent
- 2001 growth, ROS, RONA all well below industry five-year averages
- Questionable strong projections for 2002 (see Strengths)

Industry Characteristics

- Industry growing at moderate pace
- Continued moderate growth driven by increased government regulation and growing public concern for environmental issues
- Many medium-sized competitors, but the industry was dominated by one large firm
- Increased competitive intensity
- Price competition increasing pressure on cost structure
- No real price increases since 1996
- Slight diseconomies of scale for companies with annual revenues above $75 million
- Significant economies of growth
- Slow and steady decline in industry returns since 1998
- Industry RONA: Five-year average 5.6 percent; high 11.4 percent in 1998; low 3.2 percent in 2000

STRATEGIC SUMMARY

Business Strengths

Lewis Corporation was a firm that relied on past successes which had not left it well equipped to compete in the changing filtration equipment industry. The company had very strong brand recognition in its core lines of business, which included gas and air, chemical, and engineered systems. In these lines, the company held either the number one or number two positions. With an overall market share of 13.4 percent and revenue of approximately $100 million, it was among the largest firms in the filtration systems industry. Despite lackluster performance in 2001, projections for 2002 indicated that growth, ROS, and RONA would all exceed industry averages. A strong brand combined with a leading market position and capable management supported the optimistic outlook portrayed by 2002 projections.

The strengths that supported such projections belied a number of very serious problems and cast doubt on Lewis's ability to meet the revised goals dictated by the corporate office. Gross margins 35 percent below the industry average indicated fundamental inefficiencies in the cost structure. In a price-competitive marketplace, this situation pointed to continued difficulty for the company in maintaining market share leadership. A significant decline in customer confidence had followed the extended order lead times required by Lewis.

In addition, weak R&D efforts had eroded the division's traditional technology edge, and they had hampered the company's efforts to be successful in the nuclear and petroleum categories. An insufficient commitment to marketing and sales, evident in SG&A spending levels at 50 percent of the industry average, had contributed to the mediocre performance of these two product lines. Poor productivity improvement and inadequate information systems called into question the ability of Lewis's management to improve short-term performance and to attract the amount of investment required to ensure long-term competitiveness.

Overall business strength: Low to medium.

Industry Attractiveness

Moderate growth was expected in the industry after several below average years. This positive trend was expected to continue, driven largely by increased government regulation aimed at protecting the environment and greater public awareness of environmental concerns. Although growth in the industry was returning, profitability was not. Increased competitive intensity had spurred a high degree of price competition. As a result, the industry average RONA had steadily declined since 1998. Annual returns in the industry had declined from 11.4 percent in 1998 to 3.2 percent in

2000. The average RONA in the industry had been 5.6 percent over the previous five years.

As firms in the industry attempted to back away from price competition, differentiation efforts raised customers' expectations with regard to service and quality. As part of these efforts, a trend toward greater use of technology in the form of manufacturing automation and management information systems seemed likely to continue. A likely result of these changes was diminished price competition, reflected in greater operating margins, which was offset by higher levels of marketing expenditure and greater capital investment.

Overall industry attractiveness: Low.

RECOMMENDATIONS

Pelican should divest Lewis and use the proceeds to invest in the acquisition or growth of ascending businesses in industries with more attractive competitive structures.

If Retained, What Should Lewis Do?

- Improve operational performance
- Focus on cost reduction
- Explore the increased use of CNC and automation as potential sources of cost reduction
- Invest in the information systems necessary to monitor and control costs
- Emphasize customer focus to stem eroding confidence
- Increase customer contact
- Better understand customer requirements and concerns
- Improve order responsiveness
- Reduce order-to-delivery cycle time
- Improve distribution system
- Analyze and improve warehouse stocking system
- Use more advanced technology
- Employ more innovative marketing
- Support petroleum and nuclear segments with increased investment in marketing
- Explore product bundling as a means of differentiation and growth
- Improve product and process quality

- Increase use of quality teams
- Implement ISO 9002 standards

If Divested, What Valuation Could Be Expected?

Data were compiled regarding 16 transactions involving the sales of businesses comparable to Lewis during the last five years. Averages of the 16 completed transactions provided multiples (ratios) of the sales prices to revenue, total assets, net assets, and EBIT. These multiples provided a wide range of estimates for the market value of Lewis. The EBIT multiple provided a low-end estimate of $41 million, which assumed future poor performance consistent with historical levels. Asset multiples provided midrange values of approximately $60 to 80 million, and did not reflect the potential value of continued operations of the firm. A revenue multiple provided a high-end value of approximately $98 million. The best estimate of the most likely market value of Lewis was $95 million.

C A S E   11A-9

MONUMENT CORPORATION

INTRODUCTION

The GM of Monument Corporation tossed the 2002 business plan onto his desk (see Exhibit 11.14). The original plan that he had submitted to Pelican Corporation, Monument's parent company, had not satisfied Pelican's revised expectations for the division. Despite sharp government budget cuts for defense spending and industry growth rates projected to be a mere 1.1 percent for 2002, the corporation still expected Monument to improve

E X H I B I T   11.14

2002 Projection-business plan for Monument Corporation, submitted August 2001 ($ in millions).

Income Statement	2001	% of Sales	2002	% of Sales
Sales	$179.9		$172.8	
Sales Growth		N/A		(3.9)
COGS	131.5	73.1	123.6	71.5
Gross Margin	48.4	26.9	49.2	28.5
SG&A	38.6	21.5	33.2	19.2
Misc. Expenses & Income	(2.3)	(1.2)	(2.8)	(1.6)
Profit Before Tax	7.5	4.1	13.2	7.6
Taxes (35%)	2.6		4.6	
Net Income	$4.9		$8.6	
Cash Flow				**% of FA**
Net Income			$8.6	
Depreciation			2.6	12.3
Change in Working Capital			4.3	
Change in Fixed & Other Assets			(5.4)	
Cash Flow			$10.1	
Assets	**2001**	**% of Sales**	**2002**	**% of Sales**
Current Assets	$43.3	24.1	$41.3	23.9
Current Liabilities	12.6	7.0	14.9	8.6
Fixed & Other Assets	21.1	11.7	23.9	13.9
Net Assets	$51.8		$50.3	
Return on Net Assets	9.3%		17.1%	

on its earlier plan. The GM's expectation for 2002 sales was a decrease of 3.9 percent, which would allow Monument to reorganize its business, search for new customers, and develop new products.

These changes were expected to spur future growth rates of 15 percent for 2003 and 12 percent for 2004, but the GM believed that the division would require a year to readjust. He didn't want to admit to himself that part of the reason for his conservative 2002 sales figures was the corporate bonus system. The GM and the 10 members of his management team would receive a bonus only if they achieved their business plan targets.

The GM of Monument for the previous two years was in the midst of transforming the company from a government to a commercial supplier of high-technology communications equipment. Apparently, based on the corporation's more aggressive expectations for the division, this transformation would have to occur more quickly than originally planned. Pelican had experienced poor financial performance in recent years and was taking drastic steps to return to profitability. The GM therefore needed to consider revisions to his original business plan that would achieve the performance improvements required of the division. He didn't have much time, though, because his next meeting with the CEO of Pelican was scheduled for the following week.

MONUMENT CORPORATION'S PRODUCTS, MARKETS, AND PERFORMANCE

Monument designed and manufactured high-technology communication systems for several commercial business segments, serving both domestic and international markets. Historically, the U.S. Department of Defense had been Monument's primary customer, with a select base of commercial customers augmenting company sales. More recently, as defense spending decreased and competition from the large, consolidated defense contractors increased, Monument began to shift its efforts from the defense market to the commercial market. The GM was leading the charge for Monument to become the industry's most efficient producer as well as a differentiated supplier.

The company did not have far to go to achieve its efficiency goals. A study of the division's performance for the most recent five-year period compared key operating results with those from a representative set of companies in the same SIC code. The division already ranked among the most efficient manufacturers in its industry based on economies of scale in labor. At its original projected dollar sales volume, Monument required three fewer employees per $1 million of sales than the industry average. Monument had experienced above-average productivity growth, having achieved a productivity growth rate 3 percent above the industry average. Maybe additional growth in 2002 was not such a bad idea.

PELICAN'S EXPECTATIONS FOR MONUMENT

The Pelican corporate office apparently felt that Monument was capable of better performance. Monument was expected to achieve a sales increase of 1 percent above the original plan. Additionally, Monument was expected to reduce its SG&A expenses and increase its profit margin by 1 percent of sales each. The GM was surprised by these edicts because he believed that the division's original plan was based on realistic performance forecasts. To assess the impact that achieving these targets would have on the division's cash flow and net income, he performed a sensitivity analysis on these variables. Across-the-board 1 percent improvements in these variables would increase the division's net income by about $2.4 million and its cash flow by about $1.8 million.

The GM knew that Pelican was conducting a review of the viability and attractiveness of each of the 10 operating units. Although he wasn't sure which methods of analysis were being used by the corporation to assess the business strength and industry attractiveness of each unit, he was aware of the existence of a corporate strategic analysis matrix that considered several factors in performing such an assessment. He thought it would be prudent to consider how Monument would be classified using such a tool.

GROWTH OPPORTUNITIES

To achieve its ambitious growth targets, Monument would need to increase sales by protecting its current customer base while attracting new customers through market expansion or by increasing its market share at the expense of its larger competitors. One means of achieving this goal would be to decrease the time to market for new, technically innovative products. Despite budget cuts, the government would continue to require timely delivery of technologically advanced products to maintain military superiority over potential enemies. To reduce cycle time and minimize development costs, Monument could emphasize product lines that had both governmental and commercial applications, but these were not easy to find.

This need to develop "dual-use" products would diminish over time if government sales became less important to company performance. Although government and military sales accounted for 85 percent of all division sales revenue in 1997, their significance was predicted to decline to nearly 73 percent by 2002. This downward trend would accelerate over the next several years, as the investment in commercial product development would begin to attract more customers and greater profits.

Clearly, the future success of Monument hinged on its ability to develop products attractive to the commercial markets. The high cost of research and development, design, protoype, and manufacturing of new products resulted in a particularly cash-intensive business, where significant returns were often generated years in the future. Although government sales provided steady income, they did not offer the same levels of returns possible in the commercial sector. To survive and expand in the increasingly competitive marketplace, Monument would need to generate larger cash flows in the future.

Expansion into new markets would also require adapting existing technologies to commercial use as quickly as possible. Development teams were attempting to do just that within product development efforts funded as R&D projects.

POTENTIAL ACQUISITIONS

Another growth strategy was expansion through acquisition. The GM wanted to identify the best acquisition candidates based on the strengths and weaknesses of his company. He considered three distinct situations in which an acquisition could strengthen Monument's market position:

- **The acquisition candidate would need to have existing, extensive marketing and distribution channels.** Despite sizable sales revenues, Monument did not possess the expertise or the infrastructure to market its products effectively. A company with a high degree of technological experience and an existing competency in marketing and/or distribution would certainly be attractive for acquisition.

- **Ideally, it would be desirable for the acquisition candidate to have had extensive experience in international markets.** With such a small percentage of its current sales coming from international markets, Monument would logically seek a partnership with a firm with a strong technological reputation and access to international markets.

- **The acquisition candidate should offer a complementary product line.** A computer software or hardware manufacturer or distributor would fit in nicely with many of the products currently under development at Monument. Another possibility would be a manufacturer with a similar technology base.

INTERNAL OPPORTUNITIES TO IMPROVE EFFICIENCY

The GM emphasized the importance of looking inside the company for ways to increase revenues and improve company performance. Monument possessed the core competency to manufacture high-technology electronics, but the GM was unsure whether Monument had the necessary systems in place to ensure that the division could grow and control costs simultaneously. Despite the division's impressive achievements with regard to economies of scale, he was certain that there were areas in which the firm's performance could be further enhanced.

With regard to finance, Monument maintained a reliable product cost system, supported by a fully integrated material requirements planning system. This high degree of automation enabled Monument to price products accurately. Finance was the only department, however, that did not regularly exceed budgets or miss forecasts.

Monument had a powerful engineering base, but the engineers lacked commercial experience and knowledge of the customers. They were accustomed to following stringent product specifications without deviation. Cost containment traditionally was not a concern, with engineers spending hours perfecting systems to specification levels not required by the customer and not critical to the integrity of the system.

With regard to R&D, corporate pressure on cost containment had led the division's management to curtail R&D. Management had reluctantly decided to trim the budget for R&D from 10.6 percent of sales to 8 percent of sales for 2002. As a result of the company's shift in strategic focus, almost 90 percent of the reduced R&D funding was allocated to the commercial market rather than to the government sector.

In operations, the GM had recently implemented concurrent engineering, requiring that functional tasks such as product design, manufacturing, engineering, and marketing be integrated and performed simultaneously. By encouraging interdepartmental collaboration throughout the product development process, costly delays common under the traditional linear production model were minimized. Cross-functional teams worked together to identify and eliminate bottlenecks and to incorporate customer requirements into the process at the front end rather than at the back end. The GM hoped that this process would eliminate departmental boundaries and would help to establish positive relationships across the company. The operations department had completed a restructuring, reducing management by half and pushing decision-making authority down the organization to work teams. Monument also was in compliance with ISO 9001 quality standards. With the use of the full MRP system and reduced product expediting, the number of production employees (other than in management) had been reduced, resulting in a corresponding increase in productivity.

Increasing productivity per employee was not the only benefit of the operations restructuring. Scrap was 0.6 percent, well below the industry average of 1.1 percent. Inventory accuracy rose from 84 percent to 97.5 percent. And the cost of quality, defined as the aggregate cost of material expediting, production scrap and rework, engineering ordering, warranty repairs, and overdue receivables, was less than 1 percent of sales, continuing a steady decline over the past three years.

Marketing personnel, who traditionally had little experience integrating customer requirements into the product engineering cycle, had recently initiated a program designed to create such a link. The program was still in its early stages, however, and friction still existed between the engineering and marketing departments. Monument had been considering developing and selling turnkey systems, but a better understanding of customer requirements was needed before such a system was adopted.

In the past, there was no structured training program for marketing or sales personnel. As the role of marketing was expected to expand in the new commercial markets, formal training would become more important. Among the expanded responsibilities of the marketing staff would be to increase the quality and depth of direct marketing efforts and to increase participation in trade shows and industry conferences in each product area. A crucial component of expanding sales would be product demonstrations that would require the sales staff to possess thorough product knowledge.

The current compensation and incentive systems did not recognize and reward key performers or those who demonstrated the ability to adapt quickly to changing environments. The performance appraisal system was not conducted consistently, did not include career planning or feedback, and did not encourage interaction between managers and teams. Employees were hired into functional departments and were discouraged from seeking experiences in other departments within the company.

There was no formal procedure for monitoring the product development process, and it was not uncommon for design and development to be thrown off schedule. The GM saw two options for improving this process and reducing the length of the product development cycle. One option was to implement a management system for auditing the product's life cycle, monitoring the system from product design to manufacture. The other option was to hire an experienced consultant to bring Monument management up to speed on the latest project management techniques.

STRATEGIC ISSUES

As the GM weighed the strengths and weaknesses of Monument in his mind, he began to formulate options that would enable him to expand sales and grow the business while containing costs. His concern was that the results of his efforts would not be realized soon enough to appease the corporate office. He and his management team would need to discuss Pelican's new expectations and devise alternatives for achieving the new, more demanding performance goals.

STRATEGIC ANALYSIS: STRENGTHS AND WEAKNESSES

Strengths

- Efficient manufacturer of high technology products
- ISO 9001 certified
- Recently completed restructuring, reduced management by 50 percent and production full-time employees (FTEs) by 21 percent

- Scrap rate of 0.6 percent was half the industry average of 1.1 percent
- Cost of quality had been declining for three years, currently at 0.4 percent of sales
- MRP system was superior
- Inventory accuracy at 97.5 percent, up from 84 percent in 1998
- Superior productivity
  - Currently employed 8 employees per $1 million in sales, 27 percent below industry average
  - Growth in productivity was two times the industry average
  - Strong continued economies of growth were expected
- Strong technological base
- Currently served technologically sophisticated customers (government/military)
- Full pipeline of new product concepts
- Leveraged heavy investment in R&D (average 10 percent of sales)
- Established system of concurrent engineering and product development
- Strong financial management skills
- Strong industry growth projected
  - 2001: 15 percent, 2002: 12 percent
- SG&A below industry average of 25.4 percent of sales
  - 2001: 21.5 percent, 2002 projected: 19.2 percent
- ROS above industry average of 2.1 percent
  - 2001: 2.7 percent, 2002 projected: 5 percent
- RONA well above industry average of 2.2 percent
  - 2001: 9.3 percent, 2002 projected: 17.1 percent

Weaknesses

- Necessary marketing and sales experience and infrastructure were lacking
- Insufficient resources were devoted to sales
- Integration with engineering was new and tenuous
- There was no formal training program
- Salespeople lacked necessary technical/product expertise
  - Needed to develop skills in direct marketing and promotions
- Product development process
  - Engineering lacked commercial experience, had little customer contact
  - No formal auditing/monitoring system

- Lacking cost control focus
- Weak control systems
  - Product development: auditing and monitoring
  - Marketing and sales: training, personnel development
  - Cost control
  - Bonus system
- Performance appraisal
  - Compensation: Lacked pay for performance
  - Inconsistent implementation of appraisal system
  - Did not cross-train or rotate
- R&D spending was declining
  - Cut from 10.6 percent of sales to 8 percent, although devoted 90 percent to commercial
- Lacked resources and scale of larger defense firms
- Lacked leverage in government contracts
- International sales played only a small role
  - Lacked international experience and developed infrastructure
- Gross margin below industry average of 31 percent
  - 2001: 26.9 percent, 2002 projected: 28.5 percent
- Sluggish growth lags industry average of 1.14 percent
  - 2001: –4.5 percent, 2002 projected: –3.92 percent

Industry Characteristics

- Relatively large but mature market
- Declining defense spending increasing pressure to transition to commercial business
- Low growth: Five-year average of 1.1 percent
- Cyclical
- Heavily dependent on defense-related business
- Investment-intensive
- Wide swings in profit potential
- Industry RONA: Five-year average of 2.2 percent; high 46.4 percent in 1996; low –13.7 percent in 1999

STRATEGIC SUMMARY

Business Strengths

Monument was a technology and manufacturing leader in the communications equipment industry. The firm coexisted with many medium-size firms and several large defense conglomerates. It had a distinctive advantage in the productivity of its manufacturing operations, having recently restructured to remove excess labor and overhead costs. In addition, with above average rates of productivity improvement, Monument seemed well positioned to remain a manufacturing leader. Its expertise in the service of technologically demanding defense customers had given the company a well-stocked pipeline of new commercial product opportunities, and it had begun to transition toward the commercial sector.

Over the past several years, RONA had been extremely high and was projected to be almost eight times the industry average in 2002. Return on sales had increased from the industry average to a projected level almost 2.5 times the industry average. During this period, the company had seen top line revenues shrink as their dependence on defense sales had declined. Management expected strong future growth as the commercial reorientation was completed. Although size represented a disadvantage for Monument, growth through acquisition offered an attractive solution.

Overall business strength: Medium to high.

Industry Attractiveness

The communications equipment industry had been undergoing a dramatic transition because of shrinking defense spending. This trend had led to a stagnant growth rate in the industry. The industry was highly cyclical, driven by the the political process and by the economic climate that affected the level of investment in this capital- and cash-intensive industry. As a result of these factors, industry profitability had varied widely over time. Averaging only a 2 percent RONA over the previous five years, the communications industry had been boom or bust for decades.

Despite these wide swings, the industry offered a relatively steady, albeit declining, flow of business from the defense sector, which brought with it experience in leading-edge technologies. These technologies provided an attractive foundation for success in the commercial market. Firms that succeeded in balancing these two business sectors would enjoy technological leadership along with reduced exposure to wide profit swings.

Overall industry attractiveness: Medium to high

RECOMMENDATIONS

Pelican should retain Monument and invest in developing or acquiring a marketing and sales infrastructure, improving control systems, and establishing an international presence upon which success in the commercial sector could be built.

If Retained, What Should Monument Do?

- Focus on continued shift from government to commercial business
- Build marketing and sales infrastructure
- Strengthen international presence
- Develop and implement improved control systems
- Improve product development management
- Initiate R&D cost control
- Improve performance appraisal and bonus/incentive system
- Leverage technology leadership position
- Develop "dual-use" products that appeal to commercial customers
- Continue investment in R&D
- Leverage manufacturing excellence
- Develop low-cost-producer status
- Reduce development time for new products
- Improve integration of the marketing/sales and engineering functions
- Evaluate potential acquisition targets with the following:
  - Existing, extensive marketing and sales capabilities
  - Experience in international markets
  - Complementary product lines such as computer software or hardware

If Divested, What Valuation Could Be Expected?

Data were compiled on transactions involving the sales of comparable companies during the previous five years. Averages of the 11 completed transactions provided multiples (ratios) of market prices to revenue, total assets, net assets, and EBIT. These multiples provided a wide range of estimates for the market value of Monument. Asset multiples provide low-end values of approximately $60 million to $90 million and did not reflect the potential value of continued operations of the firm. The revenue multiple provided a high-end value of approximately $147 million and assumed future performance consistent with historical levels. Very few data points were available for the EBIT calculation. The GM considered the most likely market value for Monument to be around $135 million. He also thought he might be able to put together a leveraged buyout of the division by the management if Pelican decided to sell the company.

C A S E   11A–10

CONCORD CORPORATION

INTRODUCTION

The president of the Concord Corporation had just received the reaction of the parent company, Pelican Corporation, to his division's business plan for 2002 (see Exhibit 11.15). The business plan had been returned with notes expressing the corporation's revised expectations for Concord in terms of annual revenues and cash flows. He wondered how the senior executives had derived these numbers. And more importantly, how was he going to turn these numbers into reality?

E X H I B I T   11.15

2002 Projection-business plan for Concord Corporation, submitted August 2001 ($ in millions).

Income Statement	2001	% of Sales	2002	% of Sales
Sales	$126.3		$133.5	
Sales Growth		N/A		5.7
COGS	121.4	96.1	102.8	77.0
Gross Margin	4.9	3.9	30.7	23.0
SG&A	19.4	15.3	21.3	15.9
Misc. Expenses & Income	0.4	0.3	0.0	0.0
Profit Before Tax	(14.1)	(11.2)	9.4	7.1
Taxes (35%)	(4.9)		3.3	
Net Income	($9.2)		$6.1	
Cash Flow				**% of FA**
Net Income			$6.1	
Depreciation			0.7	31.8
Change in Working Capital			12.8	
Change in Fixed & Other Assets			(0.2)	
Cash Flow			$19.4	
Assets	**2001**	**% of Sales**	**2002**	**% of Sales**
Current Assets	$39.2	31.0	$38.4	28.7
Current Liabilities	2.5	2.0	14.5	10.9
Fixed & Other Assets	2.1	1.7	1.6	1.2
Net Assets	$38.8		$25.5	
Return on Net Assets	(23.5%)		24.2%	

It seemed as though the Pelican senior management had not remembered anything he had presented the previous month at the corporate planning session. True, the day was long, but he had thought his presentation was flawless. He made sure the executives knew that he had spent considerable time in developing the three-year plan for Concord and that he was extremely confident of his estimates. How could he focus on his current day-to-day operations if he constantly had to redo business plans that he felt had already been completed?

The corporation's revised expectations were for Concord to provide a 1 percent (of sales) improvement in sales, gross margin, and SG&A expenses over the proposed 2002 plan. A sensitivity analysis of these variables demonstrated that achievement of these enhanced goals would increase net income by $1.8 million and cash flow by $1.4 million. He grimaced at the thought of agreeing to numbers he was not sure his division could achieve. He thought that he had better get to work and once again review the direction of his division. He either had to commit to achieve these new numbers or prepare and submit alternative ones.

CONCORD CORPORATION'S PRODUCTS, MARKETS, AND PERFORMANCE

Concord designed, produced, installed, and maintained all types of alarm systems for industrial, commercial, and residential customers. The division operated numerous distribution offices located throughout the United States and international offices located around the world. More than half of Concord's international business was managed through its European operations, with the remainder managed from the international headquarters in the United States. Customer service provided the greatest single source of revenues, generating 43 percent of the division total. Contracting accounted for 40 percent of the business, and international sales made up the remaining 17 percent. Fabrication facilities included a domestic facility and an international shop.

The division faced strong competition in the fast growing but difficult alarm industry. Although an important portion of its business came directly from its service operations, the majority of new business came from the construction industry. Division management did not expert this situation to continue, as it hoped to make the service product line its core business.

In the international arena, the next three years would prove to be critical for several division initiatives. The GM anticipated expanding operations to cover all of Europe. The Pacific Rim also would receive increased attention, as the division planned to staff its Pacific Rim office with design capability and additional sales personnel to market to the entire region. The Middle East and Canada also presented growth opportunities.

The influence of the construction industry on Concord's business had been seen very clearly during previous years, when a weak regional construction market impacted the division's business dramatically. A recent upturn in the construction industry, however, had led to more optimistic business projections, especially if inflation should hold at 3 to 4 percent a year. Although these developments boded well for the division, they did not signal that competition would lessen.

PELICAN'S EXPECTATIONS FOR CONCORD

As the GM gazed at the revised corporate sales expectations, he thought back to the conversations he had had with several corporate executives during the past few weeks. He also was aware that the corporation was considering the possible divestiture of several of the operating divisions. He wondered how to interpret the revised performance expectations, considering the corporation's current situation.

Although he wasn't sure which methods of analysis were being used by the corporation to assess the business strengths and industry attractiveness of each of the 10 operating units, he was aware of the existence of a corporate strategic-analysis matrix that considered several factors in performing such an assessment. He thought it would be prudent to consider how Concord would be characterized using such a tool.

PROBLEMS AND OPPORTUNITIES

Because Concord was one of the largest alarm companies, the GM believed that his division possessed strong brand equity in its small, but growing, niche. The division possessed a reputation for expertise in the alarm market, which was expected to grow in the future. In addition, management acumen was strong, with dedicated, highly qualified personnel located in all functional areas of the company. A few key individuals had recently left the company, however, and these people would need to be replaced.

Although domestic business was important, international operations also were critical. Concord had shifted its resources accordingly to spur growth in this area. In fact, the level of success achieved in international markets was a model for domestic employees. Sufficient control systems existed to identify, monitor, control, and correct any process or system deficiencies.

Offsetting these divisional strengths were several important weaknesses. Although the control systems were excellent, the division lacked enough qualified and knowledgeable personnel to carry out the programs in place. Company communications were inefficient, leaving many individuals unaware of the impressive capabilities that existed within the division's business systems. Additionally, project management expertise was lacking. As a result, Concord's contract product lines had suffered, labor overruns had occurred, and costs had risen out of control on several key projects. These underlying weaknesses caused morale problems within the division and resulted in lost revenues.

Areas Targeted as Priorities

As he thought about the challenges facing Concord, the GM decided to write down those tasks that he felt would be helpful in improving the overall operation of the division. His list included the following priorities:

- **Concord should maximize profitability in the service business.** Improved margins on the service side of the business would translate directly to a more favorable bottom line. Additionally, the service business did not require Concord to enlist subcontractors. Elimination of the subcontractors would improve margins and customer service as well.

- **The division should continue to expand its international business.** It was no secret that international business was critical to the success of the division. Resources should be allocated accordingly, to ramp-up sales efforts outside the United States.

- **Concord needed to maximize the profitability of the domestic contracting business.** Several opportunities existed to improve the margins in this line of business. Unfortunately, controlling labor costs and managing subcontractors would be difficult without first hiring qualified, experienced managers to oversee the projects.

- **The "bench strength" of the organization should be increased.** For the field offices to operate in a more efficient manner, more businesspeople would have to be added to run the offices. The GM knew that it would be impossible for his directives to be carried out if new personnel were not hired in the near future.

- **The company should control the growth of accounts receivable.** The firm's accounts receivable had been increasing dramatically over the past year. Attempts to remedy this situation had resulted in the departure of several "collectors," who complained about the stressful nature of their jobs. He would need to fill these positions immediately and decide whether to locate them in field offices or at corporate headquarters.

- **Undesirable and unprofitable accounts would have to be eliminated.** Concord had traditionally emphasized sales-volume growth over account profitability. This emphasis had led to the acceptance of business that resulted in slim or negative margins and substandard performance. The division should seek quality business contracts that would improve operating margins and add to the company's profitability.

Major Risks

Although he was optimistic about the division's ability to meet corporate expectations, the GM realized that certain risks would influence the success of his efforts. With the assistance of his staff, he identified several key areas of concern. The human resources department reported that it was experiencing difficulty replacing other key personnel who had left the organization. The GM realized that in order to meet the corporation's goals, he needed to attract and retain quality people.

Employee productivity was also an area of concern. A study of the division's operating performance for the most recent five-year period compared key operating results to those of a representative set of comparable companies. The calculation of relative economies of scale revealed that Concord had achieved productivity levels substantially better than the industry average. In addition, the analysis showed that at its projected sales growth rate, the company should continue to achieve growth rates in productivity of better than 10 percent per year. This positive trend would need to be perpetuated, but that task would be challenging.

An additional risk to be considered was the effect that unresolved legal action could have on the firm's financial performance. The GM's legal staff had informed him that pending litigation representing $2.1 million would be at risk at the end of 2001. The legal department was confident of a favorable resolution to each of these cases, but the GM knew that there was no guarantee for such an outcome. Losses in many of these cases would result in court payments that would severely impact 2002's financial statements.

Finally, the sales department had identified two major international projects that could materialize and that had not been included in the forecast for the original 2002 business plan. The first was a $12-million project and the second was a $10-million project, both in the Middle East. Decisions on the work were expected in early January 2002, with work to begin immediately upon the awarding of the contracts.

STRATEGIC ISSUES

The GM realized that he now had most of the information available to address the challenges presented to him by the corporation. If the division performed poorly, perhaps Pelican would decide to sell the division, to fund growth in divisions with more promise.

STRATEGIC ANALYSIS: STRENGTHS AND WEAKNESSES

Strengths

- Was the second-largest competitor in the industry
  - The leader was three times larger
- Had competed nationally and internationally
- Had been differentiated on the basis of its reputation for expertise
- Had a strong brand in a small growing industry
- Had a reputation for alarm-systems expertise
- The management team was good
- Their stance on use of union labor was neutral, which provided flexibility
- Had been successful in the international arena
- Cost structure: SG&A 4 percent below the industry average
- Strong productivity: 5.25 employees per $1 million in sales was half the industry average of 10.5

Weaknesses

- Was understaffed; lacked qualified and knowledgeable people in key skill areas
- Had poor attraction and retention of employees
- Had weak employee training at the field level
- Communication was poor
- Lacked project management expertise
- Had poor morale
- Profit: pretax loss of more than $11 million over previous two years
- Gross margin: 2001: 3.9 percent; 2002: projected 23 percent; both below industry average of 29.2 percent
- Revenue growth: 2002 projected growth of 5.7 percent was half the industry average of 13.2 percent, following a 9 percent decline during a slow-growth market in 2001
- 2002 projected ROS of 4.6 percent was well below industry average of 5.8 percent; potential sales growth and cost reductions could improve ROS to 8.5 percent
- 2002 projected RONA of 24.2 percent seemed unachievable, given that the industry average was 9.8 percent

Industry Characteristics

- Relatively small market
- Modest growth: Five-year average of 13.2 percent
- Highly competitive industry
  - Dependent on construction industry for most of growth
- Sensitive to interest rates and inflation
- Significantly threatened by legal liability; Concord Corporation currently involved in $2.1-million litigation
- Moderate profit potential
- Industry RONA: Five-year average of 9.8 percent; high 14.5 percent in 1997; low 1.0 percent in 1998

STRATEGIC SUMMARY

Business Strengths

The division was the second largest national alarm systems provider. With projected growth rates below the industry average, the company's strength in productivity would only deteriorate. It had a strong national and international reputation for expertise, but it lacked qualified people in key skill areas and had difficulty attracting and retaining the quality people necessary to continue this reputation. The division's international performance was a bright spot, providing growth opportunities over and above those incorporated into the 2002 proposal.

Concord had been unprofitable for the previous two years but believed that it would be profitable in 2002. Its poor performance stemmed from an inflated cost structure (cost of goods sold) and was evident in gross margins well below industry average. Labor cost overruns had played a significant role in the poor gross margins, and highlighted Concord's lack of project-management experience.

Overall business strength: Medium to low

Industry Attractiveness

The alarm systems industry was relatively small and fragmented. Competition was intense, with resulting low levels of profitability. The industry had averaged sales growth of 13.2 percent over the past five years, with returns of 5.8 percent on sales and 9.8 percent on net assets. Size provided insignificant economies of scale; rapid growth did afford beneficial learning curve effects, however. The alarm systems industry was cyclical in nature

and closely followed the construction industry, with attendant sensitivity to inflation rates. Legal liability was a constant threat to industry profitability.
Overall industry attractiveness: Low

RECOMMENDATIONS

Pelican should divest Concord and use the proceeds for debt service at the corporate level and for selective investment in the growth of stronger and more attractive divisions.

If Retained, What Should Concord Do?

- Hire qualified people to fill critical skill deficiencies
  - Project management: deal with labor issues, control costs
  - Business management: field offices
  - Financial management: improve working capital management
- Evaluate proposed focus on service business and in-house technicians for impact on cost structure
- Cut costs:
  - Eliminate marginal offices
  - Manage labor costs better
- Improve management of working capital (accounts receivable, payable)
- Increase margins
  - Drop low-margin accounts
- Focus on profit improvement rather than revenue growth
- Improve project management
- Balance increased margins from in-house labor against increased cost and reduced flexibility
- Invest in international growth
  - Pursue Middle East contracts ($22 million total, 17 percent increase in projected 2002 revenue)
  - Develop infrastructure for international expansion
- Resolve pending litigation

If Divested, What Valuation Could Be Expected?

The GM enlisted the help of his financial department to prepare an estimate of the market value of the division. The valuation method relied on financial data regarding the sales of 16 comparable companies during the previous 10 years. These transactions provided multiples (ratios) of market prices to revenue, total assets, net assets, and EBIT. Asset multiples provided low-end values of approximately $45 million to $55 million, and did not reflect the potential value of continued operations of the firm. Revenue and EBIT multiples provided high-end values of approximately $104 million to $124 million and assumed future performance consistent with historical levels. Based on this analysis, the market value of the division was estimated to be $115 million.

PART FIVE

STRATEGIC RESTRUCTURING FOR SHAREHOLDER VALUE

CHAPTER 12

The Restructured
Pelican Corporation

INTRODUCTION

We have reviewed the Pelican situation at the corporate level and from the perspective of each of its divisions. We see that the necessary restructuring of the corporation must consider the unique set of corporate problems and opportunities, together with the strategic positioning and opportunities of each division. At the corporate level, the most important factors affecting the need for immediate restructuring are the crash of the stock price, the urgent need to address the excessive bank debt within the allotted time frame, and the need to trim the bloated corporate staff. Clearly, some divisions would have to be divested to raise the cash necessary to deal with the debt in the time remaining under the bank terms. It also would be necessary to retain a subset of divisions that would constitute a viable new Pelican corporation. Let us review a few facts and assumptions summarized at the end of the Pelican case study.

A PLAN FOR ACTION

The CEO of the Pelican Corporation studied the summary chart showing each division's ranking on certain financial criteria (see Exhibit 11.3) and also considered the chart that showed the outside analysts' placement of each Pelican division on a widely used strategic-analysis matrix (see Exhibit 11.4). How could all of this information be used to improve the corporation's performance and meet both Pelican's short-term cash requirements and long term earnings goals?

If sales could be increased significantly, Pelican could generate some of the necessary cash to help resolve its crisis. Indeed, a few of the divisions had submitted aggressive forecasts, but could growth alone produce the cash Pelican needed to satisfy its creditors and stockholders? An attempt could also be made to generate needed cash by squeezing performance improvements in productivity, gross margin, and SG&A from some of the key divisions. Benefits from this type of initiative, however, seemed unlikely to materialize in the short time available, particularly on the scale that would be needed to satisfy the banks. As a last resort, one or more of the divisions would have to be divested to raise some of the needed funds, but which ones? The report advocated growth for some of the better performing divisions at levels that seemed possible only through acquisitions. This recommendation would require still more cash. How would it be raised?

EXTERNAL FINANCING ISSUES

Aside from short-term creditor requirements, the CEO had to consider longer-term concerns of outside investors, creditors, and analysts. Pelican's current ratio of debt to total capital was clearly unacceptable to the current stockholders and a far cry from Pelican's average in healthier times. How could Pelican's capital structure be molded to make it more attractive? The consultants' report had excluded interest charges and the allocation of the costs of a bloated corporate overhead from division performance measurement; yet at a corporate level, debt service was clearly an issue. How much debt could be afforded? How much would the investors tolerate? The company's present 15 percent interest rate on the debt indicated the market's wariness of Pelican's current structure. Should an attempt be made to raise additional equity? The banks were looking for a stable, long-term capital structure to replace the current emergency plan, and answers were needed sooner rather than later.

ASSUMPTIONS FOR THE 2002
PRO FORMA ESTIMATES

Historical and controllable factors would influence the financial performance of Pelican going forward. The following related assumptions would provide a basis for Pelican's eventual emergence from the brink of bankruptcy. The debt level of $650 million carried a stiff interest rate of 15 percent. It was assumed that the interest rates would gradually adjust to a more reasonable 10 percent if Pelican reached a debt-to-capital ratio of 35 percent. As Pelican returned to profitability, the company would benefit from a tax-loss carryforward to $270 million, a legacy from the recent collapse. This provision in the tax law would shield an equal amount of future profits and gains from corporate income taxes.

To create a corporate income statement and balance sheet from the division summary given in Exhibit 11.2, the net assets from the division summary, had to be separated into debt and equity. Corporate interest expense had to be deducted to calculate corporate profit before tax (PBT), and corporate overhead, which was currently a bloated 5 percent of revenues, also had to be accounted for. Pelican's CEO felt that the company had to move rapidly to reduce the cost of the corporate office to a more realistic 1.5 percent of revenues, consistent with well-managed corporations. By setting the example at the corporate level, Pelican corporate management could encourage the ongoing operating units to achieve improvements. Specifically, the CEO expected divisional gross margins and SG&A expenses to improve by 1 percent of sales each year until they reached a level of outstanding performance relative to their competition.

The fourth quarter of 2001 provided a window of opportunity for Pelican to effect changes allowing the corporation to go into 2002 with a drastically improved corporate structure. The achievement of that result would require decisive action on a number of issues.

THE CORPORATE PICTURE: HOW BAD WAS IT?

The first step toward understanding the depth of Pelican's crisis is to adjust the summary of the divisions' projections for 2002 to show the likely corporate financial picture. The division summary shows a robust set of division results, with revenues of almost $1 billion, net operating profit of $68 million, and net assets of almost $300 million. With an after-tax return on sales of almost 7 percent and an after-tax return on net assets of almost 23 percent, the Pelican divisions collectively constituted an enviable collection of businesses. Unfortunately, the Pelican corporate situation would only be clear when the division summary was adjusted to account for the corporate debt ($650 million), the interest expense on the corporate debt (at 15 percent), and the bloated corporate overhead (5 percent of revenues).

To study these relationships and to expedite the analysis of many strategic options, we developed a comprehensive simulation model using Excel software. This model began with a capability to represent each Pelican division for the five-year forecast period. The model could then sum these division forecasts to produce a corporate summary. Finally, the corporate financial assumptions were added to produce the likely corporate result for any strategy. The forecast growth rates for each variable could be estimated independently, which allowed forecast improvements to be studied. The model also allowed the user to simulate the divestiture of each division at the likely value estimated by the consultants—or any other estimated value. The simulation model thus provided a powerful tool for strategic analysis. It made possible a systematic and detailed study of the likely results of adopting any immediate corporate strategy.

As a first step, the model was used to transform the consolidated division summary into a corporate forecast for five years, assuming that each division would perform as forecast and adding on the corporate adjustments. Exhibit 12.1 shows these corporate results. A quick review reveals that the corporate problem was clear. When the balance sheet was adjusted to account for the debt of $650 million, the $299 million of net assets at

E X H I B I T   12-1

The forecast for business as usual ($ in millions)

Year	2001	2002	2003	2004	2005	2006
Ratios						
Sales Growth		7.7%	9.5%	10.0%	10.8%	11.0%
COGS, as % of Sales		73.5%	73.0%	72.8%	72.6%	72.5%
SG&A, as % of Sales		15.8%	15.8%	15.8%	15.8%	15.8%
ROS		(4.7%)	(4.8%)	(4.7%)	(4.6%)	(4.4%)
RONA		(15.4%)	(15.6%)	(15.6%)	(15.3%)	(14.9%)
ROE		N/A	N/A	N/A	N/A	N/A
Income Statement						
Sales	$898.2	$967.1	$1,058.5	$1,164.5	$1,290.5	$1,432.8
Gain on Sale of NA		$0.0	$0.0	$0.0	$0.0	$0.0
Profit Before Tax		($45.8)	($50.5)	($55.2)	($59.5)	($63.7)
Net Income		($45.8)	($50.5)	($55.2)	($59.5)	($63.7)
Tax Loss Carryforward	($270.0)	($315.8)	($366.4)	($421.6)	($481.1)	($544.8)
Cash Flow						
Net Income		($45.8)	($50.5)	($55.2)	($59.5)	($63.7)
Depreciation		13.6	17.5	19.1	20.9	23.0
Change in Working Capital		27.6	(16.4)	(18.5)	(21.2)	(23.5)
Change in Fixed Assets		(27.3)	(27.0)	(30.0)	(33.8)	(37.6)
Sale of Net Assets		0.0	0.0	0.0	0.0	0.0
Total Cash Flow		($31.9)	($76.4)	($84.6)	($93.6)	($101.8)
Balance Sheet						
Current Assets	$351.6	$348.5	$378.3	$412.3	$451.7	$495.7
Fixed & Other Assets	89.7	103.4	112.9	123.9	136.8	151.5
Total Assets	441.3	451.9	491.3	536.2	588.5	647.2
Current Liabilities	128.9	153.3	166.8	182.3	200.5	221.1
Net Assets	$312.4	$298.6	$324.5	$353.9	$388.0	$426.1
Debt	$650.0	$682.0	$758.4	$843.1	$936.6	$1,038.4
Equity	(337.6)	(383.4)	(433.9)	(489.1)	(548.6)	(612.3)
EXCESS CASH[a]	$0.0	$0.0	$0.0	$0.0	$0.0	$0.0

[a] Excess cash is cash beyond that required for a 0.35 debt/capital ratio.

the divisions in 2002 would result in a negative equity of –$383 million. Further, the corporate overhead expense and the interest expense on the debt would leave Pelican with an after-tax loss of more than $45 million and negative cash flow of almost $32 million in 2002. Clearly, if drastic action

E X H I B I T   12-2

The assumptions for the strategic analysis ($ in millions).

Assumptions	2001	2002	2003	2004	2005	2006
Corporate Debt	$650					
Loss Carried forward	($270)					
Debt/Capital (Goal)		0.35	0.35	0.35	0.35	0.35
COGS Improvement		1.00%	1.00%	1.00%	1.00%	1.00%
SG&A Improvement		1.00%	1.00%	1.00%	1.00%	1.00%
Corporate OH		1.50%	1.50%	1.50%	1.50%	1.50%
Interest on Debt		15.00%	12.00%	10.00%	10.00%	10.00%
Interest on Excess Cash		7.00%	7.00%	7.00%	7.00%	7.00%
Taxes		35.00%	35.00%	35.00%	35.00%	35.00%

was not taken, the company would have soon been bankrupt, as the banks would have been forced to foreclose on Pelican.

As a next step, let us examine the effect of restructuring corporate overhead to the more acceptable level of 1.5 percent of revenues that well-run companies achieve. Let us also assume that each division improved its operations by 1 percent of sales per year in revenue growth, SG&A expenses, and gross margin. These planning assumptions were input into the planning model and are summarized in Exhibit 12.2. The increase in revenue growth was input into the plans for each division.

Finally, after a number of iterative steps, it was determined that a number of divisions would have to be sold to raise the cash to deal with the emergency debt provisions. Referring to Exhibit 11.3, we can see that the best strategies involved divesting the seven marginal divisions while retaining the three highest-ranking divisions, Foxbrook, Raintree, and Monument, to provide the core for a new Pelican. Incorporating these divestitures into the model provided the results shown in Exhibit 12.3.

The fate of the divested divisions should be clarified. Occasionally, there is concern that these businesses will be disbanded, with the employees losing their jobs. This is rarely the case. Very few businesses simply shut their doors and go out of business. In fact, numerous businesses are sold by corporations every day. These businesses are sold primarily because they no longer fit the corporate strategy of their parents or because of some deep trouble in the company such as that experienced by Pelican. Such businesses are often bought or acquired by financial investors (venture capitalists), by strategic buyers (for whom the business is a strategic fit), or by management-led leveraged buyouts. Regardless of the nature of the buyer, the majority of the workers and the managers simply carry on, under different leadership and direction. There is usually some trauma in a town where such a business is located, as the local press and politicians fret about lost jobs in the event the operation is moved or closed by the new owner.

E X H I B I T   12-3

The forecast for the revised strategic plan ($ in millions)

Year	2001	2002	2003	2004	2005	2006
Ratios						
Sales Growth		(49.7%)	13.1%	13.9%	15.0%	15.0%
COGS, as % of Sales		68.5%	67.4%	66.3%	65.4%	64.7%
SG&A, as % of Sales		13.3%	12.7%	12.4%	12.0%	12.0%
ROS		68.7%	10.1%	11.8%	13.2%	14.1%
RONA		368.2%	53.8%	52.2%	39.0%	31.9%
ROE		N/A	207.6%	73.5%	48.4%	37.4%
Income Statement						
Sales	$898.2	$452.3	$511.4	$582.3	$699.7	$770.1
Gain on Sale of NA		$279.2	$0.0	$0.0	$0.0	$0.0
Profit Before Tax		$332.7	$79.3	$106.1	$135.4	$167.3
Net Income		$310.8	$51.6	$69.0	$88.0	$108.8
Tax Loss Carryforward	$(270.0)	$0.0	$0.0	$0.0	$0.0	$0.0
Cash Flow						
Net Income		$310.8	$51.6	$69.0	$88.0	$108.8
Depreciation		5.7	6.2	7.1	8.1	9.3
Change in Working Capital		(2.6)	(5.5)	(6.5)	(8.0)	(9.2)
Change in Fixed Assets		(9.7)	(12.2)	(14.1)	(16.5)	(19.0)
Sale of Net Assets		234.8	0.0	0.0	0.0	0.0
Total Cash Flow		$539.0	$40.1	$55.5	$71.6	$89.9
Balance Sheet						
Current Assets	$351.6	$98.4	$111.2	$126.6	$145.5	$167.4
Fixed & Other Assets	89.6	43.2	49.1	56.1	64.5	74.1
Total Assets	441.3	141.6	160.3	182.7	210.0	241.5
Current Liabilities	128.9	57.2	64.5	73.3	84.3	96.9
Net Assets	$312.4	$84.4	$95.8	$109.4	$125.7	$144.6
Debt	$650.0	$111.2	$70.9	$38.4	$44.0	$50.6
Equity	(337.6)	(26.8)	(24.8)	(93.8)	181.8	290.6
EXCESS CASH[a]	$0.0	$0.0	$0.0	$22.8	$100.1	$196.6

The results of the divestitures and the operational improvements at Pelican would be dramatic. As shown in the summary of corporate results for the restructured Pelican, Exhibit 12.3, revenues from operations would drop sharply as a result of the downsizing; however, all other performance measures would be greatly improved. The ROS and the RONA would be impressive, reflecting the inherent strength of the three best divisions that would be retained. Net income and cash flow would be strong and would improve each year after 2002. The combination of the large influx of cash from the divestiture of the seven divisions together with the tax-loss carryforward would allow Pelican to pay off most of the debt in the first year, eliminate the negative equity by the second year, and pass the 0.35 debt-to-capital ratio in the third year, which should provide Pelican a 12 percent interest rate in year 2 and a 10 percent rate thereafter, as shown in Exhibit 12.2.

The new, restructured Pelican consisting of Foxbrook, Raintree, and Monument, would be a much stronger company going forward, with attractive growth prospects, strong RONA and ROE capabilities, and an impressive balance sheet. Most importantly, the projected net income of $51.6 million in year 2 would provide an earnings per share for the 18.1 million shares outstanding of $2.85, which would support a stock price recovery to approximately $22 per share, based on the stock price multiple of 8 enjoyed by the company before the collapse. Referring to the corporate results in Exhibit 12.3, the same logic would support a stock price of $30 per share by the end of year 3, $39 per share by the end of year 4, and $48 per share by the end of year 5. Thus, there would be a higher share price by the end of year 5 than the highest price enjoyed prior to the collapse. This strategy would provide a likelihood that the share price could be brought back from disaster to at least its previous level by year 5.

Many additional strategic options remain for Pelican. In the next chapter, we will investigate several of these strategic options to examine their potential to hasten the recovery of the stock price or even provide greater returns for the shareholders in the short term.

Review Questions

1. What was the first threshold criterion that Pelican's CEO had to deal with?
2. What changes had to be made to the divisional summary to produce valid corporate financial statements?
3. How bad was the situation from both the corporate and the divisional perspectives?
4. How did the CEO determine which divisions would be divested in the restructuring of Pelican?
5. What happens to businesses that are divested?
6. Does the likely recovery of the share price constitute a positive result of the debacle and the restructuring?

CHAPTER 13

A Final Strategy for Pelican Corporation

INTRODUCTION

The strategy devised and analyzed in Chapter 12 resulted in a corporate forecast that would eventually, over a five-year period, regain or improve upon the stock price Pelican enjoyed before the collapse. The strategic plan proposed dealt with the emergency bank loans, paid off the excessive level of debt, resulted in a stronger, more focused company, and would restore investor confidence in the company, the board of directors, and the new CEO. But problems are always accompanied by opportunities. Could a corporate strategy be found for Pelican that would bring prosperity even more rapidly? The prospect of working the next five years just to reach the previous level of market acceptance would be less than stimulating to the executive staff. Previously awarded stock options would be "underwater," or worthless. The most talented staff might be tempted to seek their fortunes elsewhere.

Consider again Exhibit 12.3, the final forecast for the restructured Pelican Corporation. That strategic plan would restore profitability immediately, pay off most of the debt, eliminate negative equity by the end of year 2, and create a capital structure compatible with a AA bond rating (a debt-to-capital ratio of at least 35 percent, along with excess cash) by the end of year 3. That strategic plan called for the divestiture of seven divisions, with Pelican retaining the three most attractive businesses: Foxbrook Corporation, Raintree Corporation, and Monument Corporation. Each of these divisions was its industry leader, had impressive growth opportunities, was very profitable, and produced cash beyond its needs for supporting its own growth. In fact, Exhibit 12.3 shows that by the end of year 5, at which time Pelican would likely have passed its precollapse stock price, the company would have excess cash of almost $200 million beyond that needed for optimal operations and to maintain its recovered capital structure. In the final three years of the five-year plan, the buildup of excess cash would, in fact,

221

lower Pelican's returns on investment, because the 7 percent return on excess cash would be significantly less than the greater-than-30 percent return on equity forecast to be earned overall. (It was assumed that Pelican would invest its excess cash in low-risk investments, such as marketable securities.)

Most of us would consider the divestiture of 7 of the 10 divisions to be drastic, to the point of being unthinkable. But corporate strategies frequently involve thinking the unthinkable. As we described in Chapter 2, the greatest unknowns in strategy formulation, and in decision making in general, are the likely actions or reactions of competitors and our own ability to execute. Anything Pelican does will be carried out in an atmosphere of intense reaction by competitors and a risky internal morale climate. Let us examine some additional strategic options that Pelican should consider. The strategic objective would be to further enhance shareholder value beyond that forecast by the three-division strategy derived in Chapter 12. Pelican needs to consider carefully the following five strategic options for further enhancing shareholder value:

1. The board could consider selling the whole of the remaining Pelican Corporation.
2. The board could consider selling one or more of the remaining divisions.
3. Pelican could seek to buy back a portion of its outstanding shares.
4. Pelican could spin off one or more of the remaining divisions, transferring the shares of the spun-off company to its shareholders.
5. The company could pursue some combination of the above strategies in various sequences.

As we begin to consider these additional strategic actions, recall the situation in which Pelican would find itself with the company trimmed down to the three premier divisions. The emergency debt would have been taken care of but the remaining debt would still be more than $100 million, and equity would be negative (debt would be greater than the net assets of the company) in year 1. Shareholders' equity would turn positive in year 2, and excess cash would appear in year 3 (indicating a strong capital structure), growing to $197 million by the end of year 5.

Apparently, additional shareholder value would be locked up (unrealized) by the diversified nature of Pelican's divisions. As mentioned earlier, financial analysts who have a lot to say about the price-to-earnings multiple at which stocks trade prefer focused businesses to diversified businesses, on the premise that they are easier to understand. Furthermore, analysts and investors typically prefer to construct their own portfolios by holding the shares of focused companies rather than own shares in a diversified company. This is a powerful driving force within the investment community and can be demonstrated by Pelican itself. The Pelican case noted that the highest stock price achieved by the company prior to the collapse was a multiple of eight times the earnings per share. This relatively low multiple of share price to earnings reflected the risk analysts felt to be inherent in the highly diversified Pelican Corporation.

One of the strategic questions asked about each division of Pelican was the likely market value of that business if it were to be sold, say, by auction. The market values, based on recent transactions involving the sales of similar businesses, for the remaining three Pelican divisions were $355 million for Foxbrook Corporation, $405 million for Raintree Corporation, and $135 million for Monument Corporation. The net income for 2002 was forecast to be $21.6 million for Foxbrook, $15.1 million for Raintree, and $8.6 million for Monument. If we divide Foxbrook's market value of $355 million by its expected net income of $21.6 million, we calculate an implied stock price-to-earnings multiple of 16.4. Similarly, the multiple for Raintree is 26.8 and for Monument, 15.7. All are significantly greater than the highest multiple of eight times earnings enjoyed by the precollapse Pelican.

ANALYSIS OF THE STRATEGIC OPTIONS

It was suggested in Chapter 12 that the stock price could well recover to a price of $48 per share by the end of year 5 with proper management of the restructured, three-division Pelican Corporation. This would imply a market capitalization (value) of approximately $870 million at the end of year 5. The same logic would estimate a market value of $413 million at the end of year 2, based on an estimated earnings per share of $2.85, a stock price-to-earnings multiple of 8, and 18.1 million shares outstanding. But the estimated market values for the three divisions, based on the prevailing multiples for each industry, total almost $900 million immediately. This estimate is a strong suggestion that the company might be worth significantly more broken up than as an ongoing whole.

Considering the first two strategic options described above, we might conclude that the option to sell the whole company would be worth less to shareholders than selling off one or more divisions individually. This follows from the brief valuation estimates derived above. Now consider the third option, that of Pelican buying back a portion of its outstanding shares. In general, this option has strong advantages because reducing the shares outstanding mathematically increases the earnings per share, and therefore the share price, thus creating value for the shareholders. Moreover, the buying back of shares is a nontaxable event. This is also a better option than holding "excess cash" at the corporate level because of the low return earned by the corporation on excess cash. Recall that we assumed earlier that excess cash would be held in low-risk, marketable securities. It is less than prudent, and some might argue inappropriate, for a corporation to engage in risky investments when it has excess cash. One reason for this is that the negative consequences of adverse results could be devastating. For instance, when a number of major companies were unfortunate victims of market reverses while they held "derivatives," the criticism from analysts and the adverse effects on their stock prices were dramatic.

Thus, there appears to be no better option for the use of excess cash than buying back the company's shares. This is, in fact, a practice now widely employed by companies that find themselves with levels of cash beyond what they need for the business. Pelican, however, would be unable to buy back shares before year 3, because a company is precluded from buying back shares when it has negative equity. Management should also prefer to defer the buying back of shares until the firm's debt-to-capital ratio reached the preferred 35 percent level, consistent with an AA bond rating. As a result, this strategic option would have to be put on hold for Pelican until it paid down its debt and restored a strong capitalization.

The fourth strategic option mentioned was the possibility of spinning off one or more divisions. Spin-offs have come to be very popular vehicles for breaking up unnatural alliances of businesses, the most obvious of which is the situation in which two businesses are worth significantly more separated than together. If one of the businesses is sold, the gain on the sale is a taxable event. Additionally, any dividends paid to shareholders of the after-tax proceeds from the sales would be a further taxable event to the shareholders. With the proper structuring of the spin-off transaction, wherein the parent company is deemed to have divided its assets (and value) between two securities, instead of its original security, the shares of the spin-off company can be distributed to the shareholders as a tax-free transaction. For tax purposes, the company is considered to be substituting two securities for one, with the same total value. Of course, such spin-off transactions have often significantly increased the value of a company's shares.

The final strategic option for Pelican was to undertake some combination of the other possible actions, which included selling one or more divisions, buying back shares, or spinning off one or more divisions. Remember that the option to sell one or more divisions was a logically dominant alternative to selling the whole company, because the breakup value exceeded the value of the company as a whole. Given that the divisions were worth much more than the company as a whole, and given that the low current stock price was expected to prevail for two or three years, Pelican might benefit by selling another division at the outset to produce "excess cash" immediately, which could be used to buy back a portion of the company's outstanding shares. The final strategic action would then be to spin off one of the remaining two divisions, creating two strong surviving public companies and leaving behind the debacle of the collapse, which the financial markets would have a hard time forgetting.

Let us consider the impact of these interconnected strategic moves. We should remember that in the initial divestiture stage of the recovery, there were literally hundreds of combinations of feasible subsets of divisions that could be sold. The overriding concern was to have the surviving Pelican Corporation capable of going forward as a viable company. As we have seen, keeping the Foxbrook, Raintree, and Monument divisions provided a solid base for the gradual recovery of Pelican over five years. Their selection for retention was no accident, because they were the three most highly ranked divisions in the table shown in Exhibit 11.3. At this stage in the strategic analysis, however, which division should be sold or which one should be subsequently spun off is not immediately clear.

Let us go back to the simulation model that produced Exhibit 12.3. The model was run again in three iterations, in turn, in which each of the three divisions was assumed to be sold. Referring to Exhibit 13.1, the sale of Foxbrook Corporation would leave Pelican with a strong company, consisting of Raintree and Monument. The model output shows that Pelican would have $142.1 million in year 1 for use in buying back shares, which would be desirable given the current low share price and the long time frame that would be required for Pelican to regain its credibility. Now consider Exhibit 13.2, which provides a portion of the model output which would result from a sale of Raintree, with the remaining Pelican Corporation consisting of Foxbrook and Monument. Again, this shows a very strong company and estimates that Pelican would have excess cash in year 1 of $189.7 million. Finally, Exhibit 13.3 shows the results of retaining Foxbrook and Raintree and selling Monument. This run projects excess cash of only $5.9 million in year 1, which would result from the relatively low selling price (market value) of Monument.

SUMMARY

And so we come to the final strategic decision for Pelican Corporation. Selling Monument Corporation would not meet the strategic objective of providing immediate cash (in year 1) to repurchase outstanding shares. Either of the other two divisions, Foxbrook or Raintree, would provide a large measure of cash ($142.1 million and $189.7 million, respectively) for buying back the shares while the markets are waiting to see Pelican's recovery solidify. One additional factor might help make the final choice of the division to be sold. In the matter of spin-offs, the new (spun-off) company must hold existing shareholders and attract new ones. Inertia among existing shareholders will cause many of them to hold the original shares. But they must be motivated to hold, not sell, the new shares they receive in the new company.

Therefore, the logically dominant alternative would be to sell Raintree, which would bring in the most cash for buying back shares. The plan would then be to buy back as many shares as possible prior to spinning off Foxbrook to the remaining shareholders. At an average share price of $20, this plan would allow Pelican to buy back approximately half of the 18.1 million shares outstanding. By year 2 this strategy would have Pelican earning $5.40 per

E X H I B I T   13-1

The forecast with the sale of Foxbrook ($ in millions).

Year	2001	2002	2003	2004	2005	2006
Ratios						
Sales Growth		(61.4%)	12.5%	13.5%	15.0%	15.0%
COGS, as % of Sales		73.3%	72.3%	71.2%	70.2%	69.2%
SG&A, as % of Sales		13.7%	13.3%	12.8%	12.4%	12.4%
ROS		152.3%	9.2%	10.4%	11.5%	12.3%
RONA		242.8%	13.9%	15.0%	15.8%	16.1%
ROE		276.4%	15.8%	16.9%	17.6%	17.9%
Income Statement						
Sales	$898.2	$347.2	$390.5	$443.3	$509.8	$586.3
Gain on Sale of NA		$625.8	$0.0	$0.0	$0.0	$0.0
Profit Before Tax		$668.2	$55.1	$70.8	$90.0	$111.0
Net Income		$528.8	$35.8	$46.0	$58.5	$72.1
Tax Loss Carryforward	$(270.0)	$0.0	$0.0	$0.0	$0.0	$0.0
Cash Flow						
Net Income		$528.8	$35.8	$46.0	$58.5	$72.1
Depreciation		4.7	4.9	5.6	6.3	7.3
Change in Working Capital		(3.9)	(5.4)	(6.4)	(7.8)	(9.0)
Change in Fixed Assets		(7.0)	(9.6)	(11.2)	(13.2)	(15.1)
Sale of Net Assets		243.2	0.0	0.0	0.0	0.0
Total Cash Flow		$765.8	$25.7	$34.0	$43.8	$55.3
Balance Sheet						
Current Assets	$351.6	$80.6	$90.8	$103.1	$118.6	$136.3
Fixed & Other Assets	89.7	35.2	39.9	45.5	52.3	60.2
Total Assets	$441.3	$115.8	$130.7	$148.6	170.9	196.5
Current Liabilities	128.9	40.2	44.9	50.8	58.5	67.2
Net Assets	$312.4	$75.6	$85.8	$97.8	$112.4	$129.3
Debt	650.0	26.5	30.0	34.2	39.3	45.2
Equity	(337.6)	191.2	227.0	273.0	331.5	403.6
Excess Cash	$0.0	$142.1	$171.2	$209.4	$258.4	$319.5

share, which, with a weighted-average multiple of 15, would support a share price of $80. This price would be far superior to the $48 share price likely by the end of year 5 with the first restructuring moves. The final act would be to change the name of Pelican to Monument Corporation, giving investors a new stock, without the baggage of the recent collapse.

E X H I B I T   13-2

The forecast with the sale of Raintree ($ in millions).

Year	2001	2002	2003	2004	2005	2006
Ratios						
Sales Growth		(61.1%)	15.0%	15.0%	15.0%	15.0%
COGS, as % of Sales		63.7%	62.7%	61.7%	60.9%	60.3%
SG&A, as % of Sales		15.9%	14.9%	14.2%	13.7%	13.7%
ROS		203.5%	15.2%	16.6%	17.8%	18.4%
RONA		227.3%	16.2%	16.7%	16.9%	16.6%
ROE		248.0%	17.6%	18.1%	18.2%	17.8%
Income Statement						
Sales	$898.2	$277.9	$319.6	$367.5	$422.7	$486.0
Gain on Sale of NA		$666.7	$0.0	$0.0	$0.0	$0.0
Profit Before Tax		$724.7	$74.8	$93.9	$115.4	$137.7
Net Income		$565.6	$48.6	$61.0	$75.0	$89.5
Tax Loss Carryforward	$(270.0)	$0.0	$0.0	$0.0	$0.0	$0.0
Cash Flow						
Net Income		$565.6	$48.6	$61.0	$75.0	$89.5
Depreciation		3.6	4.3	4.9	5.6	6.5
Change in Working Capital		5.6	(4.1)	(4.7)	(5.4)	(6.2)
Change in Fixed Assets		(8.1)	(9.1)	(10.4)	(12.0)	(13.8)
Sale of Net Assets		252.3	0.0	0.0	0.0	0.0
Total Cash Flow		$819.0	$39.7	$50.8	$63.2	$76.0
Balance Sheet						
Current Assets	$351.6	$59.0	$67.9	$78.0	$89.8	$103.2
Fixed & Other Assets	89.7	31.9	36.7	42.2	48.6	55.9
Total Assets	441.3	90.9	104.6	120.2	138.4	159.1
Current Liabilities	128.9	31.9	36.6	42.1	48.5	55.7
Net Assets	312.4	59.0	68.0	78.1	89.9	103.4
Debt	650.0	20.7	23.8	27.3	31.5	36.2
Equity	(337.6)	228.0	276.6	337.6	412.6	502.1
Excess Cash	$0.0	$189.7	$232.4	$286.8	$354.2	$434.9

As was stated in Chapter 2, the mirror images of problems are opportunities. And the catastrophic problems faced by Pelican Corporation led to a thorough strategic analysis that produced unexpected positive outcomes. No wonder so many corporations are rethinking their strategies of diversification and decentralized operations.

E X H I B I T   13-3

The forecast with the sale of Monument ($ in millions).

Year	2001	2002	2003	2004	2005	2006
Ratios						
Sales Growth		(68.9%)	11.9%	13.2%	15.0%	15.0%
COGS, as % of Sales		67.3%	66.0%	64.9%	64.0%	63.4%
SG&A, as % of Sales		10.2%	9.9%	9.9%	9.9%	9.9%
ROS		130.8%	14.5%	15.8%	16.9%	17.8%
RONA		913.6%	52.2%	38.8%	32.0%	27.7%
ROE		1301.3%	61.7%	43.3%	34.8%	29.6%
Income Statement						
Sales	$898.2	$279.5	$312.7	$353.8	$406.9	$467.9
Gain on Sale of NA		$362.3	$0.0	$0.0	$0.0	$0.0
Profit Before Tax		$417.0	$69.5	$86.2	$105.9	$128.4
Net Income		$365.6	$45.2	$56.0	$68.9	$83.5
Tax Loss Carryforward	$(270.0)	$0.0	$0.0	$0.0	$0.0	$0.0
Cash Flow						
Net Income		$365.6	$45.2	$56.0	$68.9	$83.5
Depreciation		3.1	3.3	3.7	4.2	4.8
Change in Working Capital		(7.0)	(1.5)	(2.0)	(2.8)	(3.2)
Change in Fixed Assets		(4.3)	(5.6)	(6.6)	(7.8)	(9.0)
Sale of Net Assets		286.7	0.0	0.0	0.0	0.0
Total Cash Flow		$644.1	$41.4	$51.1	$62.5	$76.1
Balance Sheet						
Current Assets	$351.6	$57.1	$63.7	$72.0	$82.8	$95.2
Fixed & Other Assets	89.7	19.2	21.5	24.4	28.0	32.3
Total Assets	441.3	76.3	85.2	96.4	110.8	127.5
Current Liabilities	128.9	42.3	47.3	53.6	61.7	70.9
Net Assets	312.4	34.0	37.9	42.8	49.1	56.6
Debt	650.0	11.9	13.3	15.0	17.2	19.8
Equity	(337.6)	28.0	73.2	129.2	198.1	281.6
Excess Cash[a]	$0.0	$5.9	$48.6	$101.4	$166.2	$244.8

As noted in the preface, we are in the midst of an unprecedented era of divestiture and refocus for the preponderance of diversified, decentralized corporations. These firms, hastened by market forces, have engaged in a flurry of tracking stocks, sales, spin-offs, and carve-outs. The preference of investors and influential analysts for focus and corporate clarity has recently spurred many firms to divest varying portions of their businesses, which has unlocked extensive value for their shareholders. In our next chapter, we will reflect on a collection of thoughts related to the ongoing operations of these firms as well as their activities in the realm of restructuring.

Review Questions

1. Is it likely that the CEO would have considered the wide array of corporate strategic options if the company hadn't teetered on bankruptcy?
2. How would you rank the strategic options listed? Are some more preferable to the others, from a shareholder perspective?
3. Are some of the strategic options logically dominant over or preferable to others?
4. How did the CEO determine which specific businesses should be sold or spun off, and in what order?
5. Is there a paradox in selling off some businesses and then having strong prospects for the share price to recover well?

CHAPTER 14

Final Thoughts

ADDITIONAL NUANCES OF STRATEGY

In keeping with the purpose of this work addressing corporate strategy, lessons related to strategic issues have been covered in the chapters and the case studies of this book. A few are listed here to remind us that strategy is an art as well as a science and that strategies are unique to a company only so long as they remain confidential.

SUSTAINABLE COMPETITIVE ADVANTAGES

Let us return to the analogy between strategy in the business context and the ultimate weapon in the military context described in the preface. Competitive advantages based on strategies almost always are short-lived, as most are readily copied. A well-thought-out strategy may provide a temporary competitive advantage, but creating a sustainable competitive advantage requires effective, supporting functional strategies in marketing, operations, and finance. Such sustainable competitive advantages often are brought about by systematic application of the winner's cycle, in which a firm achieves a position as the low cost producer in its market segments and reinvests a portion of its high margins into price reductions or other "investments" intended to gain volume and market share, placing steady pressure on competitors. The long-run application of effective functional strategies can lead to a position as the low-cost producer, which together with steady price reductions, eventually will lead to dominance of the industry's market segment.

STRATEGIC OPPORTUNITIES

Success often comes to managers as a result of luck, or *fortuna*, as described by Macchiavelli,[1] in which managers must act rapidly to seize temporary

---

1 Niccolo Machiavelli, *The Prince* (1532) from *The Portable Machiavelli*, edited and translated by Peter Bondanella and Mark Musa, Viking Penguin, New York, 1979, 159–162.

windows of opportunity that occur. Consider the following example. A CEO invites his or her counterpart from the firm's largest competitor to lunch. At the lunch, it is explained to the competitor CEO that the company has decided to concentrate on fewer core competencies (focus) and thus intends to sell one or more of its operating divisions. The object is to receive the highest possible price for the units to be divested. In most cases, the competitor (a strategic buyer) has the most to gain from an acquisition and thus can afford to pay the highest price for the divisions. Upon hearing this news, the competitor CEO has a very short time frame in which to react to the opportunity. No amount of strategic thinking on his or her part could have created such an opportunity, but the unexpected appearance of the opportunity must be met with speed and flexibility, or the window will close and the possible deal will vanish.

Such lunch meetings have led to numerous deals that proved to be in the best interest of both firms because the buyer, for whom the acquisition would be most valuable, was able to react rapidly and decisively. No degree of strategic planning or analysis can substitute for the willingness to act when *fortuna* appears. The best strategists are opportunists. They know the capability of their management and technical teams and are bold when strategic opportunities appear.

RETAINING ACQUIRED MANAGERS: ADVANTAGES AND PITFALLS

The steady activity in acquisitions and divestitures among large numbers of firms raises the question of whether managers of acquired companies should be retained or let go. Some acquired managers are outstanding and many have gone on to become CEO of the acquiring company. One major corporation on the Fortune list of the 100 largest U.S. firms was led by three consecutive CEOs who had come to the company as managers of acquired businesses. Despite such exceptions, the retention of acquired business unit managers is a risky process. Many have become wealthy in the process of selling their companies. Many have no desire to change their modes of operation to accommodate the preferences of an acquiring company. And many, having been their own bosses for many years, have little interest in being subordinates to other CEOs. To quote Machiavelli: "And one should bear in mind that there is nothing more difficult to execute, nor more dubious of success, nor more dangerous to administer than to introduce a new system of things."[2] A CEO who had consummated approximately 15 acquisitions over a 30-year period, reported that for the first two or three transactions he had hoped to succeed in having the acquired CEOs become full-fledged team members. At some point, he realized that they had no intention of "joining his team," thus leading him to conclude that in the

2 Machiavelli, *The Prince*, 94.

remainder of the acquisitions, an understanding was reached that the CEO would not stay with the business. He reported that the attempt to assimilate the CEOs had cost the company millions of dollars and delayed progress for years, until the expectations of assimilation were abandoned.

UNDERSTANDING THE MARKET VALUE OF A FIRM'S ASSETS

In valuing acquisitions and divestitures it is crucial to understand the market value of a firm's assets. In many situations, the sellers of a business may have scant knowledge of the true value of the firm's assets. Consider the case in which well-maintained plant facilities may have a market value (or replacement value) in their intended use much greater than their depreciated book value. In other cases, a buyer may intend that the assets be employed in a different way, which, in turn, may lead to much greater market value than the seller appreciates. Such a case may occur when a seller of a company views its land holdings in terms of its historical use, and the land's book value may be carried at the land's original cost. The purchaser may envision other uses of the land, with values many times the value based on the historical use. This duality of vision is the essence of entrepreneurship—the ability to see value beyond the traditional view.

THE EGO OF THE CEO

At times, the ego of the CEO of a company, especially one with control (ownership of more than 50 percent of the shares of the company), may get in the way of what is best for the minority shareholders. For instance, a number of CEOs have rejected highly favorable bids for their companies largely because they personally preferred to continue as the publicly visible CEO of the company. Some of these companies have subsequently gone bankrupt, costing all of the shareholders a great deal of money. While under our legal system, a majority shareholder is assumed to sustain more damage than anyone else in such a sequence of events, the minority shareholders are the unwitting victims of the CEO's ego.

CASH IS KING

As we saw in several of the Pelican Corporation case studies in Chapter 11, cash is the fundamental driver of a firm's viability. Almost no firm can ensure that its cash generating capability will match its cash needs. There invariably will be too much or too little cash, with cash flow and growth seldom in balance. If a firm has an optimal capital structure in which it has strong revenue and profit generating capability, then its long-term ability to grow at the rate of its market or better, without diluting its ownership, depends on its rate of "retained earnings to equity." If its earnings rate is greater than its nominal growth rate (real growth plus inflation), then the firm can continue indefinitely without seeking external funding. Similarly, if the growth rate and the earnings rate are reversed, then the firm continually will have to seek outside funding for its growth. Cash is indeed king.

MACHIAVELLI AND CORPORATE RESTRUCTURING

In the matter of the continuous restructuring of U.S. businesses that is ongoing, Machiavelli's admonition to carry out the required harsh measures as rapidly as possible is especially relevant. The quote from *The Prince* is as follows: "Wherefore it is to be noted that in taking a state its conqueror should weigh all the harmful things he must do and do them all at once so as not to have to repeat them every day, and in not repeating them to be able to make men feel secure and to win them over with the benefits he bestows upon them."[3] In the case of mergers or the acquisition of companies large enough to be reported in the press, the reduction of employees attendant to the acquisition are often made known at the time the acquisition or merger is announced. The rapid execution of the intended workforce reductions allows those who will continue to be employed to know their jobs are secure, and the acquiring firm can get on with the assimilation of the acquired firm with a better chance to realize projected synergies.

PREMIUM CONGLOMERATES

In Chapter 1 we described the pressure financial analysts exert on companies to become more focused and less diversified. As we typically find in business, there are the usual and the unusual, the normal and the abnormal, along with the exception to the rule. While most diversified companies pay a price for their lack of focus, a few diversified firms enjoy unusually high share price-to-earnings ratios, in spite of their postures counter to the conventional wisdom. These firms are rewarded for outstanding long-term performance; some would characterize it as "off-the scale" performance. For instance, a firm that earns greater than 20 percent return on equity and sustains a compound average growth rate of profit after tax greater than 15 percent per year over a period of many consecutive years will earn a high stock-price multiple because the only thing financial analysts value more than conventional wisdom is performance. Thus, a firm that aspires to outstanding market valuations can ensure its acceptance to the group of rare, highest valuations by performing superbly in defiance of the conventional wisdom. It also is likely that a firm could not perform at such a level consistently if it were hiding many imperfections.

---

3 Machiavelli, *The Prince*, 106–07.

STRATEGY AND FOREIGN COMPETITION

Foreign competitors have advantages and disadvantages when competing with U.S. firms. For example, foreign countries, especially European countries, have extremely restrictive laws regarding the ability of companies to adjust their work forces. In many countries, the act of laying off workers is financially akin to retiring them. Foreign governments have tweaked the laws relating to employment to achieve something close to a guarantee of lifetime employment. As we discussed extensively in Chapters 5, 6, and 7, work force adjustments in growing firms often allow both increased employment levels and productivity improvements. But the majority of firms are not growing as rapidly as their productivity needs to improve in order to preserve their competitive positions. In such firms, the legal and sociological norms that permit firms to take the actions needed to remain competitive, even if they result in workforce reductions, are distinct competitive advantages for U.S. firms.

DIFFERENCES IN VALUATIONS BETWEEN CASH FLOW ANALYSIS AND MARKET MULTIPLES

The two basic approaches to the valuation of a firm, the NPV of the cash flows method and the multiples method, may lead to widely disparate estimates of value. The multiples method, described in Chapter 10 and in the Pelican Corporation case studies, usually reflects most accurately the "market value" of a firm. Using the multiples of various performance measures derived from recent transactions, the essence of the market is captured in the prevailing multiples. A firm's value in a proposed transaction is resolved through a negotiation that establishes, to the satisfaction of both parties to the deal, how the firm's performance or other attributes warrant its placement along the spectrum of values suggested by the multiples.

In an NPV analysis, however, one ceases to consider the past, which is known with some accuracy, and considers, instead, estimates of the likely cash flows across some horizon of future years, based on forecasts of literally hundreds of variables that collectively determine cash flow. Then one estimates all of the future cash flows, in perpetuity, through a process of "capitalizing" the final year's cash flow. This capitalizing often leads to very large estimates of the so-called terminal value that, even when discounted back to a present value, contributes disproportionately to the NPV of the estimated future cash flows of the firm.

This process can produce NPV estimates of a firm's value several times greater than the "multiples" or market value. On the one hand, if the larger, cash-flow-based value is accurate, then the buyer should rapidly close the deal and be well rewarded for his or her ability to identify incremental value relative to the market. On the other hand, if the cash-flow-based value is overstated, the buyer likely will pay too much for the company, a process that leads to a postacquisition analysis to try to determine why the forecast synergies didn't materialize. Buyers and sellers had best beware of the disparities that may develop from the use of these two valuation methods.

THE FALLACY OF USING THE COST OF CAPITAL AS A FIRM'S HURDLE RATE

There is an inherent problem in automatically using a firm's cost of capital as its discount rate in the analysis of capital expenditures. The basic purpose of a firm is to earn a profit greater than its cost of capital. If the firm uses its cost of capital as the discount rate and over time approves many capital projects as long as their returns meet the hurdle rate, then the average return on investment earned in the business will inevitably be eroded to the cost of capital. Such a return will not earn a premium stock price-to-earnings multiple for the company. If the firm intends to be valued as a premium investment vehicle, it must use a discount rate similar to its target return on investment.

THE DELETERIOUS EFFECT OF EXCESS CASH

Given that cash is king, the term *excess cash* seems to be an anomaly, but when a company has a proper balance sheet with a correct ratio of debt to total capital, any additional cash could correctly be termed "excess cash." The problem that arises with a firm holding excess cash is that the lower returns on cash holdings tend to lower the average return on assets of the firm. In the not-too-distant past, firms that found themselves with excess cash had few recourses for remedying the situation. The continued presence of excess cash led many firms to make ill-advised acquisitions to dispose of the excess cash. Conversely, such firms also become targets of cash-seeking raiders.

Recently, it has become quite acceptable for a firm to buy back its own shares, which is an effective resolution to the excess cash problem. Many firms currently fine-tune disparities between their available cash and their needs for cash through a program of publicly announced buy-backs of their shares. There is an associated additional positive effect of this action, in that it signals investors that the firm feels that the shares are undervalued and the shareholders are willing to buy in shares at the current price.

FINALE

We thus conclude our current take on the elusive subject of corporate strategy. As we find continually in the field of management, there are always new fads *du jour* to bring new insights regarding old and timeless dilemmas. We hope that our observations have given you new ways to think of corporate strategy, and especially the importance of "execution," in both the old and new economies.

1. How does a firm achieve a sustainable competitive advantage?
2. What role does luck play in strategic analysis?
3. How can a CEO's ego affect the share price of a public company?
4. Why is the phrase, "cash is king" so often invoked in discussions of corporate strategy?
5. Why is it so decisively important to move swiftly in strategic decisions?
6. What would prevent any company from seeking to become a "premium conglomerate"?
7. How do you reconcile the major differences between the valuations produced by the multiples method and the net-present-value method?
8. If cash is king, why is excess cash deleterious?

Bibliography

Abegglen, James C., and George Stalk, Kaisha: *The Japanese Corporation*, Basic Books, New York, 1985.

Abernathy, W. J., and K. Wayne, "Limits of the Learning Curve," *Harvard Business Review*, 52, (September–October 1974), 109–119.

Adler, Paul, "Shared Learning." *Management Science*, 36, 8 (August 1990), 938–957.

Adler, Paul, and Kim B. Clark, "Behind the Learning Curve: A Sketch of the Learning Process," *Management Science*, 37, 3 (March 1991), 267–281.

Allen, Julius W., "Increasing Productivity in the United States: Ways in Which the Private and Public Sectors Can Contribute to Productivity Improvement," in *Productivity: The Foundation of Growth: Studies/Prepared for the Use of the Special Study on Economic Change of the Joint Economic Committee, Congress of the United States*, U.S. Government Printing Office, Washington, D.C., 1980, 67–100.

Andrews, Kenneth, *The Concept of Corporate Strategy*, Irwin, Homewood, IL, 1971.

Argote, Linda, Sara L. Beckman, and Dennis Epple, "The Persistence and Transfer of Learning in Industrial Settings," *Management Science*, 36, 2 (February 1990), 140–154.

Arthur, W. Brian, "Increasing Returns and the New World of Business," *Harvard Business Review* (July–August 1996), 100–109.

Badiru, Adedeji B., "Computational Survey of Univariate and Multivariate Learning Curve Models." *IEEE Transactions on Engineering Management*, 39, 2 (May 1992), 176–188.

Baloff, Nicholas, "Extension of the Learning Curve—Some Empirical Results," *Operational Research Quarterly*, 22, 4 (December 1971), 329–340.

Baloff, Nicholas, "Estimating the Parameters of the Startup Model—An Empirical Approach," *Journal of Industrial Engineering*, 18, 4 (April 1967), 248–253.

3M, "Startups in Machine-Intensive Production Systems," *Journal of Industrial Engineering*, 17, 7 (January 1966a), 25–32.

3M, The Learning Curve—Some Controversial Issues," *Journal of Industrial Economics*, 14, 3 (July 1966b), 275–282.

Baloff, Nicholas, and John W. Kennelly, "Accounting Implications of Product and Process Start-Ups," *Journal of Accounting Research*, 5, 2 (Autumn 1967), 131–143.

Baumol, William J., and Kenneth McLennan, "U.S. Productivity Performance and Its Implications," in William J. Baumol and Kenneth McLennan (eds.), *Productivity Growth and U.S. Competitiveness*, A Supplementary Paper of the

Committee for Economic Development, Oxford University Press, New York, 1985a, 3–28.

3M, "Toward an Effective Productivity Program," in William J. Baumol and Kenneth McLennon (eds.), *Productivity Growth and U.S. Competitiveness*, A Supplementary Paper of the Committee for Economic Development, Oxford University Press, New York, 1985b, 185–224.

Blattberg, Robert C., "Managing the Firm Using Lifetime Customer Value," *Chain Store Age* (January 1998), 46–49.

Bodde, David, "Riding the Experience Curve," *Technology Review*, 78, 5 (March–April 1976), 53–59.

Bowen, D. E., "Managing Customers as Human Resources in Service Organizations," *Human Resource Management*, 25 3 (Fall 1986), 371–384.

Brodsky, Norm, "The Return of Customer Loyalty," *Inc., Magazine* (September 1997), 39–40.

Burck, Charles, "A Fresh Look at Productivity," *Fortune*, 119, 4 (February 13, 1989), 28.

Byczkowski, John, "Service Please: Industry Overtakes Manufacturing with 76% of Jobs," *The Cincinnati Enquirer*, (November 18, 1991), D1.

Carlson, John G., "Cubic Learning Curves: Precision Tool for Labor Estimating," *Manufacturing Engineering & Management*, 71, 5 (November 1973), 22–25.

3M, "How Management Can Use the Improvement Phenomenon," *California Management Review*, 3, 2 (Winter 1961), 83–94.

Cetron, Marvin J., Wanda Rocha, and Rebecca Lucken, "Think Big or Think Small," *The Futurist*, (September–October 1988), 9–16.

Chandler, Alfred, *Strategy and Structure: Chapters in the History of the American Industrial Enterprise*, MIT Paperback Press Edition, Boston, 1969.

Chandler, Alfred D., Jr., *The Visible Hand: The Managerial Revolution in American Business*, Belknap, Boston, 1977.

Chase, Richard B., "The Customer Contact Approach to Services: Theoretical Bases and Practice Extenstions," *Operations Research*, 29, 4 (July–August 1981), 698–706.

3M, "Where Does the Customer Fit in a Service Operation?," *Harvard Business Review*, 56, 6 (November–December 1978), 137–142.

Chase, Richard B., and Nicholas J. Aquilano, *Production and Operations Management: A Life Cycle Approach* (rev. ed.), Irwin, Homewood, IL, 1977.

Chase, Richard B., and Robert H. Hayes, "Beefing Up Operations in Service Firms," *Sloan Management Reveiw*, (Fall 1991), 15–26.

Christainsen, Gregory B., and Robert H. Haveman, "The Determinants of the Decline in Measured Productivity Growth: An Evaluation, in *Productivity: The Foundation of Growth, Studies/Prepared for the Use of the Special Study on Economic Change of the Joint Economic Committee, Congress of the United States*, U.S. Government Printing Office, Washington, D.C., 1980, 1–17.

Clark, Jeffrey A., "Economies of Scale and Scope at Depository Financial Institutions: A Review of the Literature," *Economic Review* (EKC) 73, 8 (September–October 1988), 16–33.

Clayman, Michelle, "In Search of Excellence, The Investor's Viewpoint," *Financial Analysts' Journal*, (May–June 1987) 68–71.

CNBC Interview, "Interview with Michael Dell," November 1998.

CNBC Interview with Ron Insana, "Market Watch," January 1999a.

CNBC Interview with Mark Haines, "Squawk Box," January 1999b.

CNBC Live Broadcast, "Chairman Greenspan Testifies Before the Senate Finance Committee," January 28, 1998.

Colarusso, Dan (1998), "Net Option Plays Stay Expensive," http//www. TheStreet.com, (December 1998).

Colley, John L., Jr. "Corporate and Divisional Strategy," Lecture, The Darden Graduation School of Business Administration, (November 1998).

3M, *Corporate and Divisional Planning: Text and Cases*, Reston Publishing, Reston, VA, 1984.

Colley, John L., Jr., Robert D. Landel, and Robert R. Fair, *Operations Planning and Control*, Holden-Day, San Francisco, 1978.

Collins, James C., and Jerry I. Porras, *Built to Last*, Harper Business, New York, 1994.

Conley, Patrick, "Experience Curves as a Planning Tool," *IEEE Spectrum*, 7, 6 (June 1970), 63–68

Conway, R.W., and Andrew Schultz, Jr., "The Manufacturing Progress Function," *Journal of Industrial Engineering*, 10, 1 (January–February 1959), 39–53.

Cramer, James J., "Recent Hop in Playboy Stock Should Give Investors Pause," http://www.TheStreet.com (December 1998a).

3M, "Measure Value by the Product, not the Price," http://www.TheStreet.com (December 1998b).

3M, "Trumping Even Great Research," http://www.TheStreet.com (December 1998c).

3M, "Ignore the .comSilliness," http://www.TheStreet.com (November 1998d).

3M, "The Truth About Lycos," http://www.TheStreet.com (December 1998).

3M, "Cramer's Rewrite of His Cashing In on Crazy Times," http://www. TheStreet.com (January 1996).

3M, "About My Schizophrenic Net Pieces," http://www.TheStreet.com (January 1999c).

3M, "Online and Offline: You Can't Have It Both Ways," http://www. TheStreet. com (January 1999d).

3M, "Take Two: Cramer's Rewrite of His 'Cashing In on Crazy Times' Piece," http://www.TheStreet.com (January 1999e).

Cushing, Woodrow W., and James E. McNulty, "The Behavior of Operating Costs at Large Commercial Banks," *The Mid-Atlantic Journal of Business*, 1 (March 1993), 27–40.

Day, George S., and David B. Montgomery, "Diagnosing the Experience Curve," *Journal of Marketing*, 47 (Spring 1983), 44–58.

Dean, Joel, "Pricing Policies for New Products," *Harvard Business Review* (November 1950), 45–53.

DeGeorge, Gail, "Sign of the Times: Help Wanted," *Business Week* (November 1997), 60–61.

Denison, Edward F., *The Sources of Economic Growth in the United States and the Alternatives Before Us*, Supplementary Paper No. 13, Committee for Economic Development, New York, 1962.

Devellis, Robert F., *Scale Development: Theory and Applications*, Applied Social Research Methods Series, Volume 26, Sage Publications, Newbury Park, CA, 1991.

Devore, Jay L., *Probability and Statistics for Engineering and the Sciences* (2d ed), Brooks/Cole, Monterey, CA 1987.

Doler, Kathleen, "A Conversation with James Cramer," *Upside* (November 1998), 70–75; 120–124.

Dow Jones Retrieval Service, Tradeline database, Fall 1993.

Dowling, Grahame, and Mark Uncles, "Do Customer Loyalty Programs Really Work?" *Sloan Management Review*, (Summer 1997), 71–82.

Doyle, Jacqueline L., "Economies of Growth: A Study of Corporate and Productivity Growth Rates in Two Service Industries," A dissertation submitted in partial fulfillment of the requirements for the degree of Doctor of Philosophy in Business Administration, The Darden Graduate School of Business Administration, The University of Virginia, Charlottesville, 1995.

Doyle, Jacqueline L., and John L. Colley, Jr., "Pizza Hut, Inc., "Darden Graduate Business School Sponsors, Darden Graduate Business School, Charlottesville, VA, UVA-OM 0698, Rev. 10/92.

Drucker, Peter, *The Practice of Management*, Harper & Row, New York, 1954.

3M, *Innovation and Entrepreneurship*, Harper & Row, New York, 1985.

Dugan, Ianthe Jeanne, "In Bull Market, The Urge to Gamble Is Rising," *The Washington Post* (February 1999), A1, A8.

Dutton, John M., and Annie Thomas, "Treating Progress Functions as a Managerial Opportunity," *Academy of Management Review*, 9, 2 (April 1984), 235–247.

Eppes, Thomas E., "Keeping Customers Is Just as Important as Winning New Ones," *Business Marketing* (November 1997), 9.

Fitzsimmons, James A., "Making Continual Improvement a Competitive Strategy for Service Firms," in David Bowen, Richard B. Chase, Thomas G. Cumming, and Associates (eds.), *Service Management Effectiveness*, Jossey-Bass, San Francisco, 1990.

Follett, Mary Parker, *Prophet of Management*, Pauline Graham (ed.), *Harvard Business Press*, Boston, 1995, released from 1920.

Fournier, Susan, Susan Dobscha, and David Glen Mick, "Preventing the Premature Death of Relationship Marketing," *Harvard Business Review* (January–February 1998), 42–44.

Freeman, R. Edward, *Strategic Management: A Stakeholder Approach*, Pitman, Boston, 1984.

Fromson, Brett D., "Big Drop in Stocks Sets Off Automatic Circuit Breakers for First Time," *The Washington Post* (October 1997) A5.

Galante, Suzanne, "The Ax: What Price Amazon, Pick One, Analysts Decide," http://www.The Street.com (December 1998).

Gardner, Davis, and Tom Gardner, *The Motley Fool Investment Guide: How the Fool Beats Wall Street's Wise Men and How You Can Too*, Simon and Schuster, New York, 1996.

Garvin, David, "Quality on the Line," *Harvard Business Review* (September–October 1983), 64–75.

Glassman, James K., "At a Loss in Valuing Internet's Darlings," *The Washington Post* (July 1998), C1.

Globerson, Shlomo, and Abraham Seidmann, "The Effects of Imposed Learning Curves on Performance Improvements," *IIE Transactions*, 20, 3 (September 1988), 317–323.

Graham, John R., "Eight Ways to Build Customer Loyalty," *Incentive* (October 1997), 124.

Graham, Pauline, *Mary Parker Follett: Prophet of Management*, Harvard Business Press, Boston 1995.

Grayson, Jackson, Jr., "The U.S. Economy and Productivity: Where Do We Go from Here?" in *Productivity: The Foundation of Growth, Studies/Prepared for the Use of the Special Study on Economic Change of the Joint Economic Committee, Congress of the United States*, U.S. Government Printing Office, Washington, D.C., 1980, 18–45.

Greenberg, Herb, "Life Beyond the Internet: Running Away from the Herd," http://www.TheStreet.com (January 1999).

Griffin, Jill, "The Internet's Expanding Role in Building Customer Loyalty," *Direct Marketing* (November 1996), 50–53.

Griliches, Zvi, "Productivity, R&D, and the Data Constraint," *The American Economic Review*, 84, 1 (March 1994), 1–23.

Griliches, Zvi, and Jacques Mairesse (eds.), *Productivity Issues in Services at the Micro Level: A Special Issue of the Journal of Productivity Analysis*, Kluwer Academic Publishers, Boston, 1993.

Gupta, Vinod K., "Labor Productivity, Establishment Size, and Scale Economies," *Southern Economic Journal*, 49 (January 1983), 853–859.

Hagstrom, Robert G., Jr., *The Warren Buffett Way*, John Wiley and Sons, New York, 1994.

Hald, A., *Statistical Tables and Formulas*, John Wiley and Sons, New York, 1952.

Hamel, Gary, "Strategy as Revolution," *Harvard Business Review*, (July–August 1996), 69–71.

Hamel, Gary, and C. K. Prahalad, *Competing for the Future*, Harvard Business School Press, Boston, 1994.

Hanley, William, "Internet Bubble at Bursting Point," *The National Post* (January 1999), D1.

Harmon, Steve, "98 Pre-Holiday Euphoria: Internet.com's IPODEX Shows Strong Demand," http://www.internet.com (November 1998).

3M, "What's Hot: Access Stocks Show Most Gains," http://www.internet.com (January 1999a).

3M, "Top 10 Web Sites Get Buy Eye Happy," http://www.internet.com (February 1999b).

3M, "The Internet Report," http://www.internetnews.com (February 1999c).

3M, "The Internet Report," http://www.internetnews.com (February 1999c).

Hart, Christopher W. L., "The Power of Unconditional Service Guarantees," *Harvard Business Review*, (July–August 1998), 54–62.

Harvard Business School, "Sustainable Growth and the Interdependence of Financial Goals and Policies," HBS Case Services, Harvard Business School, Boston, publication 9-282-045, 1982.

Hayes, Robert H., and Kim B. Clark, "Exploring the Sources of Productivity Differences at the Factory Level," in Kim B. Clark, Robert H. Hayes, and Christopher Lorenz, *The Uneasy Alliance: Managing the Productivity-Technology Dilemma*, Harvard Business School Press, Boston, 1985.

Hayes, Robert H., and Steven C. Wheelwright, *Restoring Our Competitive Edge: Competing Through Manufacturing*, John Wiley and Sons, New York, 1984.

Heaster, Jerry, "Tiptoe Through the Web Stocks," *The Kansas City Star* (January 1999), F1.

Heineke, John M., "Notes on Estimating Experience Curves: Econometric Issues," *IEEE Transactions on Engineering Management*, EM-33, 2 (May 1986), 113–119.

Heizer, Jay, and Barry Render, *Production and Operations Management: Strategies and Tactics* (3d ed.), Allyn and Bacon, Boston, 1993.

Herther, Nancy K., "The Personal Computer: Today's Workhorse Moves into the Twenty-First Century," *Online* (January 1998), 29.

Heskett, James L., "Lessons in the Service Sector," *Harvard Business Review* (March–April 1987), 118–126.

Hesselbein, Frances, Marshall Goldsmith, and Richard Beckhard, eds., *The Leader of the Future*, The Drucker Foundation, Jossey-Bass, San Francisco, 1996.

3M, *The Organization of the Future*, The Drucker Foundation, Jossey-Bass, San Francisco, 1997.

Hill, Miriam, "Amazombies Fuel Buying Frenzy for Internet Stocks," *Philadelphia Enquirer*, http://www.phillynews.com (January 1999).

Hirschmann, Winfred B., "Profit from the Learning Curve," *Harvard Business Review*, 42 (January–February 1964), 125–139.

Humphrey, David B., "Productivity in Banking and Effects from Deregulation," *Economic Review*, Federal Reserve Bank of Richmond (March–April 1991), 16–28.

3M, "Why Do Estimates of Bank Scale Economies Differ?," *Economic Review*, Federal Reserve Bank of Richmond, 76 (September–October 1990), 38–50.

Jorion, Philippe, *Value at Risk: The New Benchmark for Controlling Market Risk*, McGraw-Hill, New York, 1997.

Kachigan, Sam Kash, *Statistical Analysis: An Interdisciplinary Introduction to Univariate and Multivariate Methods*, Radius Press, New York, 1986.

3M, "Specifying the Learning Curve in Services," DSI Proceedings, November 1991.

Kaufmann, Patrick J., "Pizza Hut, Inc.: Home Delivery," HBS Case Services, Harvard Business School, Boston (unnumbered), 1987.

Kessler, Andy, "Time for Net Stocks to Put Up or Shut Up," http://www.TheStreet.com (January 1999).

Kirkpatrick, Davis, "Why Have Investors Ignored Lycos for So Long?," *Fortune* (February 1999), 150.

Kolodny, Richard, Martin Laurence, and Arabinda Ghosh (1989), "In Search of Excellence . . . for Whom," *Journal of Portfolio Management* (Spring 1989), 56–60.

Kotter, John, *Leading Change*, Harvard Business School Press, Boston, 1996.

Kuhn, Susan, "Why You Should Own Tech Stocks," *Money* (May 1997), B15.

Lardner, James, "Ask Radio Historians About the Internet," *U.S. News and World Report* (January 1999), 48–52.

Lee, Jeanne, "Net Stock Frenzy," *Fortune* (February 1999), 148–150.

Lee, L. Douglas, "Productivity, Inflation, and Economic Growth," In *Productivity: The Foundation of Growth, Studies/Prepared for the Use of the Special Study on Economic Change of the Joint Economic Committee, Congress of the United States*, U.S. Government Printing Office, Washington, D.C., 1980, 46–57.

Leftwich, Richard H., *The Price System and Resource Allocation* (rev. ed.), Holt, Rinehart, and Winston, New York, 1961.

Lenz, Ralph C., and Linda L. Bricker, "Relationships Between Market Growth and Productivity," *Business Horizons* (May–June 1983), 36–41.

Levitt, Theodore, "The Industrialization of Service," *Harvard Business Review*, 54, 5 (September–October 1976), 65–74.

3M, "Production-Line Approach to Service," *Harvard Business Review*, 50, 5 (September–October 1972), 41–52.

Levy, Ferdinand K., "Adaptation in the Production Process," *Management Science*, 11, 6 (April 1965), B136–154.

Lovelock, C. H., "Managing Interactions Between Operations and Marketing and Their Impact on Customers," in David E. Bowen, Richard B. Chase, Thomas G. Cumming, and Associates (eds.), *Service Management Effectiveness*, Jossey-Bass, San Francisco, 1990.

McDonald, John, "A New Model for Learning Curves, DARM," *Journal of Business & Economic Statistics*, 5, 3 (July 1987), 329–335.

McGee, John S., *Industrial Organization*, Prentice Hall, Englewood Cliffs, NJ, 1988.

Magretta, Joan, "The Power of Virtual Integration: An Interview with Dell Computer's Michael Dell," *Harvard Business Review* (March–April 1998), 72–84.

Malkiel, Burton G., *A Random Walk Down Wall Street*, W.W. Norton and Company, New York, 1996.

March, James, and Herbert Simon, *Organizations*, John Wiley and Sons, 1958.

Meeker, Mary, "Internet Quarterly: The Business of the Web . . .," *U.S. Investment Research*, Morgan Stanley Dean Witter (September 1997).

Miller, Edward M., "Extent of Economies of Scale: The Effect of Firm Size on Labor Productivity and Wage Rates," *Southern Economic Journal* (January 1978), 470–487.

Moore, Alison, "It's Getting Harder to Beat the Benchmark Without Net Stock," http://www.TheStreet.com (February 1999).

Morris, Barbara, and Robert Johnston, "Dealing with Inherent Variability: The Difference Between Manufacturing and Service?," *International Journal of Operations and Production Management*, 7, 4 (1987), 13–22.

National Geographic Atlas of the World (rev. 6th ed.) National Geographic Society, Washington, D.C., 1992.

Pattison, Diane D., and Charles J. Teplitz, "Are Learning Curves Still Relevant?," *Management Accounting*, 70 (February 1989), 37–40.

Pedhazur, Elazar J., and Liora Pedhazur Schmelkin, *Measurement, Design, and Analysis: An Integrated Approach*, Lawrence Erlbaum Associates, Hillsdale, NJ, 1991.

Peles, Yoram C., "On Deviations from Learning Curves," *Journal of Accounting, Auditing & Finance*, NS6 (Summer 1991), 349–363.

Peters, Thomas J., and Robert H. Waterman, Jr., *In Search of Excellence*, Warner Books, New York, 1982.

Pine, B. J., *Mass Customization*, Harvard Business School Press, Boston, 1993.

Porter, Michael, *The Competitive Advantage of Nations*, The Free Press, New York, 1980.

Quinn, James Brian, and Penny C. Paquette, "Service Technologies: Key Factors in Manufacturing Strategy," in David Bowen, Richard B. Chase, Thomas G. Cumming, and Associates (eds.), *Service Management Effectiveness*, Jossey-Bass, San Francisco, 1990.

Reis, Dayr A., "Learning Curves in Food Services," *Journal of the Operations Research Society*, 42, 8 (August 1991), 623–629.

Roberts, H. V., Statistical Versus Clinical Prediction of the Stock Market," Paper presented to the Seminar on the Analysis of Security Prices (May 1967).

Roser, Sherman R., and Lawrence C. Sundby, "Learning Curves and Inflation," *Cost & Management* (July–August 1985), 30–34.

Roth, Aleda V., and Marjolijn van der Velde, "Operations as Marketing: A Competitive Service Strategy," *Journal of Operations Management*, 10, 3 (August 1991), 303–328.

Rudestam, Kjell Erik, and Rae R. Newton, *Surviving Your Dissertation: A Comprehensive Guide to Content and Process*, Sage Publications, Newbury Park, CA, 1992.

S&P Industry Surveys, March 11, 1993, L45.

S&P Industry Surveys, November 12, 1992, B15.

Samuelson, Paul A., and William D. Nordhaus, *Economics* (14th ed.), McGraw-Hill, New York, 1992.

Sasser, W. Earl, and William E. Fulmer, "Creating Personalized Service Delivery Systems," in David Bowen, Richard B. Chase, Thomas G. Cumming, (eds.), *Service Management Effectiveness*, Jossey-Bass, San Francisco, 1990.

Sasser, W. Earl, R. Olsen, and D. Daryl Wyckoff, *Management of Service Operations: Text, Cases and Readings*, Allyn and Bacon, Boston, 1978.

Scherer, F. M., *Industrial Market Structure and Economic Performance* (2d ed.), Rand McNally College Publishing, Chicago, 1980.

Schonberger, Richard J., *Japanese Manufacturing Techniques*, The Free Press, New York, 1982.

Schonfeld, Erick, "Schwab Puts It All Online," *Fortune* (December 1998), 94–100.

Schroeder, Roger G., *Operations Management: Decision Making in the Operations Function* (3d ed.), McGraw-Hill, New York, 1989.

Scism, Leslie, and Rebecca Buckman, "High Price of Amazon.com Is Raising Some Eyebrows," *The Wall Street Journal* (July 1998), C1.

Seymour, Jim, "Nine Trading Principles for '99, http://www.TheStreet.com (January 1999).

Shabelman, David, "CMGI's Stance on Lycos Deal Shakes Stocks," http://www.TheStreet.com (February 1999).

Shapiro, Benson P., Adrian J. Slywotzky, and Stephen X. Doyle, "Strategy Sales Management: A Boardroom Issue," *Strategy and Business*, (Third Quarter 1997), 29–46.

Shiller, Robert J., *Market Volatility*, The MIT Press, Cambridge, MA, 1989.

Simons, Davis, "Amazon's $10 Billion Understanding," http://www.TheStreet.com (December 1998).

Skinner, Wickham, "The Productivity Paradox," *Harvard Business Review* (July–August 1986), 55–59.

Sloan Alfred, *My Years with General Motors*, Anchor Press Doubleday, New York, 1972.

Smith, David B., and Jan L. Larson, "The Impact of Learning on Cost: The Case of Heart Transplantation," *Hospital & Health Services Administration*, 34, 1 (Spring 1989), 85–97.

Smith, Delos R. "How the Heirs of Sloan and Dupont Are Faring," *Across the Board*, May 1986.

Staff, "A Banner Day for the Biggest Tech Names," http://TheStreet.com (January 1999).

Staff Reports, "CMGI May Not Support Lycos Deal," http://www.InternetNews .com (February 1999).

Stewart, G. Bennett, *The Quest for Value*, Harper Business, New York, 1990.

Stobaugh, Robert B., and Phillip L. Townsend, "Price Forecasting and Strategic Planning: The Case of Petrochemicals," *Journal of Marketing Research*, 12 (February 1975), 19–29.

Stoner, A. F., R. Edward Freeman, and Daniel R. Gilbert, Jr. *Management*, Prentice Hall, Upper Saddle River, NJ, 1995.

Stultz, Rene, M., "Rethinking Risk Management," *Journal of Applied Corporate Finance* (Fall 1996), 8–24.

Stum, David L., and Alain Thiry, "Building Customer Loyalty, *Training and Development Journal* (April 1991), 34–36.

Sudman, Seymour, and Norman M. Bradburn, *Asking Questions*, Jossey-Bass, San Francisco, 1982.

Thomas, Dan R. E., "Strategy Is Different in Service Business," *Harvard Business Review*, 56, 4 (July–August 1978), 158–165.

Tichy, Noel M., and Stratford Sherman, *Control Your Own Destiny or Someone Else Will*, Harper Business, New York, 1993.

"Bubble.com," *The Economist* (December 1998), 102.

"The Net Results," *USA Today* (January 1999), B3.

U.S. Bureau of the Census, *Statistical Abstract of the United States: 1993* (113th ed.), Washington, D.C., 1993.

3M, *Statistical Abstract of the United States: 1992* (112th ed.), Washington, D.C., 1992.

3M, *CPI Detailed Report: Data for December 1992*, Washington, D.C., 1993.

UVA-F-0910, "The Corporation's Cost of Capital and the Weighted-Average Cost of Capital," Darden Graduate School of Business Technical Note (October 1990).

Vancil, Richard F., and Benjamin R. Makela (eds.), *The CFO's Handbook*, Dow Jones-Irwin, Homewood, IL, 1986.

Wang, Nelson, "IPO Fever, Already Burning, Intensifies," http://www.internet-world.com (January 1999).

Ward's Business Directory of U.S. Private and Public Companies, Gale Research, Inc. Detroit, 1991.

Waterhouse Securities, "Choosing the Right Order," *Investing Ideas Newsletter* (February 1999a) 2.

3M, "Tactics for Trading In a Volatile Market," *Investing Ideas Newsletter* (February 1999b), 1.

3M, "Important Service Note," *Investing Ideas Newsletter* (February 1999c), 2.

Womack, James P., and Daniel T. Jones, *Lean Thinking*, Simon and Schuster, New York, 1996.

Woolley, Suzanne, "Internet Insanity," *Money* (January 1999), 94–101.

Wright, T. P., "Factors Affecting the Cost of Airplanes," *Journal of the Aeronautical Sciences*, 3 (February 1936), 122–128.

Yelle, Samuel, "Common Flaws in Learning Curve Analysis," *Journal of Purchasing and Materials Management*, 21 (Fall 1985), 10–15.

3M, "The Learning Curve: Historical Review and Comprehensive Survey," *Decision Sciences*, 10, 2 (April 1979), 302–328.

INDEX

ABOUT THE AUTHORS

John L. Colley, Jr., D.B.A., is the Almand R. Coleman Professor of Business Administration at The University of Virginia's Darden Graduate School of Business Administration. He is the author of *Case Studies in Service Operations, Corporate and Divisional Planning*, and other management-related titles and case studies.

Jacqueline L. Doyle, Ph.D., is a Visiting Assistant Professor of Business Administration and former General Motors Post-Doctoral Fellow at the Darden School. She has consulted with a variety of U.S. businesses in areas of strategy and productivity improvement, and authored or coauthored numerous cases and working papers.

Robert D. Hardie, Ph.D., is a Visiting Assistant Professor of Business Administration at the Darden School. He is also a project director for the University of Virginia, where he performs financial and strategic analyses on business and technology issues. His research has been primarily in the high-technology area.